WHY SPORT?

AN INTRODUCTION TO THE PHILOSOPHY OF SPORT

To Katie
whose strong, athletic body
may one day find its way to a sports arena

WHY SPORT?

AN INTRODUCTION TO THE PHILOSOPHY OF SPORT

Sheryle Bergmann Drewe

University of Manitoba

THOMPSON EDUCATIONAL PUBLISHING, INC.

Toronto

Information on how to obtain copies of this book may be obtained from:

Web site:	www.thompsonbooks.com
E-mail:	publisher@thompsonbooks.com
Telephone:	(416) 766-2763
Fax:	(416) 766-0398

National Library of Canada Cataloguing in Publication Data

Drewe, Sheryle Bergmann, 1964-
Why sport? : an introduction to the philosophy of sport / Sheryle

Bergmann Drewe.

Includes index.

ISBN 1-55077-130-2

1. Sports–Philosophy. I. Title.

GV706.D74 2003 796'.01 C2002-905618-7

Copy Editing: Elizabeth Phinney
Cover Design: Elan Designs
Cover photo: Allsport Concepts, Mike Powell; courtesy of Getty Images Inc..

Reader's Comments: If you have suggestions or information that might improve future editions of this book, the authors and publisher would be pleased to hear from you. Please send your comments to: publisher@thompsonbooks.com

We acknowledge the support of the Government of Canada through the Book Publishing Industry Development Program for our publishing activities. We acknowledge the support of the Government of Ontario through the Ontario Media Development Corporation Book Initiative.

Printed in Canada.

1 2 3 4 5 07 06 05 04 03

Table of Contents

Acknowledgments

I would like to acknowledge the assistance provided by the Social Sciences and Humanities Research Council of Canada, the University of Manitoba, and the Health, Leisure and Human Performance Institute at the University of Manitoba, who provided grant money that facilitated the conducting of this research.

I would like to thank my dean, Dr. Dennis Hrycaiko, who has been incredibly flexible in allowing me to arrange my teaching schedule to fit my research schedule. I would also like to thank Dr. Henry Janzen, who, many years ago, first introduced me to the Philosophy of Sport Society (now the International Association for the Philosophy of Sport), which has been my main academic venue for presenting many of the ideas in this book. I must also thank the athletes and coaches who shared their perspectives with me, as these perspectives are an integral part of Chapters 5, 6, 8, and 9.

I must also acknowledge the following journals for granting permission to republish material in some of the chapters in this book: *European Physical Education Review* 4 (1998): 5-20 (Chapter 3); *Journal of Professional Ethics*, in press (Chapter 4); *Sport, Education and Society* 4 (1999): 117-130 (Chapter 5); *Sport, Education and Society 5* (2000): 147-162 (Chapter 6); *Journal of the Philosophy of Sport* 29 (2002): 174-181(Chapter 11); *and Avante* 5 (1999): 1-17 (Chapter 9).

I must also thank my family and friends, who listen (and challenge!) many of my ideas. Finally, a special thanks to Nick, Josh, and Katie–whose existence makes me realize that there is far more to life than philosophy!

Preface

Why Sport? was written to fill a gap in the philosophy of sport literature. Although there are some good anthologies on the market, most of these books were written for a fairly advanced audience. What this text attempts to do is cover most of the same topics but at a level that is accessible for undergraduate students in an introductory philosophy of sport course. Arguments from the philosophy of sport literature are summarized and analyzed, and connections are made to the "real world" of sport. Pedagogical tools such as key concepts and review questions are included to increase the readability of the text.

Why Sport? begins with a fundamental conceptual question: "What makes something a sport?" It is important for practitioners and theoreticians to be clear on what it is they are discussing when they are examining issues in the sports world. Conceptual clarity is especially important if value claims are going to be made. An examination and critique of the values of sport is found in Chapter 2. Fundamental to the meaning of sport and to the various positions people have taken concerning the value of sport is the concept of competition. A conceptual and normative inquiry of competition is the topic of Chapter 3.

Having examined the conceptual and normative underpinnings of sport, the remainder of the text deals with particular aspects of sports, including youth sport, ethical issues, autonomy of athletes, cheating, sportspersonship, doping, violence, coach-athlete relationships, gender issues, and the aesthetic dimension of sport. Although each chapter can be read on its own, an examination of all of them will provide a fuller treatment of the multi-faceted world of sport.

Why Sport? was written primarily as a text for undergraduate philosophy of sport courses. However, graduate students and researchers in this field might find some of the chapters to be a good starting point for further exploration (since most of the chapters include references to the seminal work concerning the particular aspects under consideration). Although *Why Sport?* was written as a text, it has something to offer athletes, coaches, sport administrators, and anyone interested in a philosophical examination of the world of sport.

1

When Is Something a Sport, and Why Should We Care?

Bridge is as much a sport as some things in the Olympics. It might not be physical, but you need endurance and mental toughness to play. (Wilkes 2001)

Is hunting a sport? What about car racing? Mountain climbing? Bowling? Chess? When should we call something a sport? What is the relationship between sports, play, games, recreation, and physical education? If we can determine when something is a sport, what have we accomplished? In other words, why should we care when something is or is not a sport? These are the questions we will address in this chapter. The key concepts that will be utilized include: **necessary and sufficient conditions for sport, gross physical skills, competition, institutional condition, play, games, recreation, physical education, moral** and **social issues.**

Necessary and Sufficient Conditions for Sport

In trying to determine when something should be considered a sport, it is helpful to look for necessary and sufficient conditions. What philosophers mean by **necessary and sufficient conditions** can best be understood through an example. In examining the necessary and sufficient conditions for the concept "bachelor," one might propose the criteria of being unmarried and male. Although being unmarried and male is necessary for being considered a bachelor, these conditions would not be sufficient. We would also have to specify an age condition, since we do not typically refer to a baby boy as a bachelor. Thus the necessary *and* sufficient conditions for someone to be referred to as a bachelor would include being an unmarried, adult male. Any and only people who meet these conditions would qualify as bachelors. Philosophers of sport have proposed a number of such necessary and sufficient conditions for sport. These conditions will be considered and then tested against our intuitions concerning potential "sport" activities.

The first condition most people would agree with concerning whether something should be considered a sport is that the activity should be physical in nature. By **physical**, we are referring to a focus on the movement of the human body. However, how physical is "physical enough"? For example, is bowling sufficiently physical to be considered a sport? Even chess playing involves the movement of chess pieces on a game board. Would this "movement" count? To make sense of these examples, it is necessary to look more closely at what we mean by "physical" and "movement." Osterhoudt (1977) makes a very important distinction concerning physical movements:

> [Sports] rules embody an emphasis on the "physical" which makes the way in which movements are performed highly significant. The final outcome of these movements does not exhaust their significance, as is so in the movement of chess pieces and in other board and in card games as well. In these games, the terms of movement themselves are incidental, in any constitutive or genuinely interesting sense, as compared to the importance of the position (or state) moved from and to. In sport, however, the movements themselves are idealized and become an engaging part of the activity. (p.13)

Osterhoudt points out that "idealized" movements require great skill to perform well. In contrast, the actual movements in a chess game do not require great skill; rather, the chess player's skill is demonstrated not by *how* he or she moves the pieces but to *where* he or she moves the pieces. Bowling might be considered similar to chess in that it matters where the bowling ball ends up in relation to the pins. However, where the ball ends up *is* determined by the bowler's skill in moving his or her body before releasing the ball. Thus, under the condition of physical skill, bowling, but not chess, should be considered a sport.

The requirement of **physical skill** is also evident in Loy's (1968) conception of "the demonstration of physical prowess" as "the employment of developed physical skills and abilities within the context of gross physical activity to conquer an opposing object of nature" (p.6). Loy's condition of a "context of gross physical activity" would eliminate some activities that require physical skill, but not gross physical skill. For example, driving race cars requires skilled movements but these movements are not at the "gross" level. Using the condition of "gross physical activity," race-car driving would not be considered a sport.

Loy's (1968) conception of physical prowess also included the notion of "conquering an opposing object of nature" (p.6); in other words, another condition for something to be considered a sport is an element of competition. The root word of **competition**, *com-petitio*, means "to strive together." This striving requires an "other" to strive with. It has been argued that the "other" with which people "strive together" in *com-petitio* need not be limited to other people. Thomas (1983) alludes to this situation in her discussion of the "other" as an essential element in competition.

> There is someone or something to go against or against which to measure success. Depending on the sport or the kind of competition, the "other" can be a person, oneself, a river or mountain, time, previous performances, or a score or person in absentia such as in telegraphic meets. A related commonality is that an outcome is evident. There will be a winner(s) or loser(s), or you will either succeed or fail in the objectives that were established for the contest. (p.78)

The notion that a person can compete with oneself, a river, or a previous performance has not escaped criticism. McIntosh (1979) suggests that competing against oneself represents a conceptual impossibility: "I cannot both win and lose against myself, nor, when I improve my performance over last time, can I dissociate my present self from my previous self. Self-improvement is central to learning but it is not competition" (p.178). Keating (1973) suggests that there are other, more accurate, ways to describe what a person is doing when he or she is referring to competing against him or herself: "He is attempting to improve his skill, to learn, to develop, to grow, to actualize his potentialities. Only when he seeks to exceed, surpass, or go beyond the best efforts of others is he actually competing. Competition in all of its forms always presupposes another or others" (p.159). Kildea (1983) refers to competing against records as personal: "Attempting to beat the clock or to upend any record previously established by oneself (often referred to as the 'historic self') is an attempt toward excellence. It is personal rather than interpersonal activity. The pursuit of excellence is not competitive activity" (p.177).

Common to all of the above mentioned criticisms levied against the notion of competing against oneself, scores, or records is the distinction that is drawn between self-improvement and the pursuit of excellence, and competitive activity. However, the question must be raised concerning how people know if they have achieved excellence if not by comparison to others or to some standard. How can people speak of self-improvement if they do not have a standard by which to gauge progress? Thus, the very notion of excellence or improving oneself presupposes something by which people can compare their skills and abilities as well as the skill level they could potentially reach. This comparison requires competition because it is only in comparison to other people's skills and abilities (or records of skills and abilities set by other people) whereby a person can gauge his or her own abilities and the skill level he or she could potentially reach.

Concerning the people or objects against which one competes, a criticism can be levied against Thomas's (1983) conception of the "other" as including rivers and mountains. The critical distinction that must be made here involves the notion of intention. A fellow competitor has the intention of striving together in a competitive activity. One's previous performance or a score or record set by another person can still be perceived as having at one time involved intention on the part of someone. A mountain or a river can never involve such intention. Thus, a person and a mountain or river do not strive together in the pursuit of excellence. A mountain climber or river rafter may achieve excellence but this is not determined by comparison with the mountain or the river but rather by comparison with the performance of another mountain climber or river rafter. The fact that mountains and rivers are graded does not negate this proposition that the comparison is between mountain climbers and river rafters since the mountains and rivers are graded on a scale that recommends that a climber or rafter be at a level comparable to an expert to tackle a mountain or river with a high grade, or that a climber or rafter need only be on par with a novice to attempt a climb or river run with a low grade.

The situation where mountains and rivers are graded introduces what could be referred to as the **institutional condition** for something to be called a sport. In defining sport, Tamburrini (2000) states the following conditions: "Sport is commonly defined as a game that is (a) *competitive*, involving (predominately) (b) *physical skills* and that (c) is *widely* practiced over (d) *a long period of time*, at least long enough to develop a praxis with (e) *its own expertise, trainers, judges, institutions, etc.*" (p.3). Conditions (c), (d), and (e) will be referred to as the "institutional" condition for something to be called a sport. Osterhoudt (1977) reiterates the importance that "sport" activities be practiced widely and over a long period of time: "Such activities as barrel jumping, hurling, jai alai, hula hooping, and jousting, among similar others, have an insufficiently wide basis in our geographical-historical experience to be included" (p.13). Weiss (1969) notes the importance of a sport's history: "A single game of a particular type is not yet part of a sport, for it is not yet part of a history of games; a sport need more than one occasion when its rules are exemplified. Those occasions must resemble one another" (p.144). The necessity of an activity to have a history before being called a sport is significant in that it eliminates games children make up during play time from being called sport. The suggestion that a sport requires more than "rules" or "more than one occasion" when it is played is summarized aptly by Loy (1968):

> The formulation of a set of rules for a game or even their enactment on a particular occasion does not constitute a sport as we have conceptualized it here. The institutionalization of a game implies that it has a tradition of past exemplifications and definite guidelines for future realizations. Moreover, in a concrete game situation the form of a particular sport need not reflect all the characteristics represented in its institutional pattern. The more organized a

> sport contest in a concrete setting, however, the more likely it will illustrate the institutionalized nature of a given sport. A professional baseball game, for example, is a better illustration of the institutionalized nature of baseball than is a sandlot baseball game; but both games are based on the same institutionalized pattern and thus may both be considered forms of sport. (p.7)

Having examined the institutional condition for something to be considered a sport, we will return to the notion of intention (which arose in the mountaineering example). When animate participants are involved in a sport, all participants should have intended to be part of the sport. It is easy to think of cases where participants intend to be playing a sport, for example, two teams playing basketball, a diver involved in a diving competition, mountaineers competing against other mountaineers who have scaled a particular mountain. But what about something like a gladiator contest? Would we want to call that a sport? Or, if we can imagine a hypothetical example where an activity has developed over time where a certain group of people, let us say people taller than six feet, have to run around a course involving multiple tunnels chased by people who are shorter than five feet. This activity meets the conditions discussed thus far concerning whether something should be considered a sport: it involves gross physical skills (e.g., running and crawling); there is competition between the short and the tall people; and the activity has been institutionalized, that is, it has certain rules (e.g., participants have to crawl through every tunnel to complete the course, it has a history, and it is played in many locations around the world). However, let us say for the sake of argument that the tall people have no choice as to whether they participate in the activity; that is, every person over six feet tall in the state has to participate. Would this mandatory requirement affect our opinion as to whether this activity should be considered sport? To fully answer this question, we have to examine what it means to "play" and the relationship between sport and play.

Play

We talk about playing basketball, baseball, and soccer, but we do not talk about playing diving, swimming, or mountaineering. Is this just a linguistic anomaly or should some activities be considered play while others are not? And how does this distinction relate to sport? To understand **play** it is helpful to consider necessary and sufficient conditions. Once again, philosophers have suggested a number of such conditions. Huizinga (1950) was one of the first theorists to elaborate on the conditions of play: "First and foremost ... all play is voluntary" (p.7). The condition of voluntariness answers the question posed at the end of the preceding section. If the "short people chase the tall people through tunnels" activity is to be considered play, the tall people would have to voluntarily participate in the activity. Huizinga makes a distinction between children and adults regarding play: "[Children and animals] must play because their instinct drives them to it and because it serves to develop their bodily faculties and their powers of selection.... [F]or the adult and responsible human being play is a function which he could equally well leave alone" (pp.7-8). Thus, adults choose whether to play or not.

A second characteristic of play that Huizinga illuminates is that play is "a stepping out of 'real' life into a temporary sphere of activity with a disposition all of its own.... Not being 'ordinary' life it stands outside the immediate satisfaction of wants and appetites, indeed it interrupts the appetitive process" (pp.8, 9). Being set apart from the necessary appetites of daily life does not mean that play is not serious. As Huizinga points out, "the consciousness of play being 'only pretend' does not by any means prevent it from an absorption, a devotion that passes into rapture and, temporarily at least, completely abolishes that troublesome 'only' feeling" (p.8). Being set apart from the necessary appetites of daily life can also be understood as being set apart from all of the instrumental activities we must perform in our daily lives, such as working to feed, clothe, and shelter ourselves. Suits (1977) proposes that all instances of play are instances of autotelic activity; that is, activity valued for itself. Meier (1988) views play "simply and profitably, as an autotelic activity; in other words, an activity voluntarily pursued for predominately intrinsic reasons" (p.25).

Huizinga's third condition of play is related to the second condition of play as a temporary sphere of activity; that is, play occurs within certain limits of time and place. Regarding limits of time, play begins, and then at a certain point, it ends. "Once played, it endures as a new-found creation of the mind, a treasure to be retained by the memory. It is transmitted, it becomes tradition. It can be repeated at any time, whether it be 'child's play' or a game of chess, or at fixed intervals like a mystery" (pp.9-10). Regarding limits of space, all play occurs within a "play-ground." "The arena, the card-table, the magic circle, the temple, the stage, the screen, the tennis court, the court of justice, etc., are all in form and function play-grounds, i.e., forbidden spots, isolated, hedged round, hallowed, within which certain rules obtain" (p.10).

Within these "play-grounds," the most obvious feature of play occurs, the following of rules. "All play has its rules. They determine what 'holds' in the temporary world circumscribed by play" (Huizinga 1950, 11). Huizinga illuminates the significance of the play rules when he points out that ignoring the rules is more serious than breaking the rules.

> The player who trespasses against the rules or ignores them is a 'spoil-sport'. The spoil-sport is not the same as the false player, the cheat; for the latter pretends to be playing the game and, on the face of it, still acknowledges the magic circle. It is curious to note how much more lenient society is to the cheat than to the spoil-sport. This is because the spoil-sport shatters the play-world itself. (p.11)

According to Huizinga, the conditions for something to be considered play include voluntariness on the part of the participants, an activity "outside" normal life with time and place limitations, and the following of rules.

If we accept these conditions for something to be called "play," how do we connect them with sport? Schmitz (1979) makes an important connection when he suggests that

> sport emerges from play as from an original and founding existential posture.... Sport is in its origin and intention a movement into transcendence which carries over from the founding decision to play and which builds upon that decision an intensified thrust towards the values of self-consciousness tested through performance, competition and victory. (p.27)

The notion that sport starts as play would resonate with the "institutional" condition of sport discussed earlier. However, as sport becomes more organized, developing a history with legislated rules, it is possible that its "play" nature could disappear. Schmitz (1979) proposes three abuses that can kill the spirit of play within sport. The first abuse involves an exaggeration of the importance of victory. "The policy of winning at all costs is the surest way of snuffing out the spirit of play in sport" (p.27). The second abuse occurs when coaches push their athletes too hard. "An abstract tyranny of the possible may drive players beyond what they should be asked to give, compelling them to spend what they neither have nor can afford. Driven beyond their natural capacities, they lose the spirit of play" (p.27). The third abuse that Schmitz suggests will kill the spirit of play within sport results from the presence of spectators and the exploitation of commercial possibilities. Although the spectators may attend commercial games in the spirit of play, the players are under contract "to play." Being under contract does not necessarily kill the play spirit, but it entails motives that are in many ways antithetical to play.

> Values that lie outside the play-world include agreement to deliver services for wages earned, abiding by a contract because of fear of being sued, playing out games in order not to be barred from further league participation, finishing out a sports career in order to achieve social and economic standing upon ceasing to play. These motives are not unworthy; they are simply not motives of play. (p.29)

Although sports originated in play, one does not have to look far to see how the spirit of play has disappeared in many sporting experiences. The spirit of play seems to be something beyond voluntarily following rules in an activity "outside" normal life. Hyland (1980) seems to be referring to something like a "play spirit" when he characterizes "the stance of play" as

> a certain orientation toward those with whom we play, toward our play equipment if there be such, toward time, space, indeed toward the world, which is distinctive. It is a mode of comportment towards things, a mode of being-in-the-world which, although not utterly peculiar, is nevertheless different from our mode of comportment when we consider ourselves not to be playing. (p.88)

This "stance of play" has similarities to a "leisure mindset." This mindset will be discussed in the section examining the concept of recreation.

Games

Throughout the previous two sections, reference has been made to sport and/or play experiences. However, these "experiences" can be further distinguished. In discussing varieties of play, Schmitz (1979) proposes four general varieties: "frolic, make-believe, sporting skills and games" (p.23). In making a distinction between "sporting skills and games," Schmitz is using the term *sporting skills* to refer to activities such as sailing, horse-back riding, mountain climbing, and so on, and the term *games* to refer to, for example, baseball or card-playing. What is it that makes something a **game** as opposed to "sporting skills play"? Fortunately, philosophers have tackled this question.

Suits (1978) proposes that "the elements of game are: (1) the goal, (2) the means of achieving the goal, (3) the rules, and (4) the lusory attitude" (p.36). Regarding the goal, Suits note that there are three distinguishable goals involved in playing games. He gives the example of someone running a race. The goal of the runner might be to (1) participate in a race, (2) win the race, and (3) cross the finish line ahead of the other contestants. Winning the race should not be confused with crossing the line ahead of the other contestants since the runner could cross the finish line unfairly, by cutting across the infield. Participating in the race is not the same as winning or crossing the finish line ahead of the other contestants since a runner can participate in a race but not finish first. Suits points out that the most elemental goal is crossing the finish line ahead of the other contestants since the other goals require additional elements. Suits describes this kind of goal as "a specific achievable state of affairs ... the *prelusory* goal of a game" (pp.36, 37). He distinguishes between prelusory goals (goals described prior to, or independently of, any particular game) as opposed to lusory goals (goals such as winning, which can be described only in terms of a particular game) or goals such as participating in a game (since this goal is not really the goal of a game but more of a lusory goal of life).

Distinctions can also be made regarding the means of achieving the goal of game playing–this time, between lusory and illusory means. Suits gives the example of a boxing match, where the prelusory goal is to have your opponent "down" for the count of ten. An illusory means would involve shooting your opponent as opposed to the more legitimate lusory means involving the following of the rules of the game.

The rules of the game are also of two kinds–one associated with prelusory goals and the other with lusory goals. The rules of a game are proscriptions of means useful in achieving prelusory goals. Suits cites the race example again and suggests that it is useful but proscribed to trip a competitor in a running race. Rules such as not tripping opponents in a running race can be referred to as constitutive rules since, as Suits points out, these rules along with the prelusory goal constitute all of the conditions for playing the game. The other kinds of rules (those associated with lusory goals) are referred to by Suits as rules of skill, for example, keeping your eye on the ball or refraining from trumping your partner's ace. To break a rule of skill usually results in failing to play the game well as opposed to breaking a constitutive rule that results in failing to play the game at all. Regarding constitutive rules, Suits makes the important point that these rules are rules that prohibit use of the most efficient means for achieving the prelusory goal. For example, there would be many more efficient ways of achieving the prelusory golf goal of putting the ball in the hole, such as walking to the hole and dropping the ball into it.

The final element of games, according to Suits, is the lusory attitude–"the acceptance of constitutive rules just so the activity made possible by such acceptance can occur" (1978, 40). The lusory attitude is necessary for games to occur, since without it, people would consider using inefficient means to reach a goal to be irrational. Inefficient game means should not be viewed as irrational since games are outside the realm of ordinary life. Games are played for no purpose other than the playing of the game. This notion is similar to Huizinga's characteristic of play as "a stepping out of 'real' life into a temporary sphere of activity with a disposition all of its own" (1950, 8). The relationship between games and play will be examined in a following section, but first we must consider another context in which games are played.

Recreation

Games played in a recreational context include everything from a pickup game of street hockey to a hockey league organized by a community center or local recreation department. To understand how a recreational game of hockey differs from an elite-level or professional game of hockey, we have to clarify what we mean by recreation as well as the related notion of leisure. The term **recreation** comes from the Latin word *recreatio*, which means "refreshes and restores" (Anderson 1995, 24). What a person is typically being restored for when they are "recreating" are work obligations. Kaplan (1960) reiterates this when he writes: "Recreation has been viewed as a period of light and restful activity voluntarily chosen, which restores one for heavy, obligatory activity or work" (p.19). Anderson (1995) suggests that Kaplan's "light and restful activity" seems to have limited meaning in today's Western societies where there has been an increased commitment to individual fitness. Thus, Anderson proposes the term *recreation* for more physical activity and the term *leisure* for more "light and restful activity." Whether we agree that the distinguishing characteristic of recreation versus leisure lies in the degree of "physicalness," there are common aspects to both recreation and leisure that will help clarify their relationship to sport, play, and games.

Leisure (and recreation) has been categorized into at least three basic contexts: "time, activities, or a state of mind" (Meyersohn 1958, 46). Leisure is commonly considered to be time that is discretionary; when we are free to do whatever we choose. Anderson (1995) quotes Veblen, who states that leisure "is the time surplus remaining after the practical necessities of life have been attended to" (Veblen 1899, 40). Anderson (1995) separates time into three segments: existence (the biological things we must do to stay alive, e.g., eating, sleeping); subsistence (the things we do to make a living, e.g., work, go to school); and discretionary time (the time one chooses to do whatever one pleases) (p.15). These categories can, and do, overlap. (Should sleeping in on the weekend be considered existence or discretionary time? What if you get paid for an activity you enjoy doing so much that you would do it even if you did not get paid for doing it? What if discretionary time is forced upon someone, such as mandatory retirement?) The possibility of overlapping "times" requires that the leisure-time relationship be flexible within individual circumstances (p.16).

Categorizing leisure as "activity" also requires flexibility. As Anderson (1995) notes, "any given sport, or a variation of it, could be pursued as a leisure activity. However, there is a persistent generalization that leisure activities are normally less physical and structured than a similar activity in a physical recreation setting" (p.16). Thus, Anderson reiterates the distinction between recreation and leisure based on the "physicalness" of the activity. The common element between choosing a more passive activity or a more physical activity is the notion of an activity freely chosen during one's discretionary time. Dumazedier (1967) brings these notions together: "Leisure is activity–apart from the obligation of work, family and society–to which the individual turns at will, for either relaxation, diversion or broadening his knowledge and his spontaneous social participation, the free exercise of his creative capacity" (pp.16-17).

Recreation and leisure have also been referred to as a state of mind or a state of being "wherein activity is performed for its own sake and occupies a period of time in which an individual can experience significant positive spiritual or emotional feeling" (Anderson 1995, 18). Anderson gives the examples of the outdoor recreationalist experiencing a "oneness" with nature or the climber reaching the top of the hill to view the world below. He cites de Grazia as stating that leisure is "an ideal, a state of being, a condition of man, which few desire and fewer achieve" (de Grazia 1962, 5). Related to the notion of recreation and leisure being a state of mind is the "stance of play" discussed earlier. Recall Hyland's (1980) conception of the play stance as "a mode of comportment towards things, a mode of being-in-the-world which, although not utterly peculiar, is nevertheless different from our mode of comportment when we consider ourselves not to be playing" (p.88). Thus, recreation and leisure are related to play in the sense that they are distinct from our non-recreational "mode of comportment," that is, one's attitude or state of mind is different in a recreational context than in a work, or an elite-level or professional sport, context.

Physical Education

Having considered the concepts of sport, play, games, and recreation, it would be fruitful to examine how physical education relates to these other concepts. However, we first have to be clear on what we mean by **physical education**. Arnold (1991) utilizes a three-dimensional model in describing the movement involved in physical education: (1) education *in* movement, (2) education *about* movement, and (3) education *through* movement.

Education *in* movement refers to the practical knowledge that it is possible to acquire in physical education programs. For an activity to be considered educational, it should have something to do with the acquisition of knowledge. Much of the educational curriculum is concerned with "knowing that," for example, knowing that the earth is composed of tectonic plates, that two is the square root of four, that mixing blue and yellow colors results in green, and so on. Physical education programs offer an opportunity for students to acquire practical knowledge; that is, "knowing how," for example, knowing how to kick a ball, swing a bat, express themselves through dance movements, and so on. Physical education is unique in the educational curriculum in that its primary focus is the acquisition of practical knowledge.

Education *about* movement would involve the teaching and learning of theoretical and factual knowledge pertaining to the discipline of physical education. Munrow (1972) divides this knowledge into three categories: (1) knowledge and understanding directly relevant to the specific skills or activities being taught, (2) knowledge and understanding of how the body works, and (3) knowledge in related fields. Knowledge and understanding directly relevant to the specific skills or activities being taught would include not only the knowledge and understanding of skill technique but also, as Vanderzwaag (1972) points out, knowledge and understanding of the rules, etiquette, strategy, terminology and jargon, and the equipment and facilities necessary to partake in a given activity. The knowledge and understanding of how the body works would include:

> knowledge of procedures in the prevention and care of injuries; knowledge of the effects of exercise on the body; knowledge of mechanical principles in the performance of skills; knowledge of relevant anatomic structure and function of body systems; knowledge about methods to develop fitness and the benefits of fitness. (Martens 1986, 94)

Regarding knowledge in related fields, Zeigler and McCristal (1967) organized the academic content of physical education into six specific areas: (1) exercise physiology; (2) biomechanics; (3) motor learning and sports psychology; (4) sociology of sport education; (5) history, philosophy, and comparative physical education and sport; and (6) administrative theory. Whether this is an appropriate organizational scheme is not the issue here. Rather, we are concerned with the content of the body of knowledge of physical education. What is evident is the large body of theoretical knowledge that incorporates knowledge from related fields into the discipline of physical education.

Turning now to an examination of education *through* movement, it is important to recognize that when education occurs through movement as opposed to in movement, we are speaking of movement being used in an instrumental sense. That is, participation in movement activities is being undertaken to further purposes other than the acquisition of practical knowledge. Using movement to achieve fitness is an example of education through movement. Other examples of the instrumental value of movement would include the use of movement to contribute to the development of: self-knowledge, self-esteem and personhood, social education, health education, environmental education, moral education, and aesthetic education. As Meakin (1990) points out, "[c]entral to being a person is that one has a body. It seems reasonable therefore to claim that PE [physical education] can contribute saliently to the development of personhood by assisting pupils to develop physically" (p.115). Regarding moral education through physical education, Meakin emphasizes the moral values built into many competitive game rules: "That this is so can be illustrated by concrete examples of rules designed to promote fair play, consideration for others and more generally respect for persons" (p.118). Environmental education can be enhanced through outdoor pursuits such as hiking, canoeing, camping, skiing, and so forth. Aesthetic education can be enhanced through the appreciation of what Best (1978) refers to as aesthetic sports, such as gymnastics, diving, and figure skating. Thus, there are aspects of many physical education activities that have the potential to further other curricular purposes.

The Relationship between Sport, Play, Games, Recreation, and Physical Education

In the section examining the concept of play, it was suggested that play is the origin of sport. If one considers the conditions of play proposed by Huizinga, that is, voluntariness on the part of the participants, an activity "outside" normal life with time and place limitations, and the following of rules, one can see how these conditions are necessary but not sufficient for something to be considered a sport. As well as voluntarily following certain rules in an activity "outside" normal life, a sport must also involve gross physical skills in a competitive context, a context that has become institutionalized to a certain degree. Thus, not all play occurrences would be considered sport and, as discussed in the section on play, not all sport experiences occur within a spirit or "stance of play."

Regarding the relationship between play, sport, and games, it would appear that not all play or sport involves games, and not all games should be considered sport or even play. Philosophers have used various schematic aids to clarify the relationship between play, sport, and games. Vanderzwaag (1972, 72) presents the relationship along a continuum:

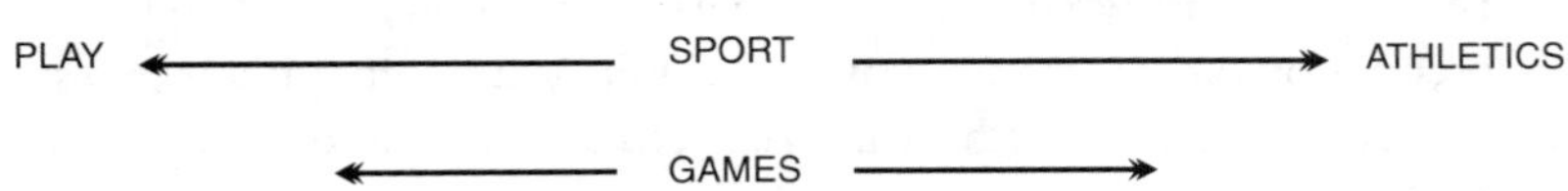

Vanderzwaag views sport as a more advanced form of play and athletics as a more organized and structured form of sport. The concept of games does not fit on the continuum since, according to Vanderzwaag, games are found in play, sport, and athletics.

Suits (1988) proposes a more complicated relationship between play, sport, and games.

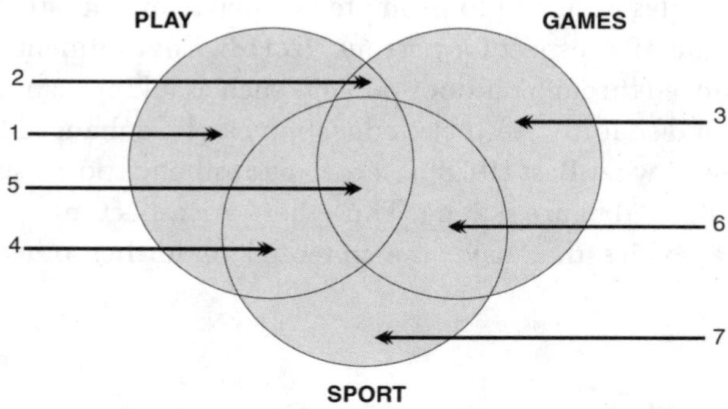

To understand Suits's schema concerning the relationship between sport, play, and games, we have to look at each of the areas in the Venn diagram. Area 1 represents what Suits refers to as primitive play. An example he cites of primitive play is that of a baby playing in a bathtub. When the baby splashes water, he or she is pleased with the consequence and continues to splash. With time, the baby becomes more skilled at water splashing. However, the baby is still involved in primitive play, because the skills learned are not the pay off the baby is seeking. Primitive play "is not concerned primarily with the exercise and enjoyment of skills but with the introduction of new experiences that arise, usually serendipitously" (1988, 2). If the skills learned become valued for their own sake, Suits argues that the activity has moved from primitive play to more sophisticated play.

Area 2, where play and games overlap, is the game instance of sophisticated play, for example, a recreational game of soccer. Area 3 does not overlap with play or sport so activities in this area would include professional non-physical activities such as professional bridge and poker. Area 4, where only play and sport overlap, but not games, would be instances of physical performances. Suits makes a distinction between games (essentially refereed events where "artificial barriers are erected just so they can be overcome by the use of rule-governed skills") and performances (essentially judged events where "there are rules, to be sure, but not only are they *not* the crux of performances, they usually take the form of applying to the participants *outside* the arena of contention") (p.5). Examples of physical performances would include diving and gymnastics.

Area 5 is the area where play, games, and sport overlap. Examples of activities in this area would be amateur games such as university-level volleyball. Area 6 includes the overlap of sport and games, and this is where we find professional sports such as those of the National Hockey League. Area 7, the area of sports that are neither games nor play, would include professional physical performances, such as professional figure skating.

Suits's schematic representation of the relationship between sport, play, and games has been criticized by Meier (1988) who proposes the following relationship:

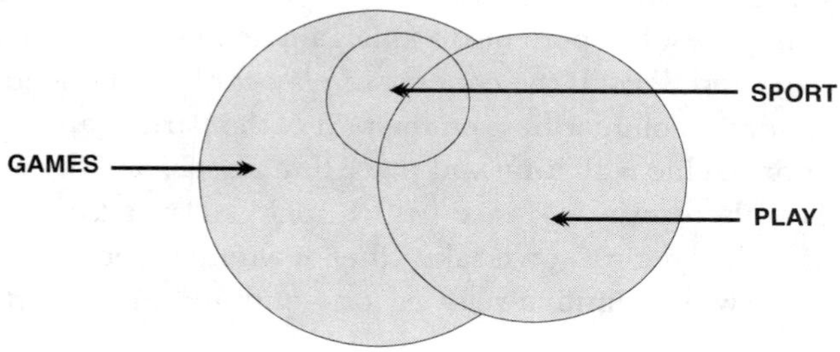

Meier agrees with Suits's suggestion that sports and games may or may not be considered instances of play. However, Meier departs from Suits's scheme in that Meier considers all sports to be games. He disagrees with Suits's distinction between games (essentially refereed events where "artificial barriers are erected just so they can be overcome by the use of rule-governed skills") and performances (essentially judged events where "there are rules, to be sure, but not only are they *not* the crux of performances, they usually take the form of applying to the participants *outside* the arena of contention") (Suits 1988, 5). Meier is critical of Suits's suggestion that events such as diving and gymnastics only have rules that apply to the participants *outside* the arena of contention and "once a performance is under way, there are no rules, or scarcely any, that need enforcing" (ibid.). Meier points out that in a gymnastics competition, if a gymnast fails to "stick the landing" and it is noticed by the judges, there will be a specific deduction in points. "Thus it may be contended that athletic performances have event rules of a regulative variety" (Meier 1988, 20).

Meier goes further to suggest that even more convincing than the existence of regulative rules in performance events is the fulfillment of Suits's games condition of the existence of constitutive rules that prohibit use of the most efficient means for achieving the prelusory goal. Meier points out that this condition is fulfilled by Suits's performance events. Meier gives the example of gymnastics where the prelusory goal is to perform an interrelated series of stipulated compulsory moves a specific number of times. "It is readily apparent that achieving the goal of demonstrating the required physical actions would be made considerably easier if the gymnast were to be permitted to perform on the floor, or even if the beam itself were anchored directly to the floor" (p.21). Thus, using Suits's conditions for determining when something should be designated a game, Meier concludes that performance events should be considered games, thus collapsing Suits's distinction between games and performances.

In considering the different representations of the relationship between sport, play, and games, it is possible to amalgamate the schemas proposed by Vanderzwaag and Suits. If the concept of play can be separated into an activity that involves voluntariness on the part of the participants, an activity "outside" normal life with time and place limitations, and the following of rules, with a play spirit or stance (which includes an attitude that the activity is being played for its own sake), then it would be possible to present a continuum with primitive play on one end and elite sport on the other.

PRIMITIVE PLAY	SOPHISTICATED PLAY	RECREATIONAL SPORT	ELITE AND/OR PROFESSIONAL SPORT

Regarding the play spirit or stance, this could appear anywhere along the continuum. The play spirit must accompany primitive play by virtue of the definition of primitive play. However, as soon as skills become valued for something other than the intrinsic pleasure they provide, there is a danger of losing the play spirit.

Games have not been placed on this continuum. Meier's notion that all sports should be considered games can be questioned. Although he gives examples of gymnastics and diving events that have regulative rules during the performance and constitutive rules that result in inefficient means, it seems counterintuitive to consider other activities that we classify as sports as games. For example, the mountain climbing example referred to earlier met the conditions for something to be considered a sport; that is, it involves gross physical skills, there is competition between different climbers, and the activity has been institutionalized (mountain climbing has a history, people climb mountains all over the world, and mountains are graded depending on the difficulty they present). Rather than call an activity that appears to meet the conditions of a sporting activity a game, when doing so seems counterintuitive, the term *game* should be reserved for sports such as basketball, soccer, volleyball, and so on, and the term *contest* (a term Weiss [1969] also uses) for sports such as mountain climbing, sailing, foot racing, and so on. Thus, similar to Vanderzwaag's scheme, games would run parallel to the play-sport continuum.

Physical education has also not been placed on the continuum. If physical education is understood as the teaching of activities geared toward the learning of physical skills, then physical education would run parallel to the continuum, starting at the sophisticated play end. Although athletes involved in elite and professional sports would most likely no longer be involved in physical education, we could consider that coaching sessions involve the teaching of physical skills, albeit at a high level. Thus, the overlapping continuums showing the relationships between sport, play, games, recreation, and physical education would look like the following:

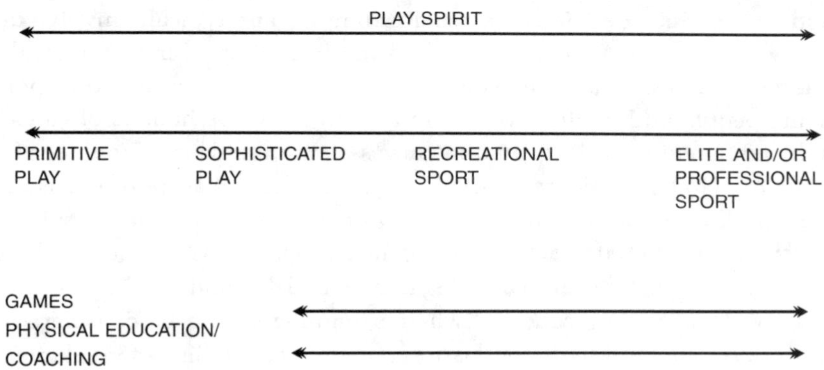

Having analyzed the necessary and sufficient conditions for the concepts of sport, play, games, recreation, and physical education, as well as the relationship between these concepts, we are left with the question: "What have we accomplished as a result of this analysis?"

Why Should We Care?

Before answering *why* we should care when something should be called a sport and when it should be called something else, we might want first to ask *who* should care about clarifying the concepts of sport, play, games, recreation, and physical education. Researchers, administrators, recreation personnel, physical educators, and anyone involved in sport (either as participants or spectators) would benefit from becoming clear on what we mean by sport and related activities. There are two main reasons why those involved in sport (whether the involvement be practical or theoretical) should be interested in the analysis presented in this chapter: (1) conceptual clarity is needed if those involved in sport are to disentangle the moral and social issues that are part of the sporting experience, that is, we need to be clear on what we are talking about if we are to effect change (or if we are to justify what is happening if we are happy with the status quo); and (2) categorizing activities as sport, play, games, recreation, or physical education has important practical implications for people designing programs and/or curricula (e.g., what sort of activities should be included in a recreational sport program as opposed to a physical education class?).

The need for conceptual clarity in disentangling moral and social issues in sport and related activities becomes evident when we consider some examples. First, however, we must clarify what we mean by moral and social issues. **Moral issues** involve decisions having to do with what is right and wrong. Such decisions are usually complex and typically involve the consideration of competing factors. In the beginning of the chapter, the question was asked as to whether hunting should be considered a sport. Some people find hunting to be morally wrong, while hunters obviously hold a different view. By examining necessary and sufficient conditions for something to be considered a sport, it was suggested that sport had its origins in play, and an important condition for something to be considered play was the voluntary participation of the participants. One would be hard pressed to say that the animals being hunted had "volunteered" for such an activity. Thus, a clarification of whether hunting should be considered a sport raises an important moral issue concerning the killing of involuntary participants. A similar example concerning human participants is found in boxing, where the morality of boxing has been questioned based on whether boxers really do make autonomous decisions to box or whether their economic situation leaves them no choice (see Dixon 2001a). Another example of questionable voluntariness on the part of athletes concerns child athletes, that is, whether children are able to make autonomous decisions regarding their sport "career."

When looking at the relationship between sport and play, additional moral issues become evident. Gerber (1972) recognizes one of these issues when she notes that "if professional sport is sport a new frame of reference for the morality of sport should be delineated, which will affect the practice of high-powered collegiate and scholastic sport" (p.14). A contemporary example of the need to distinguish between professional sports (which no longer exhibit the autotelic nature of play) and elite sport (which seeks excellence in the internal rather than external goods of the game) is the taking of performance-enhancing substances. Although the taking of drugs is widespread in professional leagues, drugs bans are severely enforced in elite sport competitions such as the Olympics. A conflict arises when professional athletes compete in elite sport competitions. Either distinct frames of references have to be upheld, or the banning of substances in elite sport has to be re-evaluated. Either way, clarifying distinctions between professional and elite sport requires a rethinking of the moral issues involved in the taking of performance-enhancing substances.

As well as moral issues, social issues become evident when concepts such as sport, play, games, recreation, and physical education are clarified. Social issues are not always moral issues (although some social issues do involve moral considerations). **Social issues** involve decisions having to do with social priorities, for example, the social status and prestige of certain activities. Gerber (1972) cites the example of "Red Auerbach who expressed shock at the selection of Arnold Palmer as the most outstanding athlete of the '60's, commenting that golf is a game, not a sport" (p.14). The relegation of activities to a "game" category as opposed to a "sport" category creates social divisions in a number of contexts. People who compete in games in a recreational context are not given the same recognition as athletes competing in elite sport (even though the recreational athletes may be competing for respectable reasons, such as fitness-related or social-related reasons). Along with recognition, certain categories of sport, such as those at an elite level, are typically given more funding than sport played at a recreational level. Also, certain activities that have not met the conditions to be considered a "sport" by sport-governing agencies suffer from lack of funding. These examples lead us to the second reason for justifying the conceptual analysis of sport and its related activities; that is, the categorizing of activities as sport, play, games, recreation, or physical education has important practical implications for people designing, funding, and implementing programs and/or curricula.

Whether it be the granting of money by sport-governing agencies, or the designing and implementing of recreation programs or physical education curricula, the classification of an activity as a sport has important practical applications. As Gerber (1972) points out, "karate, yoga and flycasting are among activities frequently excluded from school programs because they are not considered sport in the manner of basketball and tennis" (p.14). However, these activities are included in recreational programs because recreation programs typically encompass activities that fall outside a strictly "sport" category. Whether this distinction between recreation programs and physical education programs is a good distinction leads us into questions of the differing value of sports, play, games, recreation, and physical education. These questions will be examined in the following chapter. It is hoped that the preceding conceptual analysis might encourage researchers and practitioners to clarify what they mean when they speak of sport, play, games, recreation, and physical education and then to take the next step in clarifying the value of these activities.

Conclusion

A number of questions were asked at the beginning of the chapter, such as whether hunting, car racing, mountain climbing, bowling, or chess were sports. By looking at the necessary and sufficient conditions for sport, we are in a better position to answer these questions. For an activity to be considered a sport, the suggestion was made that the activity should include: gross physical skills, competition, and institutional aspects; that is, rules, history, and a wide geographical base. Chess and car racing would not appear to have the gross physical skills required by a "sport" activity. Although bowling is not as physical as basketball, it is more physical than chess and car racing. Regarding the condition of competition, it was noted that *com-petitio* (the root word of competition) means "to strive together." Although philosophers have questioned whether a person "strives together" with an inanimate object such as a mountain or a river, one could consider the "striving together" to take place between other mountain climbers or river rafters. Regarding the question of whether hunting is a sport, it is important to consider the "play" origin of sport and the voluntary nature of play.

The questionable nature of perceiving hunting as a sport ushers in the moral issues that become evident when attempting to clarify the concept of sport (and the related concepts of play, games, recreation, and physical education). Other moral issues that arise in this clarification involve the different expectations of different levels of sport; that is, professional versus elite, the taking of performance-enhancing substances, or the issue of autonomy when child athletes make decisions regarding their "careers." Social issues also arise in the process of clarifying the relationship between the concepts of sport, games, recreation, and physical education. For example, is professional or elite sport a higher priority than recreational sport and should it therefore receive more public funds, and so on. Recognizing and addressing the moral and social issues that arise when examining the concepts of sport, play, games, recreation, and physical education helps to answer the questions of "when is something a sport and why we should care."

CHAPTER REVIEW

Key Concepts

- necessary and sufficient conditions for sport
- gross physical skills
- competition
- institutional condition
- play
- games
- recreation
- physical education
- moral and social issues

Review Questions

1. What does it mean to specify the necessary and sufficient conditions of a concept? Give an example.
2. What are the necessary and sufficient conditions for something to be called a sport?
3. What are the necessary and sufficient conditions for something to be called play?
4. Describe the elements of a game as proposed by Suits.
5. Explain how leisure can be described as time, an activity, or a state of mind.
6. Explain how physical education involves education *in* movement, *about* movement, and *through* movement.
7. Reproduce the schematic representation of the relationship between play, sport, and games as proposed by Vanderzwaag, Suits, Meier, and this text.
8. What are some of the moral and social issues that can be disentangled by clarifying the concepts of sport, play, games, recreation, and physical education?

2

Why Sport, and What Role Should It Play in Society?

Permian got the ball back at its own 26 with 2:55 left in the game, but instead of confidence in the huddle there was fear. Chavez could see it in the eyes of the offensive linemen. He tapped them on the helmet and said, "Com'on, let's get it, this is it." But he could tell they weren't listening. The game was slipping away. They were going to lose. They were goddamn going to lose and everything they had worked for for the past six years of their lives, everything they cared about, was about to be ruined.... The loss to Lee sent Odessa into a tailspin, so unthinkable, so catastrophic was it. As in a civil war, goodwill and love disintegrated and members of the town turned on each other. ... When [the coach] went home late that night, several FOR SALE signs had been punched into his lawn, a not-so-subtle hint that maybe it would be best for everyone if he just got the hell out of town. He took them and dumped them in the garage along with the other ones he had already collected. He wasn't surprised by them. (Bissinger 1990, 18-19, 20)

The preceding quote, based on Bissinger's experience of the trials and triumphs of a local high-school football team, is an apt illustration of the seriousness Americans grant to their sporting experiences (both as players and spectators). The fact that Americans spend almost $100 billion a year on sports (Andre and James 1991, ix) is another indication of the value sport has in American society. A daily reminder of the prevalence of sports occurs every time North Americans open a newspaper. For many North Americans (particularly males [ibid., 7]), the first section read is the sports section. The amount of money and time dedicated to sports is evidence that Americans place great value on sports. But is this value justified? Does sport deserve this degree of attention? If sport does offer important goods, is sport the only means by which these goods can be achieved? If the goods offered through involvement in sports can be achieved only through sport, the question still remains as to whether the achievement of these goods is worth the price of some of the negative aspects that accompany sport. The answers to these questions will determine the role sport should justifiably play in our society. The key concepts utilized in answering these questions will include: **intrinsic** and **instrumental values, physical competence, human bonding, respecting rules, aesthetic value, personal expression, physical** and **emotional tenderness, discipline** and **dedication, concern for**

excellence, risk taking, cognitive complexity, sensuous and **transcendental experiences, outlet for aggression** and **surplus energy, fitness, stimulating form of recreation, recreational sport, spectator sport, intercollegiate sport, elite sport,** and **professional sport**.

The Connection between Meaning and Value

Chapter 1 involved an exploration of the conceptual terrain concerning sport, play, games, recreation, and physical education. For something to be considered a sport, the activity should involve gross physical skills in some sort of competition involving certain rules. To be considered a sport rather than sophisticated play, the activity should be institutionalized (to some degree); that is, it should have a history and be played in many locations around the world. A starting point for examining the value of sport would involve identifying the goods available through each of the conditions necessary for something to be considered a sport. At this point, it is fruitful to distinguish between values that are intrinsic and values that are instrumental. Values that are **intrinsic** to sport are logically connected to sport. Intrinsic values are connected to the very meaning of sport. Values that are **instrumental** to sport are values that are not logically tied to sport but can be consequences of participating in sport.

For example, the condition of sport involving gross physical skills could be deemed valuable because of the physical competence that can be developed through participation in sport. By **physical competence** we mean the ability to use one's body in a competent manner. From the person involved in recreational sport to the elite athlete, participation in sport can help develop physical competency. Andre and James (1991) appear to include the spectator in their exultation of the physical competence value: "One fundamental good in sport, then, is its pursuit and development of bodily competence, which is to say, human competence. At its richest, this bodily excellence includes an aesthetic and intellectual appreciation of sport, of its history, its cultural structure, perhaps its philosophy and literature" (p.5). Thus, one's physical competence and appreciation thereof can be developed by participating in, as well as watching, a variety of different levels of sport. When spectators watch competent athletes, they can develop an appreciation for the physical competence attainable by humankind.

The competitive condition of sport furthers the value of the development of physical competency in that competing with others motivates athletes to push themselves in their development of the physical skills required in their sport. (In Chapter 3 we will examine the root word of competition, *com-petitio*–to strive together–in an attempt to understand how competition helps athletes in their pursuit of excellence.) Competitors help motivate athletes, for if the competitors are more skilled than the athletes, they provide ideals for the athletes to strive for. The key here is that athletes "strive together" in their pursuit of excellence. This striving together requires co-operation and as Andre and James (1991) point out, "sports are essentially cooperative, and human bonding is intrinsically good" (p.5). By **human bonding**, we are referring to the bringing together of humankind, resulting in the recognition of our shared humanity.

The good of human bonding can also be evidenced in the institutional condition of sport. The fact that sport has a history and is played in locations around the world could result in a bonding experience for large numbers of people. "Even televised sport lets people feel, for a time, drawn out of themselves and connected with others. The United States, a nation of immigrants and subcultures, unites to watch the Super Bowl. If we share no other topics of conversation, we can at least talk about last night's game" (Andre and James 1991, 6). The condition of sport requiring rules would not appear to be an intrinsic good. But as Andre and James (1991) point out, **respecting the rules** is an essential means to the intrinsic goods of physical competence and human co-operation, so obeying the rules is at least instrumentally good (ibid.). Additional goods, both intrinsic and instrumental to sport, have been proposed by other theorists.

Other Values Proposed by Theorists

Hatab (1991) agrees with the value of physical competence as intrinsic to sport, but he also adds aesthetic value:

> The aesthetics of the human form and physical motion is often among the finer levels of appreciation in athletic events.... But, more importantly, athletics is a theatrical metaphor for the drama of human pursuits, struggles, and achievements in the lived world. Accordingly, it expresses certain meanings and truths about human existence. (p.38)

The notion that sport has aesthetic value is reiterated by many sport philosophers. In referring to sport as **aesthetic**, philosophers are noting the form and beauty observed in sport, as well as the expressive nature of sport. Kupfer (1991) refers to the "drama" of sport: "Among its more subtle aesthetic charms, sport offers the spectator its own brand of drama. Its drama emerges from human confrontation.... The drama of sport emerges from the story-like dimensions it shares with such narrative arts as novels, plays, and films" (p.109). Kretchmar (1994) reiterates the expression of "meanings and truths about human existence" when he refers to games as "wellsprings of meaning and stories" (p.216). (The aesthetic value of sport will be examined in more detail in Chapter 12.)

Whitaker (1991) proposes a number of values found in sport, including drama, competence, limitation, and co-operation (which have already been discussed). She also suggests the additional values of personal expression, physical and emotional tenderness, risk taking, cognitive complexity, sensuousness, and transcendental experience. By **personal expression**, we are referring to how we express ourselves as individuals. Whitaker posits that sport "provides us with the opportunity to express sides of our personality that we have little chance to reveal elsewhere" (p.82). She cites as examples: our instrumentalism, our physicalness, our competitiveness, and our adventurousness. Whitaker also suggests that "sport provides us with a chance to be different, to express our individuality by placing the personal stamp of our own style on our activities.... Our uniqueness is expressed in our choice of sport [and also] in our style of play" (p.83).

The value of **physical tenderness** that Whitaker attributes to sport is exhibited in the delicate skills necessary for success in many sports, for example, the putt in golf and the bunt in baseball. Regarding **emotional tenderness**, Whitaker (1991) notes the camaraderie among teammates and opponents: "Mutual encouragement, shared victories, consolations in defeat, and comfort in injury are all features of the compassionate side of sport" (p.83). Cohen (1991) also extols the compassionate side of sport and goes so far as to say that this capacity of sport has its source in the capacity that makes morality possible:

> When the pure condition happens–if ever it does, in morality or in sports appreciation–a person succeeds in attaching himself to a team in such a way that its success brings him pleasure and its failure is a source of pain, and these feelings are not mediated by any vested interest. This is a marvelous achievement. Think of what it means that a person is able to do this. It means that one of us can be moved by good or bad fortunes that is not our own. (p. 131)

The suggestion that sport has moral values that can affect prevailing societal values is also put forward by Simon (1991). Simon cites the values of discipline, dedication, respect for rules, and concern for excellence as being central to sport. **Discipline** and **dedication** refer to the commitment required to perform well in a given sport. The athlete's **concern for excellence** is the reason he or she commits him or herself to the training and practice routines necessary to do well in a particular sport. Goods that are so intimately connected with sport that they cannot be understood independently of the activity are referred to by Simon as internal goods or values. "For example, the value of being a skilled playmaker cannot even be understood without some understanding of the constitutive rules of basketball and appreciation of the strategies and nuances of the game" (p.190). Weiss (1969) also elucidates the value of excellence internal to sport.

"Young men [and women] are attracted by athletics because it offers them the most promising means for becoming excellent" (p.17). (The pursuit of excellence in sport will be examined in more detail in the section "The Role Sport *Should* Play in Society," below.)

Whitaker (1991) suggests that **risk taking** is the reason some people become involved in sport. As well as obvious high-risk sports, for example, mountain climbing, sky diving, and ski jumping, she suggests that most sports have some degree of physical, strategic, and emotional risk–physically, a softball batter risks being hit by a pitch; strategically, rushing the net in tennis is risky; and emotionally, all sport participants risk the embarrassment of a poor performance (p.83). Some people need the challenge of risks, be they as serious as putting one's life on the line or the less serious risk of failure to perform in front of spectators and/or competitors, to give them the adrenaline rush they desire.

Cognitive complexity is another value Whitaker elucidates, although she focuses only on strategy in her reference to the cognitive values connected with sport. However, sport offers *many* opportunities for the development of cognitive involvement. There is the possibility of acquiring practical as well as theoretical knowledge regarding sport, as well as many opportunities for athletes to develop critical thinking skills (Bergmann Drewe 1999; Bergmann Drewe and Daniel 1998). Critical thinking plays an important role in learning specific sport skills.

> For example, learning to serve a tennis ball requires the learner to be able to analyze the movements involved, compare and/or contrast his or her performance attempts with a model, sequence movements appropriately (swing the racket with the toss of the ball), predict where the ball will land in the opponent's court, decide if the serve was successful, and evaluate the effectiveness of the trial in preparation for future attempts (Schwager and Labate 1993, 25).

Critical thinking is necessary not only for learning sport skills but also for using these skills in a game situation.

> [I]n a sport such as soccer wherein the contextual circumstances involve a moving ball as well as a dispositional fluidity of players, skillfulness, at the highest level, is not so much recognized by the ability to trap, dribble, head, and lay-off the ball competently, though these skills remain important, as by an ability to utilize these acquired learnings intelligently as the game is being played. These separately acquired skills will only be of use if they serve in the development and promotion of tactical procedures and dynamic strategies. (Arnold 1988, 122)

The final two values Whitaker (1991) posits are sensuousness and transcendental experiences. By **sensuousness** we are referring to the utilization of the senses. Whitaker refers to "the visual poetry of a well-turned double play, the sound of a tennis ball on the 'sweet spot' of a racket, the smell of a good leather fielder's mitt, [etc.]" (p.85). An acute sensuous awareness is also involved in the **transcendental experiences** possible through sport. These experiences have also been referred to as "being in the zone" or "peak or flow experiences" (Csikszentmihalyi 1975, 36). Whitaker describes these experiences as "frequently characterized by feelings of total control or invincibility, of floating, of time slowing, of otherworldliness, or of supernatural ability to influence external objects and events. The sport world seems somehow to engender such transcendental experiences" (p.85).

Another sport philosopher who examines and critiques a number of potential values available through sport is Vanderzwaag (1972). He asks why people are attracted to sport (which is, in essence, asking what people perceive to be the values of sport). He proposes a number of reasons, many of which have already been discussed. Two additional reasons examined by Vanderzwaag are the potential for sport to be an **outlet for aggression** as well as **surplus energy**. Some people feel that sport provides a context where players can legitimately act aggressively. Sport has also been viewed as a context where players (often children) can let off surplus energy. Vanderzwaag also considers the supposed physical values attributed to participation in sport (this would include the value of **fitness** as well as the physical competence value discussed earlier). A final reason Vanderzwaag proposes (and the one he suggests is the most convincing) is that sport is valued as a **stimulating form of recreation**. (This reason will be examined in more detail in the section "The Role Sport *Should* Play in Society," below.)

Are These Values Unique, and Are They Worth the Price?

What are we to make of the numerous values attributed to sport? The majority of these values are not unique to sport but can be achieved just as easily (and in some cases, more easily) through other activities. To summarize, the values explicated thus far include: physical competence, human bonding (through *com-petitio* and the sharing of the institution of sport), respecting of rules, aesthetic and personal expression, physical and emotional tenderness, risk taking, cognitive complexity, sensuousness and transcendental experience, discipline and dedication, concern for excellence, outlets for aggression and surplus energy, fitness, and a stimulating form of recreation.

As mentioned previously, it is important to distinguish between values that are *intrinsic* (or as Simon [1991] refers to them, internal) and values that are *instrumental.* The only values listed that should be considered intrinsic or internal to sport would be physical competence, human bonding through *com-petitio*, and concern for excellence of particular sports. These values are logically connected to sport. If a defining condition of sport is the use of physical skills, then an internal value of sport would be achieving competency in these skills. If another defining condition of sport is competition, and we accept the root of *com-petitio* as "striving together," then competition by definition involves the human bonding found in co-operative endeavors. By concern for excellence of particular sports, we mean achieving excellence in the use of the particular skills following the constitutive rules to meet the particular goals of the particular sport in question. The intrinsic values of physical competence, human bonding through *com-petitio*, and concern for excellence of particular sports can only be achieved through participation in sport. However, whether these values are worth the price of some of the negative aspects that accompany sport will be examined in the following section.

The remaining values are instrumental; that is, they are values that are not logically tied to sport but can be consequences of participating in sport. For example, the human bonding that can result from sharing the institution of sport can also result through the sharing of other human activities. Andre and James (1991) give examples of alternative shared experiences: "Soap operas and jingoism have given Americans shared experiences and conversational topics, some of which this country would have been better off without" (p.7). It should not be assumed that sport is "above" the experiences "this country would have been better off without." It must be argued that the values of sport are worth the negative aspects that accompany sport.

Respecting rules is also an instrumental value. Although some philosophers have argued that, if you are not obeying the rules of a game, you are not actually playing the game (Wigmore and Tuxill 1995), it seems perfectly intuitive to speak of cheating while still playing the game (Leaman 1995). Although obeying the rules is important for playing sports, it must be asked if this aspect of sport is significant enough to merit the attention society grants to sport. There are many other human endeavors that require the respecting of rules, for example, functioning in a classroom, driving one's car, paying one's income tax, and so on, and these experiences may have fewer negative aspects than participation in sport.

Regarding the aesthetic value that a number of philosophers (and others involved in sport) attribute to sport, it is worth pointing out the *contrasts* as well as the commonalities between aesthetic experiences and sports experiences. Although sport can have a focus on the beautiful, this focus should be recognized as a focus on the form of the sport. A focus on the form does not necessarily make an experience an aesthetic experience. Abbs (1989b) refers to the aesthetic as "sensuous understanding," and if we are to perceive of "understanding" as a condition for an aesthetic experience, we must ask what is understood when one observes a particular form in a sport. Any understanding is purely a byproduct of the main focus that includes the skill, strategy, and so on of the game. For example, a football game involves a large degree of tension between the players of the opposing teams. However, we should not infer from this tension "theme" that, through a football game, we will come to a better understanding of the notion of tension in our world. This is not the purpose of football. However, this would be the purpose of a modern dance portrayal of the tension in a football game. This distinction is critical in making sense of the supposedly aesthetic value in sport. One is more likely to achieve the enriched understanding possible through aesthetic experience by engaging in activities whose purpose (as opposed to a byproduct) is the experience of "sensuous understanding."

Art can be a medium for aesthetic understanding as well as personal expression. Whitaker (1991) suggests that sport can also be a medium for personal expression. She proposes that sports provide the opportunity to "express sides of our personality that we have little chance to reveal elsewhere. A clear example is our instrumentalism" (p.82). Although Whitaker suggests that sport's "instrumentality need not be carried to exploitative extremes" (ibid.), it must be questioned whether the risk of instrumentality becoming exploitative is worth the opportunity of expressing one's instrumentalism. The other point Whitaker makes about personal expression through sport is that sport allows us to express our individuality through our choice of sport as well as in our style of play. However, it can be asked whether the potential for individualism is outweighed by the pressure to join particular sports to be with one's friends and to show loyalty to the team, whether this includes wearing the team jacket or getting into fights in order to a "protect" one's teammates (e.g., a common occurrence in ice hockey).

Whitaker (1991) also discusses the values of physical and emotional tenderness. Regarding physical tenderness in sport, Whitaker gives the examples of golf putts and baseball bunts. However, these skills are not the norm in sports. Recall that the conditions required for something to be called a sport included gross physical skills. The majority of sport skills are of the gross kind (e.g., golf drives and fairway shots, baseball swings, pitches, runs, and catches). If someone was interested in the value of physical tenderness, there would be far more suitable activities that would provide this value; everything from race-car driving to embroidery.

Regarding emotional tenderness, Whitaker gives the example of camaraderie among teammates and even opponents. For emotional tenderness to take place between opponents, a return to the notion of striving together would have to occur. If opponents do not "strive together," it is questionable whether the emotional tenderness that exists between teammates is worth the animosity that often exists between opponents.

When Whitaker (1991) discusses the value of risk taking in sport, she refers to fairly low-risk examples of physical, strategic, and emotional risk, as well as the high risks found in sports such as mountain climbing and sky diving. The risks involved in high-risk sports are unique to sport but low risks, such as being hit by a wild pitch, rushing the net in tennis, and the embarrassment of a poor performance, can be replicated in many other areas of life, for example, crossing the street, spending all of your money on purchasing Boardwalk in the game of Monopoly, or giving a speech in front of your classmates. Concerning the risks involved in high-risk sports, one must weigh the risk of injury and even death against the high level of arousal that such risk takers seek.

Cognitive complexity is another value attributed to sport. The cognitive aspect of sport includes the development of strategy but also, more fundamentally, the notion of practical knowledge. As discussed in the previous section, sports are an important means for people to develop practical as well as theoretical knowledge. There are, however, other areas where people can develop practical knowledge, for example, conducting scientific experiments or creating a work of art. The uniqueness of sport as opposed to science or art is that sport, by its nature, requires opponents (even if these be historic, as in the case of a record one is trying to break). Striving together with one's opponents requires respect for others that is not necessary in some of the other areas in which one develops practical knowledge. The uniqueness of sport in this regard has implications for the role it should play in schools (this will be discussed further in a later section).

The possibility of a transcendental experience (usually involving acute sensuous awareness) through sport should not be denied. However, such transcendental experiences have also been described in other areas of human experience, most notably in spiritual and aesthetic experience. The value of the transcendental experience would have to be weighed against the price one pays to achieve this experience (this would be true in the spiritual and aesthetic realm as well).

Values such as discipline and dedication (as well as a number of other "character building" values) have been espoused as a positive outcome of participating in sport. However, sport is not unique in its capacity to develop such values. People can develop discipline and dedication by immersing themselves in a field of study or in learning a musical instrument. Regarding values such as loyalty and courage (which are frequently referred to when connecting sport with values), an important question to be asked concerns the ends to which such values are employed. As Galvin (1991) points out, "bank robbers frequently exhibit a type of 'courage,' and gang members exhibit a type (albeit twisted) of 'loyalty'" (p.94). The "ends" of virtues such as "loyalty" and "courage" in sport must be explicated rather than simply assumed to be unequivocally valuable.

Sport is frequently touted as an outlet for aggression and surplus energy. However, these values would only apply to a small set of sports. Regarding aggression, it would appear that only contact sports such as football, wrestling, and hockey would provide such an outlet. To be overtly aggressive on a tennis court or golf course would result in missed shots (as well as potential penalties). Concerning the sports where aggressive behavior *is* encouraged, the question still remains as to whether sport is an appropriate outlet for aggressive behavior. It is not a large step to move from aggressive to violent behavior, and one of the ethically questionable aspects of sports such as hockey is the increased level of violence. Perhaps there would be more appropriate ways for people to release their aggression, for example, hitting a boxing bag as opposed to a fellow boxer.

Sport as an outlet for releasing surplus energy is often promoted by parents and teachers. Once again, not all sports would be appropriate for releasing energy. As Vanderzwaag (1972) points outs, "how can handball be compared with bowling as to physical-energy demands?" (p.110). In some sports, releasing energy actually creates problems, for example, golf–"anyone who has played golf recognizes that the game requires much in the way of a blend between concentration and relaxation. The individual who plays golf with surplus energy (of the tension variety) finds that he is immediately frustrated because he can neither concentrate nor relax" (ibid.). Also, depending on the demands of one's sport, there may be no surplus energy to release. As Weiss (1969) notes, "many [athletes] continue to prepare and act, well beyond the point where they have energy to spare. Sometimes they urge themselves beyond the limit of fatigue.... References to their surplus energy do not tell us how or why they make these severe demands on themselves" (pp.22-23). Once again, whether sports is the best way to release surplus energy could be called into question. If people have excess energy, perhaps this energy should be channeled into something that has significant results, for example, picking up litter in the schoolyard, building houses for the homeless, and so on.

The value of physical competence has already been discussed as an intrinsic good of sport. However, the instrumental fitness value of sport is also advocated by many involved in sport, particularly physical educators. Although by definition sports involve gross physical skills, some sports are more "physical" than others, for example, basketball as opposed to bowling, tennis as opposed to golf, and so on. Even if people play sports for their fitness value, that is, choosing more "physical" sports, the fitness value could be achieved more efficiently by simply jogging and lifting weights.

A final value of sport advocated by Vanderzwaag (1972) concerns the capacity of sport to be a stimulating form of recreation. He suggests that the characteristics of sport that people find stimulating are its activity (i.e., "we have a natural desire to move with a purpose in mind" [p.119]); concreteness (i.e., sport facilities and equipment are physically attractive to many people); challenge (i.e., "it is the challenge which makes possible the diversion because it causes people to be utterly absorbed with what they are doing" [p.12]); and competition (i.e., "the competitive element in sport is extremely visible. It is there for all to see; there is nothing hidden or submersive about sport competition" [ibid.]). Of all the instrumental values attributed to sport that can also be attained through other activities, perhaps the most plausible value for explaining why people participate in sport is the ability of sport to provide a stimulating form of recreation. Sport is engaged in as a form of recreation, that is, as a diversion from everyday work activities; it is possible to think of alternative forms of recreation, for example, card games, needlepoint, and so on. However, for some people, other activities are not stimulating enough to take their minds off their everyday work activities.

Having considered values that are instrumental and thus could be attained through other activities, it is important to ask if any of these values are worth the negative aspects that can arise from participation in sport. A glance through the sports section of any number of daily papers will reveal headlines such as "Athletes test positive for banned substances," "Hockey player injured in fight," "Coach accused of sexually abusing players," "Recruiting violations exposed at college," and so on. Sport has always had a dark side, and headlines similar to these keep reappearing in our daily papers. Sport organizations are starting to address some of the negative aspects of sport. For example, Hockey Canada has instituted a Speak Out campaign designed to create awareness of the potential for harassment and abuse in hockey. Any attempt to "clean up" sport is definitely to be encouraged, but the question may still be asked as to whether the values available through sport are important enough to risk the potential negative aspects that accompany sport.

Values intrinsic to sport also have to be weighed against the negative aspects of sport. Values intrinsic to sport include physical competence, human bonding through striving together, and concern for excellence of particular sports. The nature of an intrinsic value is such that values intrinsic to an activity are logically part of that activity. Thus, if one wants to attain such values, engaging in activities to which these values are intrinsic would make sense. What is important when seeking the intrinsic values of sport is that competition must be understood as striving together in the pursuit of excellence. If competition is understood in this way, many of the negative aspects that currently accompany sport would not exist. Many of these negative aspects of sports, for example, drug taking, fighting, and recruiting violations, occur because the emphasis is on winning and not on striving together in the pursuit of excellence. Athletes can still strive for excellence even if they lose. In fact, as Ross (1988) points out, "a loss, much more than a win, goads coaches and athletes to improved performance" (p.59). Winning will often be the result of an excellent performance, but not always. Two teams of similar skill level can both play excellently, and yet one team will lose (usually not by a great margin if the teams are comparable in skill level). The fact that athletes (and spectators) prefer opponents of similar skill levels rather than a strong opponent competing with a much weaker opponent (which usually results in a blow-out) is a good indication that winning is not the only goal of sport. If striving together in the pursuit of excellence could replace the "winning-at-all-costs" attitude that prevails in sport today, sport could have a more justifiable role in society.

The Role Sport *Should* Play in Society

As noted in the introduction, it is quite evident that sports play an important role in society. However, following the preceding analysis, we are in a better position to answer whether sport *should* play such an important role in society. A change in attitude from "winning-at-all-costs" to striving together in the pursuit of excellence would affect all levels of sport from school sports, through elite sports, to professional sports. The sport levels whose goals are not solely the pursuit of excellence are recreational and professional sport. **Recreational sport**, by its very nature, has recreation as a goal; that is, recreational sport is played as a diversion from everyday work activities. The recreational goal of recreational sport must not be replaced by the sole goal of winning. If winning becomes the goal of recreational sport, the negative aspects of sport can soon overwhelm the recreational sport experience, and if that happens, recreational sport cannot be justified since the negative aspects of a "winning-at-all-costs" attitude are not worth the diversionary value of recreational sport. **Spectator sport** can also be viewed as a recreational activity (for the spectators, not the players). Once again, if the spectators get caught up in a "winning-at-all-costs" attitude, that is, in everything from booing at opponents to starting riots, the recreational goal of spectator sport will have been lost.

The role of sport in educational institutions is another area that must be scrutinized. As sport is currently played in American secondary educational institutions, its role is questionable. Andre and James (1991) paint a bleak picture of student athletes:

> It is not surprising, therefore, that at many big-time Division I campuses few student-athletes graduate. This is not because they had better things to do: fewer than 1 percent go on to become professional athletes. A disproportionate number of these student-athletes are poor and black. Years that could have shaped their adult careers have gone for nothing–or for the fleeting benefits of campus fame. Some athletes will leave school with injuries, drug habits, or an immaturity that will cripple them for the rest of their lives. (p.2)

Although some philosophers have proposed that the values learned through **intercollegiate sports** are worth the potential risks Andre and James mention, as well as the numerous recruiting violations that continue to be exposed, one must question whether these same values could not be achieved through potentially less negative activities. Simon (1991) extols the values available through intercollegiate sport:

> At their best, intercollegiate athletics allow for development, reinforcement, and expression of desirable states of character–the virtues. In fact, the virtues promoted by athletic competition, such as dedication, concern for knowledge of self and others, and courage, are also important educational virtues. Perhaps most important, participation in the test provided by an athletic contest, as well as in the preparation for it, is itself educational in that it provides an almost unique opportunity for obtaining knowledge of oneself and others. In addition, intercollegiate sports provide an example to the rest of the community of men and women pursuing and exhibiting excellence. (p.185)

As mentioned in the previous section, virtues such as dedication, courage, and the pursuit of excellence can be developed through the pursuit of artistic or scholarly endeavors that involve endless practice as well as the exposing of one's work to an audience.

The value that Simon alludes to as being almost unique to sport, the "opportunity for obtaining knowledge of oneself and others," might be one that is worth the risk of the negative aspects that often accompany sport. Sport, in a physical education context, provides the opportunity for students to develop practical as well as theoretical knowledge (Bergmann Drewe 1999). "Knowing how" is as important a form of knowledge as "knowing that," and physical education is one area of the curriculum whose focus is largely on the development of practical knowledge.

Although other areas of the curriculum involve practical knowledge, for example, conducting science experiments, physical education also has a significant moral education dimension (due to the fact that most sports involve interaction with other people), and the development of practical knowledge along with moral knowledge should justify the inclusion of physical education in the curriculum of educational institutions.

Advocating the inclusion of physical education in the curriculum of educational institutions is not the same thing as arguing for the existence of intercollegiate sport. Throughout all levels of schooling (including post-secondary schooling), students should have the opportunity to participate in physical education programs. Students should also have the opportunity to compete in extracurricular sports, since such experiences help them further develop the skills learned in physical education programs. However, these extracurricular sport programs should be open to everyone. This is not the case in intercollegiate sports–although many students may "try out," only the "best" will make the team. This situation leaves the majority of students without an avenue to practice and develop the "practical knowledge" acquired through their physical education programs. With all students given the opportunity to play extracurricular sports, there is still the option of forming teams at different levels so that students who want to take their skills "as far as they can" will have opponents of a similar skill level. This situation may require schools competing against other schools, but intercollegiate competition does not have to result in the "big-time" athletic programs witnessed today. Division III schools in the United States may provide a model for a healthy form of intercollegiate sports:

> The educational defense of intercollegiate athletics applies largely to the kinds of athletic programs found in Division III schools of the NCCA, including the small liberal arts colleges, as well as to the Ivy League, and to institutions with similar philosophies. These colleges and universities view participants as students first and athletes second. Financial aid is given only for need and no athletic scholarships are awarded.... Recruiting is much less intense than at the major athletic powers, seasons are shorter, and the academic progress of the student is regarded as of fundamental importance. (Simon 1991, 162).

To summarize the role sports should play in educational institution, participation in sport should be part of physical education programs at all levels of schooling due to the nature of sport as a somewhat unique context to develop practical knowledge. In addition, extracurricular sport competitions should be available for any student who wishes to practice and develop their sport skills in competitive situations. Although it would be necessary to place teams in different levels, the highest level should resemble American

Division III schools, where the focus is still on the student
athlete.

Having considered the role of recreational sport and school
final levels to be examined are elite sport and professional spor
sport refers to high-level sport outside the university and/or college
text (although participants in elite sport may also be student athletes
their universities or colleges). The pinnacle of elite sport competition would be Olympic and World competitions. As proposed earlier, one of the values intrinsic to sport is the concern for excellence particular to a specific sport. Olympic athletes seemed to have replaced "faster, higher, stronger" with "gold, gold, gold" (Bergmann Drewe 1996b). When we see athletes taking serious risks, for example, Kerri Strug continuing to vault after having torn a ligament in the 1996 Olympic gymnastics competition in order to win "the gold," we have to wonder if the pursuit of excellence has been lost in elite sport. The American gymnastics team had already exhibited excellence. Did Kerri Strug have to risk a serious injury to secure a gold medal? A rethinking of the goal of elite sport is in order if elite sport is to have a justifiable role in society.

Finally, we must consider the role of **professional sport** in society. Compared to recreational, school, and elite sport, professional sport involves the greatest financial exchange. Professional athletes' salaries can run into the millions but teams are able to pay these salaries because society is willing to spend vast sums of money supporting professional teams. Concerning the value of professional sport, one can ask whether professional sport involves values intrinsic to sport, that is, striving together in the pursuit of excellence. Although professional athletes might pursue excellence, excellence is only considered to be achieved if there is a win. Professional athletes are paid to play their sport. Winning is synonymous with a pay check. If the value of pursuing excellence whether the team wins or not is not the goal of professional sports, what values *could* justify the role professional sports play in society? Two options that could possibly justify professional sports are human bonding and a stimulating form of recreation. As mentioned earlier, professional sport brings diverse groups of people together in a shared experience. The unity of fans for a particular team can be overwhelming. In 1996, when it was announced that the Winnipeg Jets had to be sold because a mid-size Canadian city could not afford an NHL franchise, the outpouring of financial support from the Winnipeg fans and local corporations was incredible. In a few short days, Winnipeg-based corporations and fans had pledged over $13 million. Although the effort on the part of the fans was not enough to "save the Jets," an important question could be asked: if people could bond together and raise

team, what would happen if people put that
child hunger in their city? The fact remains
bout watching sport than eradicating child

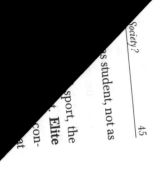

nto the second value for justifying profes-
fessional sports is a stimulating form of
though it could be argued that spending
ony concerts might be a more enriching
a football game, for many people, a sym-
ould not be stimulating enough to act as a diversion from everyday work activities. If recreational diversions are important for people, than the value of watching professional sport as a means of recreation could justify professional sport. However, it is important to perceive professional sport as a recreational outlet for which people are willing to pay, not as an activity exhibiting the value of pursuing excellence through sport. Also, even if professional sport can be justified as a recreational outlet, the potential negative aspects of professional sport must be continually kept in check if professional sport is to play a justifiable role in society. For example, a number of contact sports have become excessively violent in recent years, such as North American hockey. If the violence in hockey becomes too destructive (not only for players injured by such violence but also for young hockey players who model themselves after their NHL heroes), the value of a recreational diversion may not be worth the perpetuation of violence accompanying the sport.

Conclusion

When answering the question "Why sport?", we looked at the values available through sport. A distinction was made between intrinsic and instrumental values attributable to sport. Values that are intrinsic to sport are logically connected to sport while instrumental values are not logically tied to sport but can be consequences of participating in sport. Intrinsic values are connected to the very meaning of sport; that is, the necessary and sufficient conditions of sport. Thus, values intrinsic to sport would include: physical competence, human bonding, and a concern for excellence. Instrumental values would include: the respecting of rules, aesthetic value, personal expression, physical and emotional tenderness, discipline and dedication, risk taking, cognitive complexity, sensuous and transcendental experiences, outlet for aggression and surplus energy, fitness, and a stimulating form of recreation.

In answering the question "What role *should* sport play in society?", one has to consider different levels of sport. Sport can justifiably play a role in recreational, educational, elite, and professional contexts. People can participate in sport as a recreational diversion, both as players and spectators. In educational contexts, sports should be offered as a means for students to acquire practical knowledge. The acquisition of practical knowledge would occur most easily in a physical education program, but extracurricular sports should be offered in order to give students an opportunity to practice and develop their skills. When athletes have reached a high level of skill, elite sport competitions should be available for them. However, it is important that the goal of these competitions is the striving together in the pursuit of excellence. When athletes are more concerned with winning medals than pursuing excellence, the value of elite sports is tarnished. The pursuit of excellence may be the goal of elite sport, but in professional sport, although athletes want to be considered "excellent players," the fact that they are being paid to play adds an external monetary value to their pursuits. Professional sports can be justified as providing a recreational diversion for spectators. However, negative aspects of professional sport, such as violence, cheating, and so on, must be kept in check if they are to be outweighed by the recreational value of such sports.

CHAPTER REVIEW

Key Concepts

- intrinsic and instrumental values
- physical competence
- human bonding
- respecting rules
- aesthetic value
- personal expression
- physical and emotional tenderness
- discipline and dedication
- concern for excellence
- risk taking
- cognitive complexity
- sensuous and transcendental experiences
- outlet for aggression and surplus energy
- fitness
- stimulating form of recreation
- recreational sport
- spectator sport
- intercollegiate sport
- elite sport
- professional sport

Review Questions

1. Explain the difference between values that are intrinsic to sport and those that are instrumental.
2. Describe the values that are intrinsic to sport.
3. What are the fifteen values instrumental to sport that are described in this chapter?
4. For the fifteen instrumental values described in this chapter, suggest non-sport alternatives that could develop the same values.
5. How must competition be understood if the values intrinsic to sport are to outweigh the negative aspects of sport?
6. What are the goals of the various levels of sport, that is, recreational, spectator, intercollegiate, elite, and professional?
7. What value does Simon advocate as being unique to intercollegiate sport and how does this value relate to physical education programs?
8. What values justify the role professional sports play in society?

3

Is Competition a Good or Bad Thing?

[C]ompetition in sport is, in essence, an expression of friendship, mutuality, goodwill, in which we pay each other the high compliment of offering each other our best opposition to provide for ourselves and the other the satisfaction found in striving to do one's best. (Metheny 1977, 71)

Ironically, people are being destroyed by an extension of their own competitive ethic. They know their game of football, their game of politics, their game of life. Win in any way you can. The wholesale subscription to this principle motivates the most "savage" acts of our time. Assassins, terrorists, warriors, and war makers are not "crazy," they have merely brought the win-at-all-costs dictum whole-heartedly. (Orlick 1978, 16)

The above quotations epitomize the extreme positions people have taken regarding their conceptions of competition. What should be made of such opposing views of the virtues and vices of competition? Is participation in competitive activities a positive or a negative thing? To determine whether participation in competitive activities should be encouraged or discouraged, arguments in support of and arguments against competition must be considered. In arguing for or against the value of competition, a distinction must be made between values *resulting* from participation in an act of competition and values that are intrinsic to the concept of competition. Values resulting from participation in an act of competition are not intrinsic to the nature of competition in that these values may or may not occur, and if they do occur, they may be the result of factors other than the act of competition. However, values that are intrinsic to the concept of competition will always occur when competition takes place because these values are included among the defining characteristics of what it means to compete. Other key concepts that will be utilized in addressing the value of competition will include: **character traits, preparation for life, striving together, inequality** and **difference, "winning-at-all-costs" attitude, selfishness, causation** and **correlation, equal respect, counter-examples, contested concept, motivating influence, pursuit of excellence, respect for opponents and rules, comparable skill levels**, and **prerequisite skills**.

he virtues of competition. The sugges- a *result* of participating in competitive ied up in the often touted cliché "sports whose development have been attrib- e activities include courage, dedication, orth. Participation in competitive activi- being a necessary **preparation for life**. competitive, and thus the suggestion has titive experiences will provide the skills ete successfully in this society.

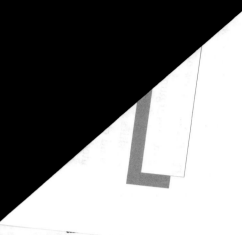

Metheny (1977) sugges "for the competitor, the *intrinsic* [emphasis added] value of competition is found in the act of competing–the striving, the doing, the satisfaction of using himself fully within the limits of the situation" (p.71). Hyland (1988) emphasizes the **striving together** that is evident in the root word *com-petitio*. "It is a questioning of each other *together*, a striving *together*, presumably so that each participant achieves a level of excellence that could not have been achieved alone, without the mutual striving, without the competition" (p.236). Simon (1991) proposes that when such competition is engaged in voluntarily as "a *mutually* [emphasis added] acceptable quest for excellence through challenge" (p.23), then its position is ethically defensible.

The Negative View of Competition

Once again, a distinction must be made between the negative consequences that could result from participating in competitive activities and the suggestion that competition is intrinsically negative. A potentially negative consequence of competitive activities results from the generation of **inequalities**. In Simon's (1991) words, "[Competition] divides us into winners and losers, successes and failures, stars and scrubs" (p.28). It is the fact that "someone has to lose" that has led many educators to criticize participation in competitive activities. If participants in competitive activities are continuously losing, a "self-fulfilling prophecy" often results and these participants will drop out, feeling that they can never win. Of course, this situation works both ways–participants who continuously win will be motivated to keep playing. However, it is the situation of the losers that is focused upon by those holding a negative view of competition. Fait and Billing (1978) suggest that "we must work against any situation which produces large numbers of failures and thus expectations of failure. Possibly then we can stop our unintentional, but nevertheless detrimental, division of students into winners and losers" (p.101). A point could be made here that, if there is a large number of failures, the losers feel "average" and the winners feel "good," as opposed to the situation where there is a small number of failures and the losers feel "bad" and the winners feel "average." However, Fait and Billing advocate against a situation where losers feel bad at worst and only average at best.

Other negative consequences that could result from participation in competitive activities are related to the **"winning-at-all-costs" attitude** that often accompanies the act of competing. In the drive to win, many participants have resorted to cheating. Cheating occurs in many forms, including intentional fouls and intentional injuries. The "winning-at-all-costs" attitude might not always result in the extreme consequence of cheating, but the price paid in participants' drive to win might be the sacrifice of their individual identities, their education, or their health. Some critics feel that involvement in competitive activities may not only limit the educational opportunities of participants, but that competition and education are actually antithetical. In Campbell's (1974) words, "Kids in our society may always engage in some competition, but it is not the teacher's job to promote it, for it has nothing to do with education" (p.145). Grinski (1993) suggests that "competition is a noneducational practice for children: an exclusive, not inclusive, practice that limits learning opportunities for most students" (p.11).

Besides the negative consequences of inequalities, cheating, and the potential tension with educational opportunities, some critics of competitive activities (Fielding 1976; Kohn 1986; Schaar 1967) have suggested that competition is intrinsically negative. As Kohn (1986) points out, "we must recognize that the problem rests squarely with the structure of mutually exclusive goal attainment. We need not know anything about the individuals involved to see the destructive potential of a system that says only one of them can be successful" (p.116). Fielding (1976) writes: "Competition as a social ideal seems to me abhorrent; competition as a procedural device is morally repugnant because whatever other criteria one wishes to include or omit I would insist that part of one's characterisation contains some reference to working against others in a spirit of selfishness" (p.140). Simon (1991) states the criticism as follows: "The goal of competition is enhancement of the position of one competitor at the expense of others. Thus, *by its very nature* [emphasis added], competition is selfish. But since selfish concern for oneself at the expense of others is immoral, it follows that competition is immoral as well" (p.20). (Whether competition is intrinsically **selfish** will be addressed in the following section.)

Critique of Positive and Negative Consequences of Competition

Advocates of the positive view of competition maintain that participation in competitive activities can help develop positive character traits and that these traits, such as courage, dedication, discipline, and perseverance, along with a competitive attitude, are necessary for surviving in our competitive world. Critics, on the other hand, suggest that negative consequences such as cheating, violence, and lack of learning opportunities result from the "winning-at-all-costs" attitude that is promoted in competitive activities as a result of the negative consequences of losing. What are we to make of these supposed consequences resulting from participation in competitive activities?

First, a distinction must be made between **causation** and **correlation**. That is, if participants in competitive activities exhibit particular traits, be they negative or positive, it cannot be assumed that it was the competitive situation that caused these traits to develop. For example, people exhibiting dedication and perseverance would be the kind of people who would find competitive activity attractive. Coakley (1994) illustrates this situation, and although he discusses physical traits, his argument is equally applicable to character traits.

> For example, if participants in youth sport programs were stronger, faster, and more coordinated than nonparticipants, would it be reasonable to conclude that strength, speed, and coordination among athletes were solely a result of their involvement in sport? Obviously, it would not. It is rather clear that children with certain physical attributes will be attracted to sport, and, once involved, they will be continually encouraged by peers, parents, and coaches. Furthermore, children who lack strength, speed, and coordination would be less likely to try out for competitive teams. (Coakley 1994, 94).

Thus, a distinction must be made between viewing participation in competitive activities as *causing* the development of "strong" personalities with the possibility that these personalities are the type who excel in competitive situations. Likewise, the negative consequences of cheating to ensure a win may not be caused by the competitive situation as much as by the ethics of the offending participant. Not all participants in competitive activities cheat, and those who do cheat might also exhibit such cheating behavior in other areas of their lives, for example, in academic tests, lying to parents, and so forth. Although such correlations are an empirical matter, it is important to point out that the claims made regarding the positive values and negative consequences of participation in competitive activities must not be considered as simply being *caused* by the act of competition.

The claim that participation in competitive activities is important as preparation for life must also undergo closer scrutiny. There are two points at issue here. Firstly, it may be questionable as to whether competitive attitudes *are* necessary for survival in our world and, secondly, *if* this claim is accepted, *who* in fact is best prepared for life as a result of participation in competitive activities? The question regarding whether a competitive attitude is necessary for surviving in our world is, to a certain extent, an empirical question.

> For example, many managers have discovered that using competitive reward structures among employees often subverts the relationships the employees need to have with one another to perform their jobs efficiently. Success in today's world often depends much more on a person's ability to cooperate and to maintain intrinsic sources of motivation than on the ability to compete and the desire to dominate others. Those who are motivated only to outdo others often cut themselves off from the allies they need to become successful. (Coakley 1994, 100)

Coakley cites examples of professionals such as doctors and lawyers forming organizations that restrict competition in their work lives, and leaders in the business world who, although proclaiming the merits of competition, get together to devise ways of concealing trusts, monopolies, and other anti-competitive practices so that they can increase profits while avoiding government sanctions. Thus, it is questionable whether a competitive attitude is as important as it is often claimed to be for surviving in our world.

A point related to whether a competitive attitude is necessary for surviving in our world concerns the desirability of a competitive world in the first place. As Bailey (1975) notes,

> the important point is that even if a given society can be shown to be highly competitive what can an educator deduce from this about what he ought to do and what he should teach? Surely it is still an open question whether children should be taught to "fit in" to the prevailing or majority ethos, or be taught to resist or at least be critical of such an ethos? The mere fact of a majority attitude accepting competition proves nothing. (p.45)

If, for the sake of argument, a competitive attitude *is* accepted as necessary for survival in our world (whether this *ought* to be the case will be left unexamined at present), the question arises as to who is best prepared for life as a result of participation in competitive activities. Those best prepared are those who frequently win. Fait and Billing (1978) would concur with this answer: "[C]ertainly there is value in experiencing both success and failure when striving for a goal, but it is extremely doubtful if those students with a steady diet of failure learn better how to compete; rather, they learn how to avoid failure through withdrawal, compensation, and rationalization" (p.101). Thus, one could argue that a consequence of participating in competitive activity is better preparation for life in a competitive world, but in this situation, a positive consequence for the winner is a negative consequence for the loser.

A discussion of winners and losers once again ushers in the issue of the inequality generated by competitive situations. Before accepting this inequality as a negative consequence of competition, a distinction must be made between inequality and difference. Dworkin (1977) makes a distinction between the right to equal treatment, "which is the right to an equal distribution of some opportunity of resource or burden," and the right to treatment as an equal, which is the right "to be treated with the same respect and concern as anyone else" (p.227). Dworkin cites the example of giving medicine to a child who is sick and one who is well. To treat the children as equal would require giving half of the medicine to one child and half to the other child. However, giving all of the medicine to the sick child would be compatible with **equal respect** and concern for both children. Thus, the children are treated differently but they are both being shown equal degrees of respect. Simon (1991) moves this distinction into the realm of competitive activities. "Accordingly, even though competition in sports may lead to unequal treatment, such as different assignments of playing time to better and worse players on a team or to a distinction between winners and losers of a contest, this is not sufficient to show that competition in sports is inequitable or unjust" (p.30). Likewise, in the realm of academics, it would not be considered unjust to award a high grade to an excellent paper and a lower grade to a poorer paper. What is critical to consider in this discussion of inequality is the equal respect shown to participants in competitive activities.

Critique of the Intrinsically Positive and Negative Views of Competition

It is in examining the intrinsic value of competition where the positive and negative views of competition "collide head on." Those espousing a positive view of competition maintain that the very nature of competition involves striving together in the pursuit of excellence. Critics of competition maintain that competition is intrinsically selfish. In dealing with this dilemma, one must examine and evaluate counter-examples to each of these claims. **Counter-examples** are examples that appear to contradict the thesis of the proposed argument. It would seem quite simple to produce an example where the striving to pursue excellence in a competitive activity does not exhibit Hyland's (1988) conception of "competition as friendship" (p.236). The intentional harming of an opposing player in order to give one's team an advantage would be a good counter-example to the "competition as striving together" view.

However, one must make a distinction here that parallels Searle's (1995) distinction between "regulative" and "constitutive" rules. Some rules regulate antecedently existing activities, for example, "driving on the right-hand side of the road" regulates driving, but driving can exist prior to the existence of that rule. Other rules also create the very possibility of certain activities, for example, the rules of chess do not regulate "people pushing bits of wood around on boards in order to prevent them from bumping into each other," but rather "the rules are *constitutive* of chess in the sense that playing chess is constituted in part by acting in accord with the rules" (pp.27-28).

"Striving together" is constitutive of participating in a competitive activity, and if regulative rules such as "not intentionally injuring an opponent" are broken, the potential "striving together" that constitutes competitive activity is not destroyed. Ideally, teachers (and society in general) should work against the breaking of regulative rules in order that what constitutes the competitive situation can flourish untarnished. In Arnold's (1988) words, "Whether or not this ideal is lived out as a part of a young person's upbringing is largely, if not entirely, a matter of how competitive sport is promoted and taught in schools. What then is being rejected, both on conceptual and historical grounds, is the view that competitive sport is inherently and therefore necessarily immoral" (p.60). Examples of "non-friendly" acts as they are currently practiced do not destroy the constitutive "striving together" involved in competition. To suggest that the breaking of regulative rules by some competitors destroys the possibility of "striving together" would be, in Dunlop's (1975) words,

> As unfair and inappropriate as judging philosophy from the betrayal of intellectual values that sometimes occurs among professional philosophers. Soccer violence and hooliganism is not a logical working out of the "essence" of a competitive game; rather as Bailey himself points out, a symptom of the general moral state of society. (p.159)

Critics of competition argue that competition lends itself to "violence and hooliganism" because of the selfish nature of competitive activities. To examine the claim that competition is intrinsically selfish requires an elucidation of the concept of "selfishness." As Simon (1991) points out, "if we define selfish behavior as self-interested behavior, then the pursuit of victory will be selfish, because we have stipulated it to be so by definition" (p.28). He proceeds to cite two examples to which the concept of selfishness might be applied:

> 1. Jones is playing in a touch football game with friends. Jones says, "I'll be the quarterback." The others declare that they too want to be quarterbacks and suggest the position be shared. Jones replies, "It's my football! If you don't let me play quarterback, I'll take my ball and go home!"

> 2. Jones is in a spelling contest between two teams in her fifth grade class. She correctly spells a difficult word. As a result, her team wins and the other team loses. (p.28)

These examples would seem to be of two different kinds. As Simon (1991) points out, "if there is an important difference between trying to defeat an opponent within a mutually acceptable framework of rules and simply disregarding the interests of others, then there is a significant, ethically relevant difference between athletic competition and selfishness" (p.28). Thus, the first example is a demonstration of selfishness since Jones is disregarding the interests of her teammates by demanding that she be allowed to be quarterback. In the second example, Jones is not disregarding the interests of her classmates when participating in the spelling contest. In fact, she is *respecting* the interests of her classmates by playing according to the rules, thus allowing the constitutive "striving together" of the competitive activity to occur in a *non-selfish* manner.

One further counter-example to the claim that competition is intrinsically selfish involves the necessity of opponents having to co-operate in order to participate in a competitive activity. Opponents must *co-operate* in their agreement to compete if competition is to occur. Perry (1975) notes that "competitions require us to assume the capacity to cooperate if they are to run at all" (p.128). Not only do opposing participants have to co-operate to "get a game off the ground," but members of the same team in a team sport must co-operate if they are to be successful in playing the game. It would seem logically inconsistent that co-operative behavior is a necessary component of an activity that is intrinsically selfish.

Excellent Ends Justify Competitive Means

The intent of the preceding discussion was to demonstrate that "competition" should not be viewed as a contested concept. A **contested concept** is a concept for which there is no agreement as to a shared understanding of the concept. In critiquing the positive and negative consequences of participation in competitive situations, neither those propounding the positive nor the negative consequences of competition appear to provide convincing arguments one way or the other. However, when analyzing the views as to whether competition is intrinsically positive or negative, the former is a far more persuasive stance than the latter.

Regarding the positive and negative views concerning the consequences of participating in competitive situations, it does *not* appear that the arguments in favor of competition are more convincing than the arguments against competition or vice versa. Recall the distinction made between causation and correlation as an attempt to dispel the claim that participation in competitive activities necessarily develops positive or negative traits in the participants. By suggesting that only the winners really enjoyed the benefits of preparation for life in a competitive world (if it be the case that competitive attitudes are truly necessary or desirable for surviving in our world), it would appear that a positive consequence for the winner is a negative consequence for the loser in competitive situations. By making a distinction between inequalities and differences, participants may have different experiences, for example, one team wins and one team loses, but this does not have to imply that the losing team is treated with an unequal degree of respect, thus lessening the negative consequences for the losers in a competitive situation.

Although in actual practice participants do not always treat opponents or rules with respect, this situation does *not* negate the striving together that constitutes competitive activity. Although critics of competition have suggested that competition is intrinsically selfish, a distinction can be made between disregarding the interests of an opponent on one hand, and on the other, trying to defeat an opponent within a mutually agreed upon framework of rules. Agreeing to play within a framework of rules requires the co-operation of all participants. The necessity of co-operating in order to pursue a competitive activity is a persuasive counter-example to the argument that competition is intrinsically selfish. The argument that competition is intrinsically positive, when conceived of as a "striving together," can withstand the counter-argument concerning the disrespect for rules and opponents that occurs because such an occurrence is not necessarily entailed by the competitive situation. The "striving together" that constitutes participation in competitive activities is not negated by the disrespecting of regulative rules. The onus is on coaches and teachers to work toward upholding respect for opponents and rules, and thus allowing the "striving together" involved in competitive activities to flourish untarnished.

To propose a persuasive argument in favor of competition requires not only an argument that competition is not intrinsically negative but also a demonstration that competitive situations provide an opportunity to grow, develop skills, and so on, which cannot be achieved without an element of competition. In order to demonstrate this, a revival of the root word *com-petitio* (to strive together) must take place. It is in the notion of "together" wherein lies the opportunity provided by competitive activities for participants to grow and develop, which cannot be experienced without an element of competition. It is only through comparison with something outside of themselves that people are able to evaluate their skills and abilities, and it is only through continued "striving together" with that "something" that people are able to realize their potential. Comparing one's skills and abilities with one's competitors provides a **motivating influence**.

The necessity of the "other" for realizing the potential for growth and development through competitive activity receives support from the work of social psychologists in the area of social comparison and social facilitation. Social comparison theory was originally formulated by Festinger (1954), who hypothesized that

> (1) there exists, in the human organism, a drive to evaluate his opinions and his abilities ... (2) to the extent that objective, non-social means are not available, people evaluate their opinions and abilities by comparison respectively with the opinions and abilities of others ... [and] (3) the tendency to compare oneself with some other specific person decreases as the difference between his opinion or ability and one's own increases. (pp.117-120)

The hypothesis that people prefer to compare themselves with others who have about the same ability level has found empirical support in other social psychological work (Dakin and Arrowood 1981; Gastorf, Suls, and Lawhon 1978; Suls and Miller 1977). This finding has important implications for coaches and teachers in their deployment of competitive situations, and these will be examined in the final section of this chapter. Social psychologists have attempted to explain this motivating influence of others performing the same task. Zajonc (1968) hypothesized that the presence of others increases one's level of arousal. Baron, Moore, and Sanders (1978) further developed this theory and suggested that it is the conflict produced between the tendency to pay attention to the task being performed and the tendency to direct attention to the "other" that is arousing. Groff, Baron, and Moore (1983) found that this conflict produces increased performance with simple tasks but decreased performance with more complex ones. This finding has important implications for the timing of introducing competitive activities, and these will be discussed in the final section of this chapter.

When competition is viewed as a striving together in a pursuit of excellence, the "winning is everything" mentality dissipates somewhat. That is, people can still be developing in their **pursuit of excellence** even if they do not win a particular competition. As Weiss (1969) points out, "even the defeated gain from the game. They benefit from the mere fact that they have engaged in a contest, that they have encountered a display of great skill, that they have made the exhibition of that skill possible or desirable, that they have exerted themselves to the limit, and that they have made a game come to be" (p.183). Losing can also motivate players to improve their performance. Ross (1988) proposes that "a loss, much more than a win, goads coaches and athletes to improved performance" (p.59).

Although competitors do not deliberately seek to lose (in an attempt to improve performance), teams will play superior teams, knowing the odds of losing are great. "Indeed, far from *avoiding* fixtures with teams to whom they are likely to lose, many clubs eagerly seek out such 'superior' opponents, since to play against a better side is usually more exciting and worthwhile, and tends to raise one's own game" (Dunlop 1975, 154). Thus, even though it is a logical necessity that the product of a competition is a winner (or perhaps a draw), it is obviously not the only reason people have for competing against others. As Arnold (1989) points out,

> *[t]rying to win* then may be considered a necessary feature of competing but this is not to be confused with a person's *reason* or *motive* for playing. For many school children (as well as for many adults) winning is a prospect rarely achieved but this does not prevent them wanting and continuing to compete and trying to win. Their reason for playing may be to do with fun, fitness, therapy, friendship, sociability, or the *pursuit of excellence* [emphasis added] rather than winning in order to "demonstrate their superiority over others." (p.20)

Shields and Bredemeier (1995) reiterate the notion that to win is not the only reason for competing. "When the internal aim of competition – winning – is not the exclusive aim of the participant, competition can be a mutually enjoyable and satisfying means of *improving abilities* [emphasis added], challenging boundaries, and expressing one's affective need for exhilaration, joy, and community" (p.218). If winning *was* the only reason people competed, they would deliberately seek out weak opponents to play against. However, spectators and players alike enjoy the challenge of a "close" game. It is that "challenge" that epitomizes the striving together in pursuit of excellence, which is made possible through competitive situations.

In summary, it might be helpful to look at the issue of competition in an ends-means light. That is, the gain of pursuing excellence with the heightened arousal attributed to the competitive situation justifies the means of participating in competitive activities that will sometimes result in losing. The gain of excellence is also worth the risk of a disregard for regulative rules, which arises as a result of living in a society that attaches such a negative stigma to losing. Although coaches and teachers may not be able to change societal values regarding winning and losing, they can make progress in striving to defuse the "winning-at-all-costs" mentality by stressing the striving together in the pursuit of excellence.

Implications for Coaches and Teachers

Having explicated and critiqued conceptions of "competition" in their positive and negative forms, it was proposed that the ends of pursuing excellence justified the means of competitive activity. However, a distinction was made between the "striving together" that constitutes competitive activity and the regulative rules that, if broken, do not negate the possibility of striving together in the pursuit of excellence. However, "striving together in pursuit of excellence" suffers abuse when competitors do not respect each other and the rules by which they have agreed to play. In order to avoid potentially disrespecting an opponent, some people advocate competing against oneself or other standards as opposed to competing against other people. Yet, rather than avoiding competition with others because of the potential of disrespect for the opponent, coaches and teachers must seriously strive to foster **respect for opponents and rules**. Thus, we turn to a discussion of the implications of such a conclusion for coaches and teachers.

If the fundamental reason for avoiding competitive activity is the potential for disrespecting opponents and the rules of the activity, then it becomes incumbent upon coaches and teachers to emphasize the importance of respecting rules and opponents. How might this be done? One of the most important means by which the coach or teacher can instill a respect for opponents and rules is through example. As Arnold (1989) points out, "[the teacher] should understand that how to conduct oneself on the sports field is likely to be as much caught as taught. It is not enough then, that the teacher be a clear interpreter of the rules of sport. What is required in addition is to show himself as being genuinely committed to the forms of consideration and conduct it demands" (pp.23-24). Coaches and teachers must take seriously their position as role models and diligently respect the rules and opponents in the game.

Although "teaching through example" is an indispensable means of instilling respect in players, attention must also be given to the reasons participants give for respecting opponents and rules, and this will require more direct teaching. "[T]o be fully moral one must do the right things as well as have the right reason. Both are required" (Hamm 1989, 141). If participants respect the rules only out of fear of being caught breaking them, then problems will ensue when the referee is not looking. Thus, coaches and teachers must help players develop a respect for rules and opponents that is based on good reasons. The practice field and physical education class provide ample opportunities for the coach and teacher to stop a play and point out how a player is not receiving the respect that he or she deserves and seek reasons for why this situation has occurred and why it creates a problem. Formal as well as informal discussion should be part of the process. Meakin (1981) suggests that

> the aim would be to sensitize the developing child to the moral presuppositions of competitive sport and bring home to him that he has some degree of choice whether to abide (by them) or not.... The teacher should not only ask children whether they ought or want to behave in certain ways but, by an appeal to moral reasoning, should condemn "bad" practices and recommend "good" ones. (p.246)

Thus, through example and precept, coaches and teachers should do all that they can to instill the respect for opponents and rules that allows the competitive "striving together in pursuit of excellence" to flourish untarnished.

A criticism that is sure to arise and that must be addressed concerns the possibility of achieving competitive situations without the breaking of regulative rules in our present society. In a society that extols winners, it may not seem possible to engage in activities in which it is logically necessary to have a winner (or at least a draw) but in which winning is not necessarily the only important aspect of the activity. Since many people are unable to enjoy the valuable aspects of competition, that is, striving together to improve skill, grow, and actualize potential, because of the fear of losing, it is necessary to create situations where everyone has a chance at winning. An important factor in increasing the chances of everyone winning at some point relates to the social comparison theory discussed previously. As Delattre (1995) points out, "it is of the utmost importance for competitors to discover opponents whose preparation and skill are comparable to their own and who respect the game utterly" (p.189).

The importance of playing against people of **comparable skill levels** cannot be overemphasized. However, it would be an unusual recreation program or physical education class where the participants were all at the same level. Thus, it will be necessary to group teams with the same number of advanced and not-as-advanced players during team games. During individual activities, it is important that players are matched with someone of comparable ability. In a recreational or physical education setting, the coach or teacher may have to be innovative in creating activities in which everyone at some point will win. For example, when playing baseball, the coach or teacher should vary the pitcher so that the highly skilled pitchers are pitching to the highly skilled batters, while pitchers with slower pitches are pitching to the weaker batters.

Even when teams are paired up with evenly matched teams, members on the same team will not always have the same ability level. What often happens in games where not everyone can play at once is that the more skilled players monopolize playing time. Thus, a team may participate in a competition but not every member is able to "strive for excellence." In order that all players should receive the benefits of competing, the coach or teacher should avoid situations where students have to sit out. The teacher must ensure that all players have the opportunity to play. An example suggested by Tutko and Bruns (1976) involved children's hockey teams in Chicago where a buzzer went off every two minutes, and the coaches had to change their lineups. Another example that necessitates the involvement of more than a few players is a volleyball game where the ball has to be touched by three different players before it is passed over the net.

Not only must participants have the opportunity to play against competitors of similar ability levels, and in the case of team sports, the opportunity to have their fair share of "playing time," another consequence of the preceding discussion concerns the timing of the introduction of competitive activities. Recall the claim made by social psychologists that social facilitation increases performance of simple tasks but decreases performance of more complex ones. This claim is substantiated by researchers in the area of physical education who propose a continuum of skill development. This continuum starts from a base of body management competence, moves into the development of fundamental skills, and finally into the utilization of specialized skills (see Gallahue 1982; Pangrazi and Dauer 1992). It is only at the upper level of the continuum that students utilize their skills in a game setting. It is only after students have control of the necessary fundamental skills that the distraction of opponents is outweighed by the motivation these opponents provide. The upshot of this discussion then, is that once people have control over the skills needed for a particular activity, a competitive situation provides a heightened arousal that can result in improved performance, which captures the notion of "striving together in the pursuit of excellence."

Critics of competition raise questions such as "If the goal of competitive games is for students to compete and win, how can students accomplish either if they have not learned the prerequisite skills?" (Brown and Grineski 1992, 18). This situation does not require the removal of competitive experiences, but rather, it necessitates the teaching of the prerequisite skills. Children require not only the physical skills necessary for the competitive activity, but they must also be mentally and socially "ready" (Gallahue 1982; Hinson 1993; Wall and Murray 1994). The importance of social comparison cannot be overemphasized, as Roberts (1980) explains:

> Competition in sports is an evaluative system of normative social comparison in which being competent is important to children and to young boys in particular. Therefore, when we formalize the competitive experience as we do when we organize children's sports, we place the children in a very intensive evaluation process. For older children who are able to accurately attribute cause and effect relationships, this evaluation gives them important normative information relative to their own sport competence. (p.43)

The point that "competitive experiences give important normative information for children who are able to accurately attribute cause and effect relationships" must be reiterated. Horn (1993) is critical of competitive experiences because, in her words, "When we use competition, we are increasing this emphasis on peer comparison; [kids] then judge whether they are competent or not in an activity in terms of their peers. We are then strongly encouraging kids to look at their worth in terms of factors they have no control over (i.e., the skill of another child)" (p.8). However, if children experience progressive and age-appropriate tasks, they will learn to accurately attribute cause and effect relationships regarding their own skills and abilities, and thus, the danger of attaching one's self-worth to another child's skill level should be minimized.

Conclusion

Having considered the positive and negative views of competition, it would appear that competition might be a contested concept. When looking at the positive and negative consequences of competition, it does not appear that the arguments in favor of competition are more convincing than the arguments against competition or vice versa. The arguments that participation in competitive activities can result in either positive character traits, for example, courage, dedication, discipline, or a "winning-at-all-costs" attitude, lose some of their force when the distinction is made between causation and correlation. The suggestion that competitive activities are a necessary preparation for life in a competitive world would seem to be a positive situation for winners but a negative situation for those who continuously lose. The argument that competition generates inequalities loses some of its force when the distinction is made between inequalities and differences, and just because participants may have different experiences, for example, one team wins and one team loses, this does not have to imply that the losing team is treated with an unequal degree of respect.

Although in actual practice, participants do not always treat opponents or rules with respect, this situation does *not* negate the striving together that constitutes competitive activity. Although critics of competition have suggested that competition is intrinsically selfish, a distinction can be made between disregarding the interests of an opponent on one hand, and on the other, trying to defeat an opponent within a mutually agreed upon framework of rules. Agreeing to play within a framework of rules requires the co-operation of all participants. The necessity of co-operating in order to pursue a competitive activity is a persuasive counter-example to the argument that competition is intrinsically selfish. The argument that competition is intrinsically positive, when conceived of as a "striving together," can withstand the counter-argument concerning the disrespect for rules and opponents that occurs because such an occurrence is not necessarily entailed by the competitive situation. The "striving together" that constitutes participation in competitive activities is not negated by the disrespecting of regulative rules.

If people are to enjoy the motivating influence competitors add to the pursuit of excellence involved in participating in competitive activities, coaches and teachers must strive to create situations where opponents and rules are treated with respect. Coaches and teachers must also ensure that all players have the opportunity to compete against opponents of comparable skill levels. Finally, players must have the prerequisite skills so that the addition of opponents will not undermine their ability to play. Thus, the onus is on the coach and teacher to create situations where everyone has a chance at winning. If players experience some wins, as well as losses, the hope is that they will enjoy the competitive activity for what it was meant to be–a striving together in the pursuit of excellence.

CHAPTER REVIEW

Key Concepts

- character traits
- preparation for life
- striving together
- inequality and difference
- "winning-at-all-costs" attitude
- selfishness
- causation and correlation
- equal respect
- counter-examples
- contested concept
- motivating influence
- pursuit of excellence
- respect for opponents and rules
- comparable skill levels
- prerequisite skills

Review Questions

1. What is the difference between values *resulting* from participation in competitive activity and values that are *intrinsic* to the concept of competition?
2. What are the positive and negative views of competition?
3. What is the distinction between causation and correlation, and why is this distinction important when critiquing both the positive and negative consequences of competition?
4. What are some of the problems with the "competition is a necessary preparation for life" argument?
5. What is the distinction between inequality and difference, and why is this distinction important when critiquing the "competition generates inequalities" argument?
6. What are some counter-arguments to the argument that competition is intrinsically positive, that is, striving together, and the argument that competition is intrinsically negative, that is, selfish?
7. How can competitive activities provide opportunities to grow?
8. How is the need to play opponents with comparable skill levels and the need to have the prerequisite skills tied into the notion of *com-petitio*?

4

Organized Sport: A Necessary Part of Childhood?

One of the most difficult balancing acts we face as parents is to try to make sure that our children have safe and successful sports experiences. (Micheli and Jenkins 1990, ix)

Baseball in spring, hockey in winter, outdoor soccer in spring, indoor soccer in winter, gymnastics in winter, swimming all year round–this schedule has become a typical routine for many children in North America. Children as young as three are starting gymnastics and tee-ball classes. This situation appears to go unquestioned by many people. For example, the author of the above quotation does not even leave open the option for parents to "balance" the question of whether children should even be involved in organized sports.

Some grandiose claims are made concerning the value of children participating in organized sports–from the building of character to the learning of teamwork. However, there are some serious costs to heavy involvement in sports–from the possibilities of injuries to an overly narrow focus on few activities. In this chapter, we will examine the benefits and costs of children's participation in organized sport. What it is about organized sport that is questionable will be analyzed, and some changes to the way society organizes sport for children will be proposed. Key concepts utilized in this chapter include: **motor skills, health fitness, belonging to a team, learning socially acceptable values and behaviors, long-term skills for leisure, enhancing child-adult relationships, self-esteem, aggressive behavior, excessive anxiety, potential injury, undesirable moral behavior, overly narrow focus, internal** and **external aspects of sport,** and **autonomy.**

Benefits of Organized Sport

Advocates of youth sport extol the many benefits that can result from participation in sport. For example, "[s]ports, such as swimming, basketball, baseball, and soccer, are heralded as developing the ideals of hard work, fair play, cooperation, and teamwork through competition" (Barber

1982, 21), and "[t]hrough top-level sports children can receive the impulses and initiative to develop and to form valuable attitudes toward life" (Grupe 1985, 11). Seefeldt (1987) summarizes the benefits resulting from participation in sport as: "learning motor skills; health related and motor fitness; participating and belonging; learning socially acceptable values and behaviors; long-term skills for leisure; and enhancing child-adult relationships" (pp.5-6). Seefeldt's summary will be utilized in outlining arguments and counter-arguments for defending children's participation in sport.

Learning motor skills

Learning motor skills is an important aspect of acquiring practical knowledge (Bergmann Drewe 1999). **Motor skills** include skills such as catching, kicking, jumping, and so on. The acquisition of practical knowledge, or "knowing how" to catch, kick, or jump, is an important justification for physical education programs, since acquiring knowledge is intrinsic to what it means to be educated (Drewe 2001). However, acquiring practical knowledge may not be intrinsic to the goals of youth sport programs. It could be argued that youth sport programs provide the context in which children can practice the skills they have learned elsewhere, particularly in physical education programs. If this is the case, that is, that youth sports programs provide a context for children to practice skills learned elsewhere, than the *learning* of motor skills should not be perceived as a benefit of youth sport programs.

On the other hand, if the learning of motor skills is to be seen as a benefit of youth sport programs, then coaches must make this learning a priority. However, a potential problem exists between acquiring knowledge intrinsic to an activity, in this case, youth sport, and the instrumental reasons coaches might have for teaching children motor skills. As Coakley (1993) points out, "[t]o the extent that sport programs provide opportunities for children to master physical skills, these programs lead to positive developmental outcomes, unless the sense of mastery is minimized by a constant emphasis on long-term performance goals that children view as distant and out of reach" (p.82). These "long-term performance goals" could include winning the league playoffs as well as the more distant goal of becoming an Olympic or professional athlete. If such goals become the driving force of a coach or child, the learning of motor skills will no longer have intrinsic value, and worse, some children may not have the opportunity to learn the motor skills involved in their sport if their coach focuses attention on the "star" players needed to win the playoffs.

Another tension that exists between organized sport and the learning of motor skills is the environment within which children are expected to learn these skills. Bunker (1981) makes an important point when she states that "[w]e do not expect children to learn to read or master quantitative skills while parents and peers are watching, judging, cheering, or jeering. Similarly, children must be able to develop motor skills in the 'least restrictive,' noncompetitive environment" (p.27). Although competitive situations are important for comparing one's skill level with some standard (recall the discussion in Chapter 3), children must first acquire the necessary skills before they are placed in a competitive situation that requires them to utilize these skills.

Health-related and motor fitness

In this age of televisions, computers, and video games, the health and motor fitness of our children should be of great concern. Although advocates of youth sport espouse the ability of organized sport to counter the sedentary lifestyle of many of our children, some aspects of organized sport are not conducive to achieving both health and motor fitness. First of all, what is meant by **health fitness** includes: increased cardio-respiratory capacity, greater flexibility, stronger muscles of the stomach and back, and less body fat. What is meant by motor fitness includes: muscular strength and endurance, power, balance, coordination, agility, and anaerobic capacity (Seefeldt 1987, 7-8). Not all sports help develop both health and motor fitness. Many sports, such as baseball, require short and intense effort, for example, running from first to second base. This activity helps develop one's anaerobic capacity but not one's aerobic capacity. Thus, if a child focuses only on sports that require anaerobic capacity, he or she will not develop his or her cardio-respiratory capacity. As well, not all components of motor fitness will be developed if a child focuses on only one sport, or if he or she always plays the same position in a particular sport. For example, if a child focuses on cross-country running, he or she will not necessarily develop his or her upper body muscles; or if a child is always the goalkeeper in soccer, he or she will not develop muscular endurance.

The previous objection to developing health-related and motor fitness through participation in organized sport could be countered by encouraging children to play a variety of sports and a variety of positions. However, there is another objection to the proposed benefit of developing fitness through youth sport, and this objection has to do with the amount of activity children actually experience when involved in organized sport. In most team sports, there are usually more players on a team than there are positions open at any given time. It is quite possible that some children could spend a large part of the season sitting on the bench. If the coach is particularly concerned with winning, the chances are good that players with lesser skills will not be improving their skills nor their fitness levels.

Participating and belonging

The idea of belonging to a team and the accompanying need to learn teamwork is a value that is extolled by advocates of youth sport. There are two issues that need to be considered when looking at the notion of **belonging to a team**. First, at what age does it make sense for children to be playing as a team? Sociologists suggest that prior to the age of twelve, children do not have the social abilities to conceptually grasp competitive team strategies (Coakley 1986, 61). An example of this inability is demonstrated in what has been referred to as "beehive soccer"–twenty pairs of legs within 10 yards of the ball, behaving like a swarm of bees following their queen.

> Beehive soccer is the result of kids just being kids. The concept of "teamwork" involves a set of relationships too complex for young children to grasp. When youngsters cluster around a ball, they are all playing as individuals. To play a team game, children must understand the rules and their tasks as members of the team. They must also understand the tasks of all the other members. At a young age, these concepts are often too abstract for children. (LeBlanc and Dickson 1996, 17)

Second, can the idea of belonging to a team be pushed too far? Playing with peers is an important developmental part of childhood. "Peers provide the means for children to separate their identities from the identities of parents and other family members" (Coakley 1993, 83). However, if playing with peers becomes structured as it does in organized sport, separating from the identities of family members becomes replaced with conformity to the identity of a team. If children are in the process of becoming individuals during the preadolescence stage, then tying their identity to a particular team would seem to be counter-productive.

Another problem with belonging to a team, if this "belonging" is very intense, is that children may only associate with team members to the exclusion of other children. Griffin (1998) reports an anecdote: "Recently I was in a high school cafeteria and remarked to myself how the athletes segregated themselves by sex and by sport at the tables" (p.28). There is a high probability that team members will segregate themselves in this way whenever there is an overemphasis on "belonging to the team."

As well as excluding children outside the team, intense belonging to a team may result not only in exclusion but also ill-feelings toward children on opposing teams. Advocates of youth sport might be optimistic about relating to opposing teams; for example,

> [w]hen a barbecue is held after a Little League game, the kids have an opportunity to get to know one another personally. That's where the true spirit of youth sports can be found. Children learn to leave rivalries on the field and discover that their opponents are kids like themselves who just want to have fun in sports. (Micheli and Jenkins 1990, 29-30)

However, it would take effort on the part of the coach as well as parents to achieve a situation where children on one team would be so welcoming to children on opposing teams.

Learning socially acceptable values and behaviors

The **learning of socially acceptable values and behaviors** through sport is encapsulated in the often touted cliché "sports build character." Character traits whose development have been attributed to participation in sports include courage, dedication, discipline, and perseverance. Participation in sports has also been expounded as being a necessary preparation for life in our society. That is, Western society is highly competitive, and thus the suggestion has been put forth that early experiences in competitive sport will provide the skills and attitudes necessary to successfully compete in this society.

As mentioned in Chapter 3, the thesis that participation in sports helps children learn socially acceptable values and behaviors requires that a distinction be made between causation and correlation. That is, it might not be participation in sport that causes people to develop particular traits; those traits might already be there. For example, people who are assertive and outgoing might be the kind of people who would be attracted to sport. Thus, a distinction must be made between viewing sport as the cause of certain personalities and the possibility that these are the type of personalities that are attracted to sport in the first place. Such correlations may be tested empirically but it should not simply be assmed that the learning of socially acceptable values and behaviors are *caused* by participating in sport.

The claim that participation in sports is a necessary preparation for life in our competitive society should also not be accepted without further examination. As elaborated in Chapter 3, there are a few questions that must be asked regarding the necessity of participation in sport as preparation for our competitive society. The question may be raised concerning whether a competitive attitude is as important for our world as we typically assume it to be. Coakley's (1984) examples of professionals such as doctors, lawyers, and business leaders forming organizations that restrict competition, as well as concealing monopolies, and so on, lend credence to the answer that competition may not be as pervasive in our society as is typically assumed.

The claim that a competitive attitude is necessary for surviving in our society assumes that a competitive world is desirable. As Bailey (1975) points out, the fact that such an attitude is in the majority proves nothing. Rather than teaching children to fit into the prevailing ethos, they should be taught to be critical of it (p.45). If a competitive attitude *is* determined to be necessary and desirable in our society, the question still remains as to who is best prepared for our competitive society as a result of participation in sport. Those best prepared would be the particpants who frequently win as opposed to those who frequently lose. As Fait and Billing (1978) point out, those who frequently lose, rather than learn how to compete, learn how to avoid failure by withdrawing from competitive situations (p.101). So although particpation in sport may better prepare winners for living in a competitive society, frequent losers may withdraw from competitive situations, further reducing their chances to learn the skills necessary for surviving in a competitive world.

Long-term skills for leisure

The proposition that participation in youth sport provides **long-term skills for leisure** is one which, in most cases, will turn out to be false. That is, most children participate in sports such as baseball, hockey, soccer, and gymnastics, which require enough people for two teams and/or specialized equipment. Although it is possible in one's leisure time to gather enough people to play a pickup game of soccer, it becomes much more difficult as children enter the adult world. Thus, if youth sport is to be perceived as a training ground for long-term skills for leisure, sports should be selected that lend themselves to leisure pursuits that are fairly accessible as one grows older, for example, hiking, cross-country skiing, canoeing, and so on.

Another problem with the notion that participation in youth sport provides long-term skills for leisure is the real possibility of "burnout" among athletes. There is disagreement between researchers on the number of children who drop out of sports, as well as the reasons for dropping out, for example, lack of playing time, overemphasis on winning, dislike of coach (Orlick 1973, 12-13; 1974, 25); too much pressure, lack of fun, too time consuming (McPherson et al. 1976, 186); and conflicts of interest and other things to do (Gould 1987, 66-67). However, the fact that large numbers of children drop out of sport before they reach their teens (Loy [1973, 89] points out that the pyramid of participation drops off very rapidly once we pass about twelve to thirteen years of age) would lead one to question how participation in youth sport provides long-term skills for leisure.

Enhancing child-adult relationships

The benefit of youth sport **enhancing child-adult relationships** is not one that is free from all danger. Firstly, the child-adult relationship that is most enhanced in youth sport is the relationship between the child and the coach. Children who are intensely involved in organized sport often spend more time with their coaches than they do with their parents (assuming these children also spend a large portion of their day with schoolteachers). Thus, organized sport might enhance child-coach relationships, but when one considers the amount of time some children spend with their coaches, the enhanced relationship with the coach might come at the expense of time spent building a relationship with ones' parents.

A second concern related to the relationship between child and coach pertains to the type of coach with which the child is involved. Coakley (1993) delineates three types of influences coaches might have on their athletes: "[C]oaches can become significant in the lives of athletes in different ways. They can make athletes dependent on them, serve as exemplars or role models, or act as advisers and advocates" (p.90). When coaches exhibit dictatorial styles, athletes often become extremely dependent upon them. This dependency is not healthy as the athletes do not learn how to take responsibility for themselves. On the other hand, coaches that serve as exemplars and/or role models or advisers and/or advocates provide a much healthier situation for their athletes. However, the possibility that a child may find him or herself relating to a dictator-type coach rather than a role model or adviser makes it incumbent upon parents to be aware of the type of coach who is playing an influential role in their child's life.

A final concern regarding the child-coach relationship is the possibility of encountering unscrupulous or abusive coaches. Although we hope it is far from the norm, some sociologists have hypothesized that the youth sport scene provides an environment ripe for unscrupulous adults who wish to prey upon young people (Brackenridge 1994, 289). Again, the possibility that coaches may abuse children requires vigilance on the part of parents and sport-governing bodies.

Having critiqued the benefits that have been espoused for children's participation in organized sport, we now turn to an examination of the costs of youth sport.

Costs of Organized Sport

As noted in the previous section, many claims have been made in support of youth sport. However, there are also costs involved when children participate in organized sport. Hellstedt (1988) suggests that negative outcomes resulting from participation in youth sport fall into three categories: low self-esteem, aggressive behavior, and excessive anxiety (p.60, 62) There are also additional categories concerned with potential injury, undesirable moral behavior, and overly narrow focus.

Low self-esteem

Critics of youth sport are quick to point out the potential for youth sport to destroy children's self-esteem. By **self-esteem**, we are referring to how one thinks of him or herself, that is, how one views one's abilities and competence. "Continuous poor performance or failure leads to an impoverished sense of personal competence and ultimately to learned helplessness" (Iso-Ahola 1980, 53). "The important point is that many children engage in intense competition over extended periods of time with similar consequences potentially being repeated over and over. This repetition makes develomental considerations, such as self-esteem, relevant" (p.306).

> Children who receive negative verbal and nonverbal messages can develop low self-esteem. Some children drop out of sport altogether because they feel incompetent. Low self-esteem can also result when children fail to fulfill their parents' expectations that they become the best pitcher, goal scorer, skier, or figure skater. (Hellstedt 1988, 60)

The potential for sports destroying children's self esteem seems to result from continuous poor performance, negative messages from coaches and parents, and failure to fulfill parents' (and coaches') expectations; and because of the importance society places on sport, this low self-esteem could have long-term adverse consequences.

Although the potential for damaging children's self-esteem through sport is real, it is not inherent to the activity of sport that low self-esteem has to result. Continuous poor performance could be alleviated by increasing training in the skills being utilized as well as in competing with opponents who are more equally matched in skill level. As mentioned in an earlier section of this chapter, acquiring motor skills may be more of a goal of physical education programs than of organized sport.

The negative messages sent by parents and coaches, as well as the high expectations of parents and coaches, have more to do with an overemphasis on winning than with participation in sport. Also, the importance placed on sport by society exacerbates feelings of incompetence on the part of children participating in sport. If society would rethink the emphasis it places on sport, and in particular, winning in sport, there would be far less potential for sport destroying children's self-esteem.

Aggressive behavior

As some theorists point out, there is a fine line between appropriately assertive behavior and overly aggressive behavior in sport (Hellstedt 1988, 60). Assertive behavior typically refers to forceful and vigorous behavior while **aggressive behavior** typically refers to forceful behavior with the intent to harm or injure someone. This distinction is frequently ignored in youth sport, particularly contact sports such as hockey and football. A study of youth hockey players in Canada indicated that 58 percent of nine- and ten-year-olds approved of fighting even though it is against league rules, and this approval of fighting increased to 84 percent among older youth hockey players (Smith 1978a, 146).

It must be emphasized that the majority of sports are not inherently violent (boxing might be considered an exception). However, an overemphasis on winning is often the cause of players being taught to be violent in order to win, for example, intentionally fouling another player or starting a fight to break the momentum of a game. The fact that aggressive behavior is condoned even when it is against the rules of the game is indicative of the systemic nature of violence in sport. "[T]he current trend toward violent behaviors, where these exist, is the responsibility of sport leaders: that is, administrators, coaches, officials, physical education teachers, and parents. At all levels, athletes are not primarily responsible for violent acts; they are merely the products of the *system*" (Pooley 1989, 7). Thus, once again, the criticism that organized sport increases aggressive behavior is more a criticism of the value sport leaders place on winning and the resulting "winning-at-all-costs" attitude (one of these costs being aggressive behavior).

Excessive anxiety

It is important to distinguish between anxiety and excessive anxiety when looking at youth sport. Anxiety can be a motivator, as pointed out by sport psychologists (Hellstedt 1988). However, the "arousing" effects of playing with a competitor diminish if the player is suffering from **excessive anxiety** resulting from competitive stress. Scanlan and Passer (1981) note that children suffering from competitive stress can display nervous or jittery behavior, appetite loss, and/or disrupted sleep (p.144). Scanlan (1984) suggests that competitive stress occurs when a child perceives that the demands of the situation are greater than his or her ability to meet these demands (p.118).

If there is a positive side to competitive stress, that is, increased "arousal," then it becomes incumbent upon coaches and parents to help children avoid the negative side of excessive stress, such as nervous behavior, and appetite and sleep loss. If excessive stress results from children perceiving that they do not have the ability to meet the perceived demands of the situation, two things can be done to help alleviate the stress: help improve children's ability, and lessen the perceived demands of the situation. As mentioned earlier in the section "Learning motor skills," children must first acquire the skills required by a sport before they are placed in a competitive situation that requires them to utilize these skills.

However, even if children have the requisite skills for performing a sport, they may still perceive of themselves as incapable of meeting the demands of the situation if the demands are too great. Competitive stress could result from excessive adult pressure to win or excel. As Hellstedt (1988) points out, "[a]dults need to deemphasize winning and encourage development of individual skills. A parent or coach should positively reinforce improvement and effort" (p.69).

A counter-argument to the criticism that organized sport places excessive competitive stress on children is that this stress is no different than other stressful situations children find themselves in, for example, school tests or music festivals. However, these other situations are also in need of change if they place excessive stress on children. Whether organized sport as we know it today is conducive to parents and coaches de-emphasizing winning and encouraging effort will be examined in the final section of this chapter.

Potential injury

Critics of youth sport point out the **potential for injury** in children participating in organized sport. However, as Taft (1991) notes,

> [t]he major injuries–fractures, dislocations, and complete ligament disruptions–that are seen in organized contact sports are much the same as those seen in children who are participating in free-play activities ... [i]n fact, more children sustained major injuries falling off their skateboards, bicycles, and swings than by participating in organized sport. (p.431)

However, there are some injuries and health-related problems that are greater in children participating in organized sport than children involved in unstructured activities. Injuries caused by overuse and health-related problems such as eating disorders may interfere with the growth and development of children, and these injuries and/or health-related problems are sometimes a direct result of children's participation in organized sport. Regarding overuse injuries, Taft (1991) points out that

> [w]ithout question, the most common sports-related problems now seen in children are the overuse or abuse syndromes. These tend to develop when overanxious adults cajole children to exercise, train, and compete at a level beyond their bodies' ability to cope. The current trend in youth sports in the United States is for a child to concentrate on a single sport rather than to participate in many activities. This primarily adult-directed specialization places these children at particular risk for overuse damage caused by repetitive microtrauma of an abused part. (p.432)

Regarding eating disorders, researchers suggest that athletes participating in activities that emphasize leanness, for example, gymnastics, long-distance running, and diving are more prone to developing eating disorders than athletes in non-weight-restricting sports (Stoutjesdyk and Jevne 1993, 279). Since sports such as gymnastics require participants to begin training early, the possibility of developing an eating disorder should be a concern for parents of children in such sports.

Undesirable moral behavior

Some critics of youth sport view participation in organized sport as a cause of undesirable moral behavior. **Undesirable moral behavior** includes cheating, fighting, intentionally injuring an opponent, and so on. "If the values learned through sport transfer to other areas of society, it's possible that the epidemic of cheating in schools, and the rise of white collar crime, stemmed from participation in youth sports" (Barber 1982, 21). One should be leery about making a causal connection between participation in youth sport and a rise in white-collar crime for the same reason that the "sport builds character" position was critiqued in a previous section. It could be that people who cheat in sports might also cheat in other areas of their lives, for example, on school tests, lying to parents, and so on.

Although there might not be a causal connection between participation in youth sport and the development of undesirable moral behavior, sport may be seen as an arena for practicing undesirable moral behavior. If this sort of behavior is not discouraged (and in some sports, e.g., hockey, and with some coaches, i.e., those determined to win at any cost, undesirable moral behavior may even be encouraged), then children will no longer see such behavior as undesirable. When such behavior is not condemned in the sports arena, it may be difficult for children to change their behavior in other areas of their life. "Children who grow up believing it's all right to cheat, abuse, and threaten their opponents find it difficult in later life to compete without trying to pull the same tricks they learned in Little League baseball or high school football" (Micheli and Jenkins 1990, 138).

Thus, participation in youth sport could be seen as reinforcing undesirable moral behavior. This argument finds support in some of the empirical research conducted by Bredemeier (1988): "Participation in relatively high-contact sports was associated with less mature moral reasoning, greater tendencies to aggress physically and nonphysically in both sport and daily life, and boys' judgments about the legitimacy of injurious sport acts" (p.294). However, other research conducted by Bredemeier, Weiss, Shields, and Shewchuk (1986) found that children's moral reasoning could be facilitated during an eight-week summer camp program by training teachers and coaches to employ theoretically grounded instructional strategies designed to promote moral growth. Shields and Bredemeier (1995) suggest that

> [p]ractitioners and researchers are giving renewed emphasis to their [youth sports'] potential role in psychosocial development. Of course ... the quality of the sport experience is what matters. This quality in turn derives from the quality of the leadership, the structural qualities of the sport itself, the social milieu in which it occurs, and the characteristics of the participants, to name only the most salient factors. (p.221)

What will have to be changed to create such a sport structure will be discussed in the final section of this chapter.

Overly narrow focus

> Children and youth involved in organized sport today can spend almost every waking non-school hour training, practicing, and playing their sports. Coaches are recruiting talented children as young as eight whose after-school hours, weekends, and summer vacations are occupied by clinics, practices, tournaments, and fight-to-the-death competitions. The old childhood ideal of goofing off–what the grimmer parenting books term "non-structured play"–isn't an option.... Family holidays, including Christmas and Thanksgiving, dissolve into long treks to tournaments. (Ferguson 1999, 39)

The dangers involved in an **overly narrow focus** include limited time with family (other than driving and spectating time), limited time to pursue other interests, and limited time for unstructured play or "downtime."

Advocates of youth sport might respond that organized sport gives children and parents a shared activity. However, other than when parents coach their own children (which raises other issues, e.g., conflict of interest), most of the time parents spend with their children when their children are involved in organized sport includes chauffeuring their children to practices and games and sitting in the stands. Although spectating parents are watching their children, the time parents spend sitting in the stands might not always be positive. "According to half the players, parents 'chew them out if they play poorly'" (Iso-Ahola 1980, 52). If parents would actually *play* sports with their children, then such an experience would truly be a "shared activity."

Regarding limited time to pursue other interests as well as the possibility to enjoy "downtime," advocates of youth sport take another tack. "It [organized sport] keeps kids out of trouble and away from the TV" (Ferguson 1999, 40). Placing sports at one end of a continuum and trouble and/or television at the other creates a false dichotomy. There are many other pursuits that are important for children's development, for example, aesthetic pursuits, literary pursuits, and so forth. Children could pursue these other activities, as well as less structured sport, if less time was dedicated to sport. Spending less time participating in organized sport does not automatically mean that children will end up getting into trouble. Also, children (as well as adults) need some time to just "be"–to take a break from activity, to "goof off." It seems ironic, but in our overly structured society, we might actually have to structure in "unstructured time." Rethinking how we organize sport for children might be a step in this direction.

Changing Organized Sport

In examining and critiquing the benefits and costs of organized sport, it would appear that the costs outweigh the benefits. Furthermore, the benefits that are able to withstand critique are available to children who participate in less structured sporting activities. Sport, by its very nature, involves a certain degree of organization, for example, rules, player responsibilities, playing areas. Each sport has rules, player responsibilities, and playing areas specific, or **internal**, to that sport. There are other aspects of sport that are not sport-specific, for example, tournaments, spectators, prizes. These aspects of the sporting world are referred to as **external** to sport, that is, not necessary for sporting activities to occur. When sport is "organized," the focus moves beyond the internal to the external aspects of sport. Advocating less structured sporting activities calls for a refocusing from the external to the internal aspects of sport. Less structured sporting activities for children would involve the adoption of modified rules, player responsibilities, and playing areas, for example, smaller playing fields, lower basketball hoops, fewer rules. By modifying the internal aspects of sporting activities, children can still enjoy the challenge of *com-petitio*, striving together, to test their skills in a context that takes their abilities (and size) into account.

A refocusing from the external to the internal aspects of sport would result in a major change to the way society organizes sport for children. If tournaments and prizes were no longer emphasized, children could focus on developing skills and challenging themselves through competition with equally skilled opponents. All children could receive the health-related and motor-fitness benefits because all children would be playing–not just the "highly skilled" children needed to win the tournament. If skill development was emphasized and winning tournaments de-emphasized, there would be far less potential for sport to create excessive anxiety, encourage aggressive behavior, and/or damage children's self-esteem.

Regarding the potential for injury and the narrow focus that exists in much of today's youth sport experience, advocating a variety of unstructured sporting experiences would help eliminate the dangers of injury and an overly narrow focus. The most common kind of injuries found in organized sport as opposed to those found in unstructured activities are overuse injuries caused by continued repetitive actions. If children are playing a variety of sports and a variety of positions, this situation will not occur. The dangers of an overly narrow focus would also be eliminated by expanding the focus of children's sporting activities.

Before concluding this chapter, it is important to address the question: "What if children *want* to achieve the external aspects of sport, for example, spectators' cheers, gold medals, and so on?" Once children are old enough to make decisions in this regard, they should be allowed to make such a choice. **Autonomy** requires making free, informed choices. Enrolling a three-year-old in a gymnastics program, with his or her parents' eye on involvement in elite gymnastics, is *not* an autonomous decision on the part of the three-year-old. Advocates of elite gymnastics would say that children have to start at that young age if they are going to compete at an elite level. But perhaps the expectations of coaches, parents, and spectators have to change if we are to wait until children are old enough to autonomously choose whether and to what extent they will be involved in sports at an elite level. Changing our expectations for a sport would be worth the preservation of autonomous individuals–individuals who will be determining the future of youth sport for the next generation.

Conclusion

This chapter involved an examination of the benefits and costs of children's participation in organized sport. The espoused benefits of youth sport include: the learning of motor skills, the development of health fitness, belonging to a team, learning socially acceptable values and behaviors, acquiring long-term skills for leisure, and enhancing child-adult relationships. A number of these benefits are unable to withstand critique.

For example, the learning of motor skills does not happen for all children involved in organized sport. Typically, the children that already have the skills receive more "playing time" than the children who need the time to develop and practice their skills. Likewise, not all children will develop health fitness through organized sport. The children who spend most of the time on the bench will definitely not develop health fitness, and those who play specific positions will develop only certain aspects of health fitness. Belonging to a team may have some value but there is also the danger that this "belonging" may interfere with the development of children as individuals as well as the exclusion of children who did not "make" the team.

The learning of socially acceptable values and behaviors cannot always be assumed to have been *caused* by participation in organized sport. Children with these values and behaviors may be the type of people who are attracted to sport in the first place. The benefit of acquiring long-term leisure would seem to apply only to children involved in sports such as cross-country skiing, running, and canoeing, rather than sports such as basketball, hockey, and baseball that require lots of people and special facilities. Finally, the benefit of enhancing the child-adult relationship found in the relationship between the child and his or her coach must be weighed against the time taken from the child-parent relationship.

As well as examining and critiquing the benefits of youth sport, the costs of youth sport were explicated. These include: low self-esteem, aggressive behavior, excessive anxiety, potential injury, undesirable moral behavior, and overly narrow focus. Although children's self-esteem may be damaged by poor performance and unrealistic expectations, performance may be improved by increased training in the skills required for that sport. Aggressive behavior frequently occurs in sports such as hockey and football, but just because this behavior seems to be condoned, most sports are not inherently violent. Excessive anxiety may result from children feeling that they may fail to perform and meet the expectations placed on them. Thus, this anxiety may be lessened by making sure children have the requisite skills and that parents and coaches do not place unreasonable demands on children. Suffering an injury is a potential cost of participating in organized sport. These injuries range from overuse injuries to health-related problems such as eating disorders. Undesirable moral behavior, like socially appropriate behavior, cannot be assumed to result from participation in organized sport. Children who cheat in sports may also be the sort of people who cheat on tests or lie to their parents. Finally, an overly narrow focus may result from participation in organized sport, leaving little time for "downtime" or other interests.

It would appear that the costs of participating in organized sports would outweigh the benefits that withstood critique. However, by focusing on the internal versus the external aspects of sport, many of the costs could be reduced and children could focus on developing skills and challenging themselves through competition with equally skilled opponents. All children could receive the benefits of participating in organized sport because all children would be playing, and not just the "highly skilled" children needed to win the tournament.

CHAPTER REVIEW

Key Concepts

- motor skills
- health fitness
- belonging to a team
- learning socially acceptable values and behaviors
- long-term skills for leisure
- enhancing child-adult relationships
- self-esteem
- aggressive behavior
- excessive anxiety
- potential injury
- undesirable moral behavior
- overly narrow focus
- internal and external aspects of sport
- autonomy

Review Questions

1. What are the six benefits of organized sport discussed in this chapter?
2. For each of the benefits discussed, what are the counter-examples that could be levied against them?
3. What are the six "costs" of organized sport discussed in this chapter?
4. For each of the costs discussed, determine if the negative outcome is inherent to organized sport or if the priorities of youth sport could be changed to lessen the "cost."
5. How should the benefit of "learning socially acceptable values and behaviors" and the cost of "undesirable moral behavior" be understood in terms of the causal and/or correlative distinction?
6. Explain the distinction between the internal and external aspects of sport.
7. How would shifting focus from the external to the internal aspects of sport affect the "costs" and benefits of youth sport?
8. What role should autonomy play in youth sport?

5

What Do Athletes Have to Say about Ethical Issues in Sport?

We're not going to win this and we might as well blow it, we might as well just, just blow it to have some fun, hurt somebody. (Fifteen-year-old Double A Midget Hockey Player [Drewe Dixon 2002, 4])

The preceding chapters have all been philosophical in nature. However, examining what athletes have to say about ethical issues has an **empirical** dimension to it, that is, it involves collecting date from subjects. Philosophers typically hypothesize examples that they then analyze. To analyze actual examples cited by athletes will be an important improvement in this process. Twelve university-level athletes were interviewed and were asked to share examples of situations where they found themselves facing ethical issues. This line of questioning required the athletes to clarify their interpretation of an ethical issue. Having shared these issues, the athletes were then asked how they came to some resolution.

The second phase of this project involved interpreting the athletes' answers concerning the reasons they gave for the decisions they made when resolving ethical issues. The framework used in analyzing the words and experiences of the athletes was derived from moral philosophy. Most of the empirical research conducted in the area of sport and moral reasoning has focused on theories of moral development, for example, Piagetian or Kolbergian theories (Booth 1981; Figley 1984; Romance 1988; Brandi 1989; Shields and Bredemeier 1995), while most of the research concerned with moral theory and/or philosophy has been conceptual in nature (Arnold 1983; Fraleigh 1984; Zeigler 1984; Feezel 1986; Shea 1996). This project was an attempt to integrate empirical research with a conceptual analysis derived from moral theory and/or philosophy.

In the final section of this chapter, the implications of the preceding analysis for moral education will be examined–specifically, the possibility of moral education in sport and physical education contexts (for example programs, see Martinek and Hellison 1997; Miller, Bredemeier, and Shields 1997). An understanding of athletes' moral reasoning, or lack thereof, has significant implications for coaches who could be facilitating the development of the critical-thinking skills and dispositions required in moral reasoning. The connection between critical thinking and moral reasoning is important. As Siegel (1988) notes,

> a morally mature person must recognize the centrality and force of moral reasons in moral deliberation, and moral education must seek to foster that recognition. Such "rational virtues" as impartiality of judgment and recognition of the force of reasons, to name just two such virtues, are indispensable to moral education. They are also, we have seen, central aspects of critical thinking. (p.109)

Sport and physical education programs provide opportune contexts for developing moral-reasoning skills and dispositions in both students who will continue on in sports as well as those who will not become elite athletes. Key concepts utilized in this chapter include: **ethical issue, "doing unto others as you would have them do unto you," fairness, respecting others, not hurting the team, respect for the game, fear of getting caught, deontological theory, teleological theory, consequentialist theory, moral education, moral considerations, formal** and **instrumental, critical thinking skills**, and **example** and **precept**.

What Athletes Have to Say

In choosing the twelve athletes, an attempt was made to achieve a gender balance. However, because there were fewer women's teams than men's teams, eight of the athletes interviewed were men and four were women. An attempt was also made to achieve representation from the variety of sports teams involved in the university athletic program. This process resulted in interviews with five individual sport athletes and seven team sport athletes.

Over half of the athletes interviewed had difficulty defining an **ethical issue**. They usually ended up citing examples, for example, cheating, playing dirty, trash talking, and taking drugs. Those athletes who were able to articulate some sort of definition related ethical issues to the obedience to or the breaking of rules, for example, "a situation in which you have to weigh whether you go against what the rule is or go with the rule, because the choice is either winning or losing." Other athletes gave broader definitions, concerned mainly with doing what was right or wrong, for example: "Deciding whether it's right or wrong and what consequences you'll have to face," and "You're faced with sort of the right and wrong, the ways that you should conduct yourself, sort of the standards," and "Maybe what's acceptable or what's not acceptable." One athlete raised the notion of guilt, as well as not harming people: "Doing things that I'm not going to feel guilty about afterwards would be being ethical. And doing things that aren't going to harm people."

A few athletes' answers were concerned not with harming people, but rather harming the nature of sport, for example, "People–administrative people, coaches, doing things that isn't [sic] in the nature or spirit of sport. That would be unethical, in my opinion," and "Ethics is more like ... more of your attitude I guess, towards a sport. This is the way I think of ethics and stuff, like the way you work, things you do to get yourself ready for games and practicing situations and stuff like that," and "Something that will bring up a lot of stink in the whole ... in the whole area of sport, just anything like judges, officials, disqualifications, coaching types, coaching." An interesting perspective concerning the "nature of the sport" was raised by the answers given by the hockey players. It was interesting to note that the two hockey players interviewed did not consider the fighting involved in hockey to be regarded as "dirty play": "I mean, that's the way the game's played by nature. I mean, as a fan going to a game you want to see a good physical game where there's a lot of hard hitting," and "I can try and get other players off their game on the other team by giving them a little shot and stuff like that and a couple cheap shots, but that ... I mean that's coming back to it again, we consider that part of the game." One of the hockey players made fighting for a team sound almost ethical: "Yeah, probably when you're fighting for your team it is more ethical, or noble than when you're just fighting for yourself." It was interesting to note that the hockey players could not think of any ethical issues in their sport.

The ethical issues shared by the athletes could be grouped into those that could harm other people and those that could harm the nature of the sport. A further categorization could be made between those issues that involve preparation for the game, for example, taking drugs, and those that occur during the game, for example, playing dirty and trash talking. It should be noted that issues that occur pre-game and during the game could hurt both people and the nature of the sport.

Having shared examples of ethical issues in their respective sports, the athletes were asked how they would resolve these issues. The answers given by the athletes were surprising but encouraging. Either univerity-level athletes are unique as an athletic level, or very ethical athletes were randomly chosen, or athletes are hesitant to share unethical behavior, but all ten athletes who were able to come up with examples of an ethical issue leaned toward what most people would consider the more "positive" choice, for example, not taking drugs, not fighting, and so forth. The possibility that athletes might not represent their ways of dealing with ethical issues honestly did not really matter for the purposes of this study. What *did* matter was the *reasons* the athletes gave for making their decisions. The reasons the athletes gave could be divided into six categories: reasons concerned with (1) "doing unto others as you would have them do unto you," (2) fairness, (3) respecting others, (4) not hurting the team, (5) respect for the game, and (6) fear of getting caught. What should be noted is that these categories are not exclusive. In fact, the first three categories are very interrelated, which will become evident in the "Interpretation" section.

Four of the athletes' reasons fell under the **"doing unto others as you would have them do unto you"** category. When one of the athletes was asked if he would "fudge" his weigh-in, he responded:

> Well, that would raise a lot of concerns with me simply because by me accepting that I would fear that everyone else was doing it. When you have an honour system, it's there for a reason and that's to keep a certain balance ... to keep some fairness and incompromise and integrity in any situation. You take that away on one part, yeah, you might be burning someone else but then you can be burned back. And that's just a situation I wouldn't want to be involved in. I'd rather keep things on an even playing field.

This same athlete experienced some tension with the "do unto others" attitude:

> In the middle of a match, to be frank with you, I've attacked knees. I mean, I've got a bad knee right now. I wouldn't want it done to me at this point in the game, but it... There is ... I guess there's a line and I guess it's there.... I shouldn't say there's a line. There probably is a gray area and the way we perceive it really tends to be in the different situation.

When another athlete was asked why he would not "play dirty," his response was, "I don't know. I've just, I've always hated when people played dirty on me." The track athlete, when asked why he would not cut another runner off, responded: "I don't want to interfere with them because you don't want it to happen to yourself as well." "Doing unto others" can also apply to your own teammates. One athlete, in reference to backing up a teammate, stated that "the thing is that if I didn't back him up, the next time maybe the situation might be in my hands or I might not be able to handle someone and I might not ... and he might not even come and back me up just because the fact that I didn't do it for him before."

The second category of reasons had to do with the issue of **fairness**. Two athletes made explicit reference to the notion of fairness. The athlete quoted above, regarding the "weigh-in" system, stated: "When you have an honor system, it's there for a reason and that's to keep a certain balance ... to keep some *fairness* [emphasis added].... I'd rather keep things on an even playing field, you know." The sentiment of an "even playing field" was raised by another athlete: "You know that in a race everything's supposed to be fair to each ... each athlete, so ... all the conditions are supposed to be fair, so you don't wanna ... you know, I guess win on the ... not the same terms as everybody else."

Related to the issue of fairness is the third category of reasons given concerning the resolution of an ethical issue; that being **respect for others**. The athlete who did not want to cut another runner off did not want that to happen to him, but he also pointed out that by cutting others off "you're disrespecting other runners." The athlete who would back up his teammate (for the reason that he would want to be backed up as well) also stated that "I mean you just kind of do it out of ... out of respect for the person and just 'cause he's your teammate and you don't want him getting hurt or ... or anything."

Closely related to "respecting your teammates" (not necessarily your opponents) is the fourth reason, **not hurting your team**. As one athlete put it: "You don't do chopping in practice, cause your own teammates. You don't want to hurt your own friends, your own team." Besides not physically hurting their own teammates, some of the athletes wanted to make sure their teammates were not hurt by the opposing team.

> We've had circumstances this year where we've sent guys off the bench to go out and fight other players on other teams just to kinda get a message across. So that may be ... I mean, for me that's not really unethical. That's part of the game if the team's going after your best player, I mean, you have to do something to stop that. But for a person like yourself or a fan, you may think, "Well, he's sending him out to beat someone up! That can't be ethical." But from the player's perspective, I mean, you see that as part of the game. You don't want your best players getting injured and you have to take measures to stop that.

Protecting one's teammates need not apply only to physical protection. Some players felt that they had to protect their teammates verbally by returning trash talk being directed at a teammate.

> If someone's ... you know, going to do something to your teammate. You want to be there right behind him and back him up or something. You know, if someone's going to trash talk you, then you [sic] just gonna let it ... the same guy that's trash talking your teammate, you better tell him the same thing or give him something back.

This same athlete used an interesting military analogy: "So, it's pretty hard to win when you don't have six guys that are going to be right behind each other like, if you're going to go to war with each other on the court, you gotta have six guys that are going to go to war with each other." Another athlete shared a similar military example: "It's a team sport so if I do something that causes a penalty, my team suffers. It's like in the military. You know, one person does it and the whole platoon has to do push-ups or whatever. So it's ... it has to do with whether you're a team player or an individual, I think." Concern for the team is evident in the example of an athlete choosing to avoid a penalty: "Sometimes you think, 'Oh, I just wanna slash him,' but then I think, 'Well, then I might get a penalty and that might put my team down even worse,'" and "I mean, there's times I just lose it and I just go but most times I think you think, okay, well I mean I can't do this because it's gonna hurt my team in the long run," and "I'm a team player. I'm more concerned with my team than just me. So, I mean if somebody's giving me a cheap shot, I'll be mad, but you know I try not to do anything that'll harm my team."

The fifth reason some of the athletes gave for making the decisions they made concerning ethical issues had to do with a respect, not so much for others, but for the game and one's ability to play the game. The notion of **respecting the game** was made clear in an eloquent response by one of the wrestlers:

> It feels good to fully understand something. Like, to fully understand the sport of wrestling and like, there's all the physiological things going on, there's all the physics, the energy system parts of it. There's just a plethora of angles and everything ... like, there's math galore going on.... There's everything going on in this five-minute span and, God, I just want to be able to experience them all.

This same athlete was more concerned with improving his wrestling skills than with winning: "[My coach said], 'We'll pick things that we want you to practice and be well at, and focus on those things.' And that made me get away from wanting to win." The desire to improve skills as opposed to winning had not always been this athlete's goal. When younger, he had thought, "Winning means peers, so you wanna win." Another athlete was also not that concerned with winning, and her reasons included the enjoyment of the sport itself as well as extrinsic reasons: "Like, I don't have the big goals to win an Olympic gold medal, like, I'm more of a swimmer to swim because I enjoy it and because it has health benefits for me, it's ... I have fun, and meet friends, and stuff like that and, you know, it's not that big of a deal for me not to come home with a huge medal all the time."

Respecting the game seemed to imply respecting one's ability to play the game, that is, one's skill. In giving reasons for why she would not "trash talk," one athlete said, "I wanna be, you know respected and for what I can do, and not for what I ... how I behave like an idiot, in my opinion." This same athlete emphasized the importance of skills: "You know, I don't wanna win that way. If I'm gonna win, I'm gonna win because of how I execute my skills and that ... and not that I'm trying in someone's head, you know." Related to the use of skill was the notion of playing the game "on your own" as opposed to cheating (through the use of drugs, rule breaking, and so forth). "I don't think you get the same satisfaction out of it if you don't do it on your own," and "For me, personally, there would be no satisfaction in winning something that I cheated for." The athlete who saw no satisfaction in cheating to win summed it up: "Like, just play the game, and that sort of thing ... and I don't get the rest of it ... in my head, it doesn't make sense." Another athlete reiterated this sentiment: "You know, I just wanna play the game."

The sixth reason, **fear of getting caught**, was expressed by only one athlete, and this athlete, upon further reflection, decided she would not cheat. Regarding her refusal to use performance-enhancing drugs, this athlete responded: "But you never know, 'cause I don't know if I'm doing it because it's so much ... right to do. Maybe I'm doing it because they can test me at any time and I don't want to be caught." It is interesting to share in this athlete's moral reasoning process regarding her refusal to use drugs:

> Why do I do it? I suppose the biggest reason is being caught. But ... I don't.... I suppose there's always ways you could get around it if you really had to so I suppose I'm not doing it because it's wrong. But ... I guess it's hard until you've really been pressured to do it and someone's... So, if someone comes up to you and says, "There's absolutely no way you're going to be caught," how are you going to do it? But I don't think I would. But I suppose you really don't know until you get that chance. But I don't think I would. No. No. I think I want to achieve it on my own.

Although this athlete is sharing her moral reasoning process, some athletes said it was not possible to reason this way while playing the game:

> Especially at our level, it's very fast and very high level. It's your thinking. I find when I'm thinking out on the ice, that's when I get into trouble because ... well, I'm a lot slower. I have to go on my instincts and reactions so it's just the way it goes.... Like you do the thinking ahead of time and then when you get into the game, it's all reaction. And when you're going on reaction, sometimes anything can happen, like that's when your emotion may take over so you have to try and keep things in equal balance.

When asked whether the "pre-game thinking" involved thoughts on ethical issues, the athlete responded: "No, it's mostly just like ... breakout, forechecks, and stuff like that.... I've never thought of the ethical aspects of a ... of the game." Whether athletes *should* be thinking of the ethical aspects of the game will be examined in the final section of this chapter.

An Interpretation of the Athletes' Reasons within the Framework of Moral Philosophy

Moral philosophy is a well-established scholarly discipline, but the application of insights gleaned from a study of this discipline to the practice of sport has not received much attention in the scholarly literature. Thus, a review, albeit brief, of theories of moral philosophy is required before applying these theories to the words and experiences of the athletes interviewed.

Theories of moral philosophy have traditionally been divided into three categories: (1) deontological, for example, Kantism; (2) teleological, for example, virtue theory; and (3) consequentialist, for example, ethical egoism (Donaldson 1986, 5-7). The resolution of a moral dilemma and/or issue can be interpreted from one or another of these three perspectives. The major types of moral theories will be summarized, and then the six categories of reasons shared by the athletes will be placed into one or another of the different categories of moral theory.

Deontological theory involves moral reasoning based on principles. The major type of deontological theory has been rationalism, and the classic example of such a rationalist theory is Kant's theory of the moral law, which he called the categorical imperative. In the *Groundwork of the Metaphysics of Morals* (1785), Kant expressed the categorical imperative in two forms: "Act only according to that maxim by which you can at the same time will that it should become a universal law"; and "Act so that you treat humanity, whether in your own person or in that of another, always as an end and never as a means only." Referring to such an imperative as "categorical," Kant is emphasizing that one has a duty to follow a particular maxim unconditionally, regardless of particular outcomes.

Teleological theory considers the *telos*, meaning "the end" or "inherent nature" for which we strive in making moral decisions. The major type of teleological theory would be that of virtue theory, first proposed by Aristotle but more recently receiving renewed attention by Anscombe (1958), MacIntyre (1984), and Carr (1996). Where deontological theories focus on *doing* (based on duty), virtue theory focuses on *being*–being a certain type of person. "Human beings, like the members of all other species, have a specific nature: and that nature is such that they have certain aims and goals, such that they move by nature towards a specific *telos*. The good is defined in terms of their specific characteristics" (MacIntyre 1984, 148). There may be some disagreement on these "specific characteristics." As MacIntyre (1984) points out, "[t]his view [that there are agreed-upon characteristics] ignores the place in our cultural history of deep conflicts over what human flourishing and well-being do consist in and the way in which rival and incompatible beliefs on that topic beget rival and incompatible tables of the virtues" (pp.162-163).

However, some philosophers have proposed lists of virtues, for example:

benevolence	fairness	reasonableness
civility	friendliness	self-confidence
compassion	generosity	self-control
conscientiousness	honesty	self-discipline

cooperativeness	industriousness	self-reliance
courage	justice	tactfulness
courteousness	loyalty	thoughtfulness
dependability	moderation	(Rachels 1993, 163)

Although it is only partial (and not everyone will agree with the contents of this list), it does give us a start in attempting to analyze the reasons the athletes gave for making ethical decisions.

The third category of moral theory is the consequentialist theory. **Consequentialist theory** involves a consideration of the consequences of particular moral decisions. The major type of consequentialist theory is utilitarianism. Utilitarianism is concerned with the consequences of particular actions. Specifically, utilitarianism is concerned with achieving the greatest good for the greatest number. Utilitarianism has also been referred to as "ethical universalism" in that the ultimate end is the greatest general good. Another consequentialist theory is that of ethical egoism, which holds that one is always to do what will promote his or her greatest good (Frankena 1973, 15). The difference between ethical universalism and ethical egoism is important in analyzing the reasons the athletes gave when resolving ethical dilemmas.

In analyzing the six categories of reasons the athletes gave for making an ethical decision, it became evident that all three types of moral theory came into play. The first category, "doing unto others as you would have them do unto you," is a prime example of Kant's deontological categorical imperative: "Act only according to that maxim by which you can at the same time will that it should become a universal law." The second category concerning fairness is intimately related to Kant's categorical imperative. If some behavior would cause an element of "unfairness," then the whole construct of the game or contest is in jeopardy. As Wigmore and Tuxill (1995) put it, "To will that everyone in a game should cheat would be to render cheating impossible, as well as pointless, since cheating or unfair play is only a meaningful activity if everyone else involved is playing fair, and it is assumed that they are doing so" (p.70).

The third category involving respect for others is a prime example of Kant's second form of the categorical imperative: "Act so that you treat humanity, whether in your own person or in that of another, always as an end and never as a means only." An example of treating a person as a means, rather than as an end, would occur if an athlete decided to cheat because he or she would be using his or her opponents only as a "means" to win the game. Once more, Wigmore and Tuxill (1995) note the importance of this Kantian principle:

> Cheating, from this perspective, also involves a cognate "means-end" reversal, that constitutes a failure of respect for persons, since other players become merely means to the ends of the cheat, rather than equal participants in a joint and conscious purpose and activity; they are used as a means to an end which is not theirs and to which they have not consented.... (p.72)

It is important to point out when following the Kantian duty of respect for persons that "persons" would include not only your own teammates, but also your opponents. Arnold (1988) relates the notion of Kantian respect to altruistic behavior:

> Altruism is perhaps best understood as having to do with those forms of action and conduct that are not done merely because of what is fair and just in terms of playing and keeping to the rules but because, in addition, there is a genuine concern for, an interest in, and concern for one's fellow competitors, whether on the same side *or in opposition* [emphasis added]. (pp.51-52)

The fourth category of not hurting the team may on the surface be perceived as an example of a Kantian respect for persons. However, a distinction seemed to be made here between one's own team and the opposition; that is, the athlete would be concerned about not hurting one's own team, but hurting the opposition was not an issue. This reason is less of a respect for persons and more of an exhibition of the virtue of loyalty; thus we have an example of teleological virtue theory in action.

The teleological theory proposed by Aristotle could also be seen as applying to the fifth reason, respect for the game. Although virtue theory would seem to apply only to humans, Aristotle applied his conception of *telos*, or inherent nature, to all things, human or not (Donaldson 1986, 6). If we consider respect for the game as involving respect for the inherent nature of the game, athletes who chose to focus on improvement of skills rather than solely on winning the game would appear to be seeking the inherent nature of competitive games (note the Latin root word of *com-petitio* involving a "striving together" [Hyland 1988, 236]).

The sixth reason cited in resolving ethical issues involved the fear of getting caught. This reason would be an example of the third type of moral theory, the consequentialist theory, particularly ethical egoism. The ethical egoist would always do what would promote his or her greatest good and would refrain from doing what would not promote his or her greatest good. In most cases, "getting caught" would be an example of something that would not promote one's greatest good, and thus an ethical egoist would refrain from making a choice that could result in the possibility of getting caught.

Having analyzed the words and experiences of the athletes interviewed within the framework of moral theory, we turn now to a discussion of the implications of this analysis for the possibility of moral education in a physical education context.

Implications for Moral Education in Sport and Physical Education

The preceding discussion has important implications for the possibility of **moral education** in sport and physical education contexts in at least three ways. First of all, the responses of the hockey players interviewed open up the whole area of whether sport experiences should be subjected to the same moral considerations as other life experiences. That is, for example, should considerations of respect and fairness apply to sports as they do to other human activities? If an affirmative answer is assumed, then the possibility of providing an education in the area of moral reasoning becomes tenable. This possibility leads to the second area where the interviews with the athletes can be informative; that is, reviewing the categories of reasons cited and their reflection of moral theory can help coaches and teachers facilitate the development of moral reasoning skills in their athletes and students. Finally, the very possibility of the athletes articulating the reasons they have for making certain ethical decisions has implications for how coaches and teachers can help facilitate the development of moral reasoning. Each of these areas will be considered in turn.

The hockey players interviewed were unable to think of any ethical issues in their sport. It was not the case that they were denying that their hockey games involved fighting, cheap shots, infractions of rules, and so forth, but that these behaviors were justified because "that's the way the game's played by nature." This sentiment raises the fundamental issue of whether sport experiences should be subject to the same **moral considerations** involved in other life experiences; that is, does the "nature of the game" permit behavior that could be deemed morally unacceptable outside the context of the game? The paradigm example of this situation would have to be boxing. If the possibility of fighting was removed from hockey, we could still have a hockey game, but this would not be the case with boxing. "[B]oxing looks morally incongruous with the rest of life. Those responses to other selves, which outside the ring would be unacceptable and mystifying, are appropriate and lauded inside the boxing ring. No explanation is required for that vicious ferocity inside the ring towards another self" (Davis 1993/1994, 55).

Perhaps it is time that a civilized society seeks an "explanation" for this sort of activity. The explanation alluded to by the athletes interviewed concerned the "nature of the game." It is true that games are social constructions, involving self-contained means and ends. But does this imply that larger issues such as issues of morality should have no impact on such self-contained activity? Reddiford, in an article entitled "Morality and the Games Player" (1981), has one of his proponents make a distinction between moral rules, one of whose characteristics is the possibility of universalizability, and constitutive rules made by groups or individuals that make certain practices possible, for example, rules of games, parliamentary procedure, and wedding ceremonies. Unlike moral rules, these constitutive rules are not universal. However, Reddiford points out that

> [i]t does not follow from this distinction that there are some areas of life that are pre-eminently moral and some that are only, so to speak, derivatively so–that there is an inside/outside distinction to be made in moral matters. It is not the case that those engaged in rule-governed practices of the sorts indicated only partake of morality in some secondary sense, that when, for example, they wish to justify what they do when playing a game the players must have resort to some purer, primary, moral sphere. (p.12)

Reddiford supports this contention by making a further distinction between the **formal** rules of a game, for example, what counts as offside, and the **instrumental** activities, for example, strategy, that are not the subject of legislation. "Since games permit a wide range of instrumental actions they leave open the possibilities of acting morally or immorally" (ibid.).

Another way of looking at the moral culpability involved in human-constructed practices is to view the possible behaviors within the practice as existing along a continuum. A paradigm case here would be that of war (an analogy to sport that was actually cited by some of the athletes interviewed). The "rules" involved in the practice of war differ from the rules involved in a non-war situation, for example, it is acceptable to kill your enemy in wartime whereas it is not acceptable to kill during peacetime. However, there are still rules regarding wartime killing, for example, limits on chemicals in warfare. Returning to the boxing situation, Davis (1993/1994) questions the culpability of boxing:

> If boxing does not essentially promote violence [he supports this argument by emphasizing the disciplined and regulated nature of boxing], it is questionable whether boxing should be placed in the dock, in the case where contingent features of context allow it to play a causal role in the generation of some violence. We do not believe that beer producers are a priori implicated in alcoholism, nor car manufacturers in road fatalities, nor candy makers in premature tooth decay. (p.51)

Returning to the concept of the continuum of moral behavior, we can see that beer producers can encourage vast amount of alcoholic consumption, or they can remain silent on drinking habits, or they can promote responsible drinking (as do many beer companies in their campaigns against drinking and driving). Likewise, car manufacturers can emphasize the high speeds that their cars can reach, or they can remain silent on road safety, or they can promote responsible driving (as witnessed in the Speed Kills campaigns evident in the province of Manitoba). The analogy with boxing could suggest the possibility of "giving and parrying of light blows with no intention of striking the opponent severely" (McCormick 1962, 70), or something similar to what we see in Olympic-style boxing, or what we witness in professional boxing. Anywhere along this continuum, we might say that a "morality line" has been crossed.

Whether we argue for the applicability of moral rules to sport based upon the possibility of behaving morally or immorally during instrumental activities (as opposed to simply breaking or adhering to formal rules), or whether we take the line of argument that sport activities involve behaviors that fall along a "moral continuum" and at some point a behavior has "gone too far," athletes will encounter moments when a decision has to be made concerning whether a particular behavior would violate a moral rule or push an issue of morality "too far." In order for athletes to make such decisions, they must have some underlying moral theory to guide them. The responses provided by the athletes interviewed showed that this was the case. The analysis of the words and experiences of the athletes demonstrated that that the reasons they gave when resolving ethical issues could be interpreted as being based upon all three major types of moral theory, that is, deontological, teleological, and consequentialist theories. However, it appeared that most athletes' reasons fell under only one of each of these moral theory categories. This provides important information for the coach or teacher interested in facilitating the development of his or her students' and/or athletes' moral reasoning skills and dispositions.

If athletes (or anyone, for that matter) consider only one moral perspective when deliberating over an ethical issue, important considerations may be overlooked. Thus, it is important to have a grasp on more than one moral theory in order to give an ethical issue the most comprehensive consideration possible. As Arnold (1988) points out,

> [it] will be seen that the Kantian view of morality has a lot in common with the justice theory of sport as well as with those preconditional features of sportsmanship which are to do with fairness. In stressing the universal and impartial, however, the Kantian view seems to overlook or disregard some aspects of interpersonal relations which are as morally important in sport as in other spheres of life. I refer to such virtues as sympathy, compassion, concern and friendship.(p.51)

Thus, Arnold is arguing for a consideration of Kant's deontological theory as well as a version of virtue theory. Zeigler (1984) argues for what he calls a "triple-play approach," where someone contemplating an ethical dilemma would follow three steps: (1) Kant's Test of Consistency, (2) Mill's Test of

Consequences, and (3) Aristotle's Test of Intentions (pp.48-55). There will, of course, be moments where considering various moral theories will result in conflicting prescriptions. However, this does not mean that teachers and coaches should avoid teaching various moral perspectives. Rather, the importance of facilitating **critical thinking skills** in their students and athletes becomes apparent.

> The greater the ability to reason, the better able we will be to address moral issues. Moral reasoning is a problem-solving activity, a way of trying to find answers. It is no different than any other logical and systematic process except that it involves offering reasons for or against moral beliefs. Moral reasoning is a way to critique questions and answers. It is not limited to a defensive position of what we believe or know to be right, rather, our purpose in moral reasoning is to discover the truth. In moral reasoning, opposing positions are analyzed to decide whether we should agree or not (Lumpkin, Stoll, and Beller 1994, 5).

The ability of the interviewed athletes to articulate reasons for choosing one or another action in an ethical issue demonstrated not only which moral theory their reasons were based upon, but also the importance of discussion concerning ethical issues. This has important implications for the coach or teacher in a sport or physical education context. As discussed in Chapter 3, one important means by which a coach or a teacher can facilitate moral development is through example. As Arnold (1989) points out, the ethical way to conduct oneself on the playing field is as much "caught as taught" (p.24). Therefore, the teacher or coach must be genuinely committed to being a good sportsperson.

Although "teaching through example" is an indispensable means of instilling respect in athletes and students, attention must also be given to the reasons participants give for respecting opponents, and this will require more direct teaching. "[T]o be fully moral one must do the right things as well as have the right reason. Both are required" (Hamm 1989, 141). Meakin (1981) suggests that the teacher or coach, although acknowledging that their athletes have a choice as to whether or not to make positive ethical decisions, should still "condemn 'bad' practices and recommend 'good' ones" (p.246). Thus, through **example** and **precept**, coaches and teachers should do all that they can to help facilitate the moral reasoning skills of their athletes and students. Participation in sports can then be seen as an opportunity to practice moral behavior rather than as an occasion to practice immoral behavior, which not only impedes the participants' own moral growth but also tarnishes the possibilities inherent in sport to provide a practice field for morally appropriate behavior.

Conclusion

In determining what athletes had to say about ethical issues in sport, it was important to hear the athletes' own words concerning the ethical issues they had encountered and how they had resolved them. Ethical issues that the athletes interviewed referred to included: cheating, playing dirty, trash talk, and taking drugs. When asked how they resolved the ethical issues they encountered, the athletes' reasons fell into six categories: (1) "doing unto others as you would have them do unto you," (2) fairness, (3) respecting others, (4) not hurting the team, (5) respect for the game, and (6) fear of getting caught. These six categories or reasons can be further subdivided into the three traditional theories of moral philosophy: deontological theory, teleological theory, and consequentialist theory. Noting that most athletes reasoned from only one moral theory perspective gives the coach and/or teacher a reason to help their athletes expand their moral reasoning by discussing alternative perspectives as well as helping their athletes develop critical thinking skills. The suggestion that moral considerations play as much of a role inside the sports arena as outside should give the coach or teacher impetus to provide a moral example as well as moral education for their athletes.

CHAPTER REVIEW

Key Concepts

- ethical issue
- "doing unto others as you would have them do unto you"
- fairness
- respecting others
- not hurting the team
- respect for the game
- fear of getting caught
- deontological theory
- teleological theory
- consequentialist theory
- moral education
- moral considerations
- formal and instrumental
- critical thinking skills
- example and precept

Review Questions

1. What were some of the examples of ethical issues cited by the athletes interviewed for this chapter?
2. The reasons the athletes gave for resolving the ethical issues in the way that they did could be divided into what six categories?
3. Describe the three main theories of moral philosophy.
4. Which theory of moral philosophy best describes each of the six categories of reasons the athletes gave for resolving ethical issues?
5. What is the distinction Reddiford makes between formal rules and instrumental activities and how does this distinction relate to the "nature of the game justifies questionable behavior" argument?
6. What are some examples of the concept of a continuum of moral behavior?
7. What is problematic if athletes tend to reason from only one moral perspective, and what can the coach or teacher do to address this issue?
8. What does it mean to teach by example and precept, and how can these manners of teaching affect the moral development of athletes?

6

What Do Coaches Have to Say about Ethical Issues in Sport?

You know you are giving something up to either do something that is right by the team, player, colleague, just pure morals and ethics, you know, and you may lose out on something. You may lose out on something like winning. (University-level coach)

In the study described in the previous chapter, university-level athletes were interviewed in an attempt to ascertain what sort of ethical issues they encountered in their sport and how they resolved these issues. A topic that arose in the interviews concerned the influence of the coach on the athletes' perceptions and resolution of ethical issues in their sport. To better understand the influence of the coach, a subsequent study was conducted with university-level coaches. Six male and three female coaches at a large Canadian university were interviewed (a gender balance could not be achieved because of the small number of female coaches in Canada). The sports coached included: ice hockey, field hockey, basketball, volleyball, football, and swimming. Questions similar to those asked of the athletes were posed to the coaches–questions pertaining to examples of ethical issues and how the coaches resolved these. A further question asked of the coaches concerned the notion of autonomy: how much autonomy should athletes be given in resolving ethical issues in their sport?

In this chapter, the ethical issues shared by the coaches will be examined, including how they resolved these issues. The coaches' perceptions and resolutions of ethical issues will be compared and contrasted with the answers given by the athletes. A distinction will be made between male and female coach responses in order to determine possible gender differences. Differences between the coaches' and athletes' perceptions and resolutions of ethical issues raise questions concerning the autonomy of the athlete. Thus, a conceptual analysis of the notion of autonomy will be conducted. Different conceptions of autonomy and how each conception translates into the coach-athlete relationship will be considered. Key concepts utilized in this chapter include: **ethical issue, moral/values/ethical beliefs, concern for the individual, fairness, respect for others, gender**

differences, gender theory, autonomy, self-sufficiency, self-rule, coach-athlete relationship, and **informed consent**.

Ethical Issues Faced by Coaches

Before sharing examples of ethical issues faced by coaches and their athletes, the coaches were asked to define an **ethical issue**. The most common theme to emerge from their answers had to do with making a decision between doing something that would be better for the team, that is, a win; or doing something that would be better for the individuals involved, including the coach, whose moral principles might be compromised if the first action was chosen:

> I would define an ethical dilemma as a situation where a coach has to make a decision philosophically whether to go ahead with something where in one case it may be better for the team, but in the case of humanistic development or his philosophy in life probably goes counter to what is the norm. (male coach)

> I feel an ethical dilemma is something that I know that there is kind of two sides to it; whereby if you go one route, you know that probably you are doing the right thing, but the other side of that, which creates the dilemma, is that if you do the so called "right thing," you may not get the maybe immediate results that you need to get, and to me that is where the dilemma comes in. (male coach)

> A dilemma ... I would think ... if you do something and the end result usually it's about winning or losing ... in effect then you may be challenged as to what your... [E]thically, you may think the right choice is A, but the outcome of that choice is not what you want. (female coach)

The coaches' perceptions of an ethical issue as a choice between what would be best for the team, that is, a win, and what would be best for an individual played itself out in the examples of ethical issues shared by the coaches. One of the most recurring examples of an ethical issue shared by the coaches was whether to play an injured athlete:

> I guess one common one [ethical issue] would be a player's ability to play if injured and whether ... you always have that dilemma of ... of whether they're actually ready to play or not and it would certainly be an asset to the team if they'd play, even if they'd only play 60 or 65 percent of their capability, they'd still be an asset to the team. But it's at ... at the risk of the person's, I guess, well-being or ... their health. (male coach)

> I look on it as some sort of a struggle between, should I really play this player because it is not right for her, should I play this player because I need her to play. (female coach)

> I think of the injury situation, whereby you know a player is injured and you try to rationalize and define the injury by "Okay Joe, are you injured or are you hurt?" Well, really they are the same thing. But I know I've done it and I know a lot of coaches who use that definition in terms of injury. (male coach)

The other frequently recurring example shared by the coaches concerned whether to play a player who had missed practice:

> You have rules for teams. These rules should be consistent with all players in the program. Now, player A misses or is late for two practices and you are in a big game on the weekend and that player has a big impact. Ethically, you should not start him and should discipline him for the two practices, but on the other side are you hurting the team's chances of winning by doing that, and should you have some other form of punishment to offset that. (male coach)

> There were times in the season where the player, through no fault of his own, had to miss maybe instead of making it to three practices leading up to the weekend, could only make one. And now you have that whole dilemma of fairness on the team....[T]hose players who've been there, working hard for all three practices, this player's only been there for one practice, and yet gets to go on a road trip or gets to play their regular shift and ... and at times ... only a couple times during the year did that become a dilemma for me. (male coach)

> Anyway, so there was this dilemma: do I play them, do I not play them? Well, I didn't, but you have to weigh the effect on the entire team. Is the lesson to be learned more valuable? (female coach)

Other examples of ethical issues that were shared by the coaches included: intentionally harming opponents, pushing the rules, pushing athletes, and the potential for intimate relationships developing between themselves and their athletes. The coaches who raised the issue of intentionally harming opponents did not approve of such action but saw the issue as a grey area in that the line between hurting someone and playing hard was not always clear:

> I don't believe that I have ever asked a player to hurt anyone. I would ask them to go out and mark them really tightly and don't give them an inch, and they are going to clash at some stage. (female coach)

> If anybody's taking runs at one of our smaller players, then our bigger players, you know, nobody has to say anything, they've been brought up that way through all their [playing] that they now have to go in and make sure that doesn't happen again. It doesn't always mean they have to go in and fight. They have to go in and, face to face with that other person, say you know, basically, "Stop–don't do that again, or there will be retaliation." (male coach)

The grey area that exists between hurting opponents and playing hard also arises in the area of "pushing" the rules:

> But there are a lot of grey areas in the rules in [my sport] and those grey areas are constantly being tested by players and coaches, and it's up to the referee to, you know, make those decisions when necessary. (male coach)

> So it [ethical issue] would be something that to me, you are asking your players to do something that goes beyond the rules of the game, but it is all in context really, my asking a player to put the ball on someone's foot to win a foul or short corner is different than going and forechecking someone in hockey. But it is all relative I guess to the sport. (female coach)

As well as trying to decide how far to push the rules, some coaches had to consider how far one could ethically push their athletes:

> My job is to push them to the limit and find out what their limits are so that I don't take them over the limits. And sometimes it happens; you do take an athlete over the limit and they get hurt and ... and is that ... should I be sued for that? No, I don't think so. I think ... if then an athlete gets hurt and I continue to train them beyond that point, then I think that's a problem. But taking athletes to the point of injury, I don't think it's unethical. (male coach)

> This year, I probably let a lot go and ... and you know, I wasn't... I should have been more disciplined as a coach with... I don't know if it's making them learn, but you know, next year... (female coach)

A final potential ethical issue shared by some of the coaches was the possibility of an intimate relationship developing between the coach and the athlete. A few of the coaches saw potential issues involving how actions might be perceived by athletes or outsiders:

> You want to comfort the athlete or you wanna say, "Hey ... good job," and you pat them on the back, you put your arm around them, or grab them by the arm, whatever. It can be perceived from the outside as sexual harassment. Now from ... the person that is receiving that, that may be perceived as "Hey, the coach appreciates what I did," or it can be perceived as a very uncomfortable feeling. And that's what defines, I think, sexual harassment. (male coach)

> You know, the obvious one [ethical dilemma] ... you know, if there's an attraction one way, how do you deal with it? It has to be approached in a way that, you know, that is more than just coaching. You know, you've gotta be able to define kind of the standard that you wanna operate with, and ... explain that "Hey, you know this is ... the situation and this is... [H]ere is how it has to be." (male coach)

> What I want to say is that a potential ethical struggle I guess for all coaches is inappropriate behavior with athletes.... I think that this is a huge dilemma that many coaches will face. It is obvious that some coaches are going to be attracted to their athletes and vice versa. (female coach)

As well as examples of ethical issues faced by the coaches, a few of them shared some examples of "non-ethical issues." These "non-issues" included the use of performance-enhancing drugs as well as alcohol, and coaches belittling athletes. Regarding performance-enhancing drug and alcohol use:

> They're not gonna tell me they're doing steroids, and probably I'm not going to find out, but I may. If I find out, there's no issue. That is a rule and I have to deal with that rule. That's not debatable, you know. (male coach)

> We have two rules: number one, there is no alcohol on the plane there and back, for coaches or athletes, there is no alcohol in the hotel at anytime, for anybody–coaches or athletes no matter what ... [and] there will absolutely be no parties and no girls brought back to the hotel period.... So we are going to avoid that issue by you not being in there. Now if that issue happens, then

> there is no dilemma here. You are wrong because you violated this code and not only would you be in trouble with the university, you would be suspended by me. (male coach)

Two coaches did consider alcohol use by their athletes to be an ethical issue they had faced:

> The last night of the tournament, in fact, one of the underage players did get very drunk and I think the thing that disturbed me about that the most was that... I guess I've always been worried that they would think, "Oh God, you're just a stick in the mud." So that is a struggle whether this is a popularity contest with my players, or am I supposed to be making sure that... [A]gain that was on the last night of the tournament. (female coach)

> So when we went away and we said, "No drinking," and there's three athletes from last year's team and they're in their room drinking.... [S]o we cut her. The other two were humiliated. They, you know, they were disgusted with the way I handled it, and it was hard because they were personal friends of mine. (female coach)

It is interesting to note that the two coaches who had trouble with their athletes using alcohol were female. Possible gender differences will be examined in a later section of the chapter.

A few of the coaches mentioned an issue that should be considered an ethical issue but was one that was not relevant to their situations–the issue of belittling athletes:

> They [some coaches] belittle their athletes and sort of degrade them at times and that's been another one [ethical issue] that I've had to deal with a few times. And let the coaches who think that screaming at athletes ... and pressuring them into performance and so on come out and start shouting, "It's part of the sport." There will be a lot of coaches that will stand up and would say, "No, it's not part of the sport." And it is not ... if your philosophy is ... developed around that kind of approach, that you need to ... pressure the athlete, you need to belittle the athlete, you need to basically run him to the ground to get their performance out, then they're not gonna last very long. (male coach)

Having considered examples of ethical issues encountered by the coaches, we will now turn to the answers they gave when asked how they resolved these issues.

Coaches' Resolution of Ethical Issues

When asked how they resolved the ethical issues they faced, the coaches shared a number of factors they considered when facing an ethical decision. As to be expected, the most common factors to be considered were the coach's morals/values/ethical beliefs, as well as what was in the best interest of the individual athlete (recall the most common definition of an ethical issue was the tension between doing something that would be better for the team, i.e., a win, or doing something that would be better for the individual involved-including the coach, whose moral principles might be compromised if the first action was chosen). Regarding the coaches' **morals/values/ethical beliefs**:

> I'm prepared to lose the game rather than compromise my ethical beliefs in terms of trying to win. (male coach)
>
> I'm not a "win at all costs." I don't believe I want to be that way. (female coach)
>
> Well, you look at the balance of everything you know, and your values as a leader, a teacher, or a community figure, you look at what you think is pressing. You know, you have your code of ethics ... as a coach of course to follow and that you follow. (female coach)
>
> I keep referring back to what is it that ... what is your coaching philosophy? What are your core values? And certainly you have to be considering that. If you're going against what you believe in, then that's pretty well answering your question as to what to do in your decision-making process. (male coach)
>
> My core beliefs are always gonna remain the same, because I think that they're ... they're just ... they are things that are integral to building blocks, to everything else. And if those building blocks are gone away, the whole foundation just crumbles, and I don't want to lose the drive to instill those core beliefs because then I can't build a strong house. (male coach)

Although the coaches did not go into much detail concerning their core values, beliefs, and so forth, one could infer that one of the coaches' core values was **concern for the individual**. The coaches expressed their concern for the team, but if there was a conflict between what was best for the team and what was best for the individual athlete, the individual athlete appeared to take priority:

> The best interest of the team, the best interests of the individual ... what's best for that kid.... I think primarily I really try to take care of the individual and ... like you were them. (female coach)
>
> You have to consider what's in the best interests of the individual and also what's in the best interest of the group or the team. (male coach)
>
> I just know that I'm on the right way because I believe in ... I believe in the athlete first, and ... I believe that they will thrive out of a healthy environment. (male coach)
>
> [Factor to consider in resolving ethical dilemmas] is the feelings of the athlete, obviously ... without compromising your honesty. And you ... don't want to be abrupt about it. I think... the facts that you want to consider are just that your end result has to be that you haven't damaged your relationship at all with, you know, the athlete in terms of coach-player, and ... the mutual respect that there is between both of you. (male coach)
>
> I think each situation is different. It may be a similar situation, but each athlete has a different background, is involved in different aspects of life ... and you have to weigh the circumstances and you have to hear their side of the story. (female coach)

When asked about their core values, a couple of the coaches referred back to their own upbringing:

> For the most part, probably because of my background [upbringing]... (male coach)

> I make a lot of judgments ... just by my own morals, you know, and upbringing. (male coach)

> I was fortunate enough that my parents have taught me the basics of right and wrong, you know, it's wrong to steal, it's wrong to ... you know... (male coach)

Having examined some of the factors the coaches considered when resolving ethical issues, we turn now to an analysis of the coaches' responses compared to the responses of the athletes to similar questions.

Analysis of Coaches' Responses Compared with Athletes' Responses

The examples of ethical issues given by the coaches included whether to: play an injured player, play a player who has missed practice, intentionally harm opponents, push the rules, push athletes, and consider the potential of an intimate relationship with an athlete. The basis for resolving these issues by the coaches involved a consideration of their morals/values/ethical beliefs as well as what was in the best interests of the individual athlete. The coaches also expressed their concern for the team, but if there was a conflict between what was best for the team and what was best for the individual athlete, the individual athlete appeared to take priority.

Although the coaches did not go into much detail concerning their morals/values/ethical beliefs, there was obviously a concern for **fairness** when the issue of playing an athlete who had missed practice was under consideration. The issue of playing an injured athlete, as well as more general considerations of what was in the best interest of the individual, reflected a **respect for others**. Although the coaches did not go into much detail in sharing the reasons for the decisions they made, it should not be assumed that the coaches were not reflective regarding ethical decisions. What might account for the limited degree of detail in the reasons expressed could be that the coaches were simply making assumptions when they spoke of their morals/values/ethical beliefs, such as subsuming fairness or respect as one of their values, rather than specifying fairness or respect as a reason for resolving a particular issue.

The athletes in the study discussed in the previous chapter, on the other hand, went into much more detail concerning the resolution of ethical issues. When asked for examples of ethical issues in their sport, their responses included whether to: play dirty, fight, trash talk, backup teammates, cut off players, and take performance-enhancing drugs. Not only were there differences in the kinds of ethical issues athletes and coaches perceived in their sports, but the athletes and coaches gave different reasons for the decisions they would make regarding the dilemma. The reasons the athletes gave for the decisions they made could be divided into six categories: (1) "doing unto others as you would have them do unto you," (2) fairness, (3) respecting others, (4) not hurting the team, (5) respect for the game, and (6) fear of getting caught. Thus, there were differences in the degree of detail in the reasons expressed for resolving ethical issues by athletes and coaches, as well as differences in the kinds of ethical issues faced by athletes and coaches.

Where there was overlap in the examples of the ethical issues arising in the sport, it was interesting to note the different perceptions of these issues by the athletes and coaches. For example, where the coaches would say that they "never told [their] players to hit anyone" or "never see any situations where a team [would] send out a player to deliberately fight a better player to take them out of the game, you know," athletes would say:

> I don't try and hit anyone from behind, I usually try and hit fairly clean but the odd time, you know ... it's tough to say. It depends on the circumstances and the time frame of the game. You don't want your best players getting injured and you have to take measures to stop that. Like, if you beat up the other guy, the team's going to get all, like, pumped and everything and they'll go out and score a couple goals.

The coaches and athletes obviously had different perceptions concerning the issue of fighting or playing dirty.

The coaches did not see the issue of taking performance-enhancing drugs as an ethical one:

> It is the coach's responsibility to look after the well-being of their player and the facts are that these things are dangerous to a person's health, long term or even short term, and any gains, personal gains, that can be achieved by the use of performance-enhancing drugs are simply not worth the risk. It is the coach's responsibility to make or influence that decision. Like, I would not tolerate players doing that on my team.

The athletes, however, *did* see the taking of performance-enhancing drugs as a potential choice:

> Guys that do drugs, or whatever steroids, I think they know it's wrong. But they're ... they just wanna do whatever, like, to improve themselves. Now that they recognize the strength part of it, the sport, that's where people are coming and trying to build in that area and then that's where the effects of drugs, because you don't need as much rest. You can train constantly.

The differences between the athletes' and the coaches' perceptions and resolution of ethical issues ushers in the notion of autonomy. By autonomy, we mean the ability to make a free, informed choice. That is, if the coaches perceive something to be an ethical issue, and their players do not perceive this issue in the same way, should players be "made" to reconsider their views? Or should players maintain a certain degree of autonomy when it comes to identifying and dealing with ethical issues encountered in their sport? A topic that arose in the interviews with the athletes concerned the influence of the coach:

> Coaches have a lot of power over you. I mean, they control who plays and who does what, and if you don't like it you can quit. Like, yeah ... coaches... [Y]ou pretty much have to take what they say.... You have to have faith in the knowledge of your coach in order to get anywhere.

How a coach conceives of the notion of autonomy will affect whether the coach will allow his or her athletes to make autonomous ethical decisions. The coaches' answers to the question concerning how much autonomy an athlete should be given could be placed on a continuum. At one end of the continuum, there were coaches who wanted to "run the ship":

> The thing they need to understand, at least in our program and I'm sure it should be like that in every program, that there is one ship and one captain, and there may be some leeway, but the captain will eventually run the ship. And that's the way it goes. They don't have to like it, but that is the way it is going to be. (male coach)

At the other end of the continuum, there were coaches who did not think the coach should be single-handedly "running the ship":

> The traditional problems I believe will happen if you have just one coach and that coach drives the ship and nobody else has input into the programming. That's where ... I think teams are open to ... and athletes are open to abuse. (male coach)

> I think that the value of having team meetings to set goals and write some dos and do not's is valuable.... I think there is value in looking at it holistically in terms of the whole team. (female coach)

> Now, being an athlete you can feel totally intimidated ... so we approached the captain and assistants and we had a good long chat with them and we got them involved in a lot of our decision making ... and they ... you know, they respected us. (female coach)

> I think the athlete should have a ton of autonomy in terms of ethical decisions. I mean ... they should know, really understand how important doing the right thing is and understand the consequences of doing the right thing, like, in a positive way.... [T]hey should also understand the consequences of the negative things… (male coach)

> The choice is always hers [the athlete's]. It's a hundred percent, don't you think?... You may feel that doing something is a bad choice ... you can try to influence, but the choice is always theirs. (female coach)

In between the extreme ends of the continuum, there were coaches who would give their athletes a certain degree of autonomy, but who still wanted a certain amount of input:

> Well, they should have about 50 percent of that ... the decision making. You know, I think you owe them as a coach.... If he thinks a certain way, I think if you sit down with that athlete ... I think that you have to make him sort of swing to your thinking, if you think it's unethical. But they should have, I think, about 50 percent of the say and you should be able to swing it over so that a proper ethical decision [is made] ... by the time the conversation's over, you know. (male coach)

> Well, if it's a case of the injuries and their desire to play, then I ... think that the player should, you know, have autonomy. In other situations that involve ethical dilemmas, then ... no question that the coach should play a role in at least informing the individual to make sure that they're aware of all the facts, all of the consequences, repercussions of their decision. (male coach)

It is interesting to note that all three female coaches fell on the "autonomous athletes" end of the continuum. This situation raises the possibility of gender differences between male and female coaches.

Possible Gender Differences

Having interviewed only nine coaches and not having achieved a gender balance, one should be leery about making too many comments about possible **gender differences** between male and female coaches. However, a few interesting observations could be made that might stimulate future research. First of all, given the gender ratio between the male and female coaches, it was surprising that there was little difference in the number of quotations from the coaches regarding definitions of ethical issues as well as the example issues of: playing an injured player, playing a player who missed practice, intentionally harming an opponent, pushing the rules, pushing athletes, and the potential for intimate relationships between coaches and athletes. An example of an ethical issue that was different for the female coaches concerned the use of alcohol by their athletes. Where two male coaches viewed the use of alcohol and/or drugs as "non-issues," two female coaches had experienced ethical issues involving the use of alcohol by their athletes. It is interesting to note that both female coaches struggled with upholding rules against the use of alcohol with the desire to "win a popularity contest" or remain friends with the athletes. This situation could be explained by the realization that both coaches were coaching athletes with whom they had previously played.

> I think the biggest one [ethical issue] was me playing and having to coach this year, and having players that I've played with for the last four years now they gotta sit and listen to me. (female coach)

> For some of the coaches here, perhaps who have been established and are quite removed from their players, in terms of their seniority, have never played with their athletes on the field or the court, I think that those kind of things are definitely different than my experience where I have coached and played on the same team. (female coach)

One could conjecture that female coaches would find themselves in the situation of coaching former teammates more often than male coaches because women's sport is relatively new compared to men's sport, and thus more time has elapsed for the development of male as opposed to female coaches.

Regarding the coaches' resolution of ethical issues, once again there was little difference between the male and female responses. Both male and female coaches referred to their morals/values/ethical beliefs as well as what was in the best interest of the individual athlete as factors to consider when resolving ethical dilemmas. The only difference appeared to concern the notion of "core values." When the coaches were asked to expand upon their core values, the males referred back to their own upbringing. The female coaches, on the other hand, spoke less of core values and more of specific situations.

> I also think that there is probably value in terms of a coach and athlete talking about it [an ethical issue] on an individual level ... so there should be room for individuality in the team. (female coach)

> Do I treat my athletes the same? No, I treat each one of them differently ... but I need to. (female coach)

This focus on the individual by females as opposed to core values by males may be a reflection of what feminists have referred to as **gender theory**. Harding (1982) summarizes gender theory in the following manner:

> Gender theory shows how the different experiences male and female infants have of the division of labor by sex/gender with which they interact accounts for the reproduction generation after generation of certain general and nearly universal differences which characterize masculine and feminine senses of self, others, and the appropriate relationship between self and other.... The infant's experience of this division of labor by sex/gender creates an "objectifying" sense of self in men and a "relational" sense of self in women. (p.233)

The "objectifying" sense of self in men is a result, suggest gender theorists (e.g., Chodorow 1978; Flax 1978) of the male's separation and individuation from a kind of person whom he cannot biologically become. However, the process by which female infants experience separation and individuation is not so critically tied to their gender identity. This results in a more "relational" sense of self in women.

Gender theory may also explain the differences in the female and male coaches' responses to the question of autonomy. In conceptualizing the coaches' responses as a continuum, all three female coaches' responses fell on the "autonomous athlete" end of the continuum. However, much more empirical research would be required to make more conclusive comments regarding gender differences concerning the notion of autonomy. The rest of the chapter will involve a conceptual analysis of the notion of autonomy and an application of the different conceptions of autonomy to the coach-athlete relationship.

Conceptions of Autonomy

Although the coaches in the study were not asked for their conceptions of autonomy, one can infer their underlying conceptions from the answers they gave concerning the question of how much autonomy athletes should be given. If coaches held a large degree of power over their athletes, it would appear that the possibility of autonomy on the part of the athletes is limited. However, it may be possible for a coach to be in a position of power but still allow his or her athletes a certain degree of autonomy. This possibility requires an examination of differing conceptions of **autonomy**.

A number of philosophers (Kupfer 1987; May 1994; and Meyer 1987) make a distinction between two fundamentally different notions of autonomy. In Meyer's (1987) words,

> The first view might be called negative autonomy: an autonomous person is *not* directed by another. The second view could be called positive autonomy: an autonomous person *is* actively self-directed. One might better distinguish these two positions by noting that negative autonomy is a social conception, a conception of liberty. On the other hand, positive autonomy involves having a certain relationship with the "natural" world of one's own emotions and desires. (p.267)

As Kupfer (1987) puts it, "[i]t is not enough simply to be free from others' interference; autonomy requires awareness of control over one's relation to others, including their access to us" (p.82). May (1994) refers to these different notions of autonomy as "autonomy as autarkeia [or self-sufficiency]" and "autonomy as self-rule" (p.134). **Self-sufficiency** refers to a person being free from others' interference while **self-rule** refers to managing one's affairs while still incorporating external influences. According to May (1994), the notion of autonomy as autarkeia has a long history, going back to Aristotle, then Kant, and more recently Joel Feinberg, John Rawls, and Robert Paul Wolff. Aristotle saw autarkeia, or self-sufficiency, as the primary good and chief aim of a city-state: "Besides, the final cause and end of a thing is the best, and to be self-sufficing is the end and the best" (Aristotle 1941b, 1129). Kant ([1785] 1959) discusses autonomy in terms of moral value. He viewed the presence of the will as not being dependent on external considerations for its moral value. "Autonomy of the will is the property the will has of being a law to itself (independently of any property of the objects of volition)" (p.59).

The Kantian view of moral autonomy as autarkeia has influenced more recent work on the topic. May (1994) notes that Feinberg's (1986) four related meanings of autonomy–the capacity to govern oneself, the actual condition of self-government, an ideal of character derived from that condition, or the sovereign authority to govern oneself–involve the core concept of self-sufficiency.

> That the idea of self-sufficiency could be seen as a core concept is particularly plausible when one considers that Feinberg especially stresses self-sufficiency in his discussion of autonomy as an "actual condition" and as an "ideal of character." This is important, since it seems that it is the actual condition of autonomy that the other uses of autonomy revolve around. For example, a capacity for autonomy is a capacity to realize the actual condition of autonomy; [t]he sovereign authority, or right to autonomy is a right to the actual condition of self-government; and the ideal of character is described by Feinberg as derived from the actual condition of autonomy. Thus, the "actual condition" of autonomy plays a central role in all four concepts, and the emphasis on self-sufficiency here should carry over to the other concepts as well. (pp.137-138)

Rawls (1971) also places an emphasis on "self-sufficiency" when he proposes that one's life should be governed by judgments that are "independent of natural contingencies and accidental circumstances" (p.515). Hence, he proposes that people test their actions against principles adopted behind the "veil of ignorance" (p.136). Finally, Wolff (1970) states that "[t]he autonomous man, insofar as he is autonomous, is not subject to the will of another. He may do what another tells him, but not *because* he has been told to do it" (p.14).

In contrast to the notion of autonomy as autarkeia or self-sufficiency, the notion of autonomy as self-rule allows for the incorporation of external influences into a person's determination of action. John Macken (1990) traces the use of the term *autonomy* to the Greeks who would denote certain rights to the city-state even when the city-state was dependent on a mother-city or outside power. This notion of "autonomy" remained throughout the Enlightenment when reference was made to the rights of individuals to manage their own affairs within the limits of a larger framework set by law. The word *autonomy* is actually derived from the Greek words *autos* and *nomos,* which mean "self-rule." It is ironic that Aristotle, who claimed that autarkeia, or self-sufficiency, is the primary good and chief aim of a city-state, presents an analogy of city-states as ships, with the citizens being sailors and the ruler the helmsman (Aristotle 1941b, 1180, 1185). May (1994) argues that the analogy of ship and helmsman (helmsperson) is an apt analogy for the notion of autonomy as "self-rule." What distinguishes Aristotle's use of the ship analogy from May's is the issue of how the helmsperson reacts to external factors.

Aristotle, unlike Kant, admitted that external factors are incorporated into the determination of moral duty. Returning to the ship analogy, these external factors would be comparable to weather and currents, and so forth. Aristotle did not see these external factors as threats to one's ability to rule as long as one acted according to practical wisdom. As May (1994) puts it,

> [t]o understand practical wisdom in Aristotle is to understand determination of virtuous action as involving a guide to action in relation to the external considerations of one's own capabilities and characteristics, as well as the situation at hand. Practical wisdom determines virtuous action but does so in the context of the circumstances of the individual. (p.139)

In Aristotle's own words:

> The general account being of this nature, the account of particular cases is yet more lacking in exactness; for they do not fall under any art or precept but the agents themselves must in each case consider what is appropriate to the occasion, as happens also in the art of medicine or of *navigation* [emphasis added]. (Aristotle 1941a, 953)

Thus, according to Aristotle, external influences would not determine behavior, but rather affect how one rules. However, May (1994) points out that some external influences have more "influence" than others, for example, a gunman putting a gun to the head of a victim and ordering her to walk across the street. Aristotle (1941a) also acknowledges such situations (in keeping with the ship analogy): "Something of the sort happens also with regard to the throwing of goods overboard in a storm; for in the abstract no one throws goods away voluntarily, but on condition of securing the safety of himself and his crew any sensible man does so" (p.964). Thus, we have a standard of autonomy. In May's (1994) words:

> Nonetheless, a standard does exist: does the behavior reflect the agent's evaluative assessment, or are the circumstances such that no sensible man could choose otherwise, so that the determination of action reflects the circumstances more than the agent's evaluative assessment. If it is the former, the agent acts as helmsman. If it is the latter, the ship's course reflects more the external circumstances than the agent's practical wisdom. (p.141)

This standard differs from the notion of autonomy as autarkeia in that the determination of one's action is not made in a detached or self-sufficient manner. As May (1994) puts it, "[a]utonomy does not require detachment from external influences. Rather, it requires that the agent actively assess these influences rather than simply react to them. External influences do not *cause* action, but rather provide information that the agent, as 'helmsman,' then steers according to" (p.141). Accepting the notion of autonomy as self-rule as opposed to self-sufficiency does not achieve Kant's desire to view people as purely ends and not means, but it does not leave us as means in a Humean "slave to the passions" vein. Once again, in May's words:

> By positing man's judgment as helmsman, we understand the action as a means to an end whose direction is set by the agent himself. While this direction is set in light of considerations many of which are beyond the agent's control, the direction itself is not simply a product of these factual considerations, but a product of the agent's active assessment of factual information. This is all we require for a plausible conception of autonomy. (p.142)

May's notion of autonomy as self-rule is a plausible conception of autonomy and such a conception has significant implications for the coach-athlete relationship.

Implications for the Coach-Athlete Relationship

How a coach conceives of autonomy will affect how much autonomy the athlete holds in the **coach-athlete relationship.** The coach might conceive of autonomy as self-sufficiency, and thus deny his or her athletes any degree of autonomy. Or the coach may conceive of autonomy as self-rule with the athlete being the "helmsperson" and the coach being one of the external considerations the athlete must take into account when making ethical decisions. Each of these conceptions of autonomy will be considered as well as how they translate into the coach-athlete relationship.

It is ironic that the coaches in this study who did not want to grant their athletes much autonomy also used the ship analogy:

> The thing they need to understand, at least in our program and I'm sure it should be like that in every program, [is] that there is one ship and one captain, and there may be some leeway, but the captain will eventually run the ship. And that's the way it goes. They don't have to like it, but that is the way it is going to be.

What is important to remember here is that the "helmsperson" is the coach, not the athlete. In fairness to the coaches who would adopt this conception of autonomy (or rather, lack thereof, on the part of the athlete), we would be justified in assuming that the athletes' interests and desires would be considered as one of the external factors examined in making ethical decisions (recall that the most common definition of an ethical dilemma was the tension between doing something that would be better for the team, that is, a win, or doing something that would be better for the individuals involved. However, the coach would have the "final say" under this conception of autonomy as "self-sufficiency."

If coaches adopted the conception of autonomy as "self-rule," with the athlete as "helmsperson," the situation would be quite different:

> I think the athlete should have a ton of autonomy in terms of ethical decisions. I mean ... they should know, really understand how important doing the right thing is and understand the consequences of doing the right thing, like, in a positive way.... [T]hey should also understand the consequences of the negative things.

In the situation of athlete as "helmsperson," the coach would be one of the external considerations the athlete would take into account when making ethical decisions. But as May (1994) suggested, the agent (in this case, the athlete) would actively assess the influence (in this case, the coach's influence) rather than simply react to it. "External influences do not *cause* action, but rather provide information that the agent, as 'helmsman,' then steers according to" (p.141). One of the coaches interviewed acknowledged the role of the coach as "information provider":

> So I think the coach certainly has a role to play ... a huge role there to play in providing information. And then it's up to the ... I think the player should have that autonomy.

Viewing the coach as "information provider" parallels the situation of informed consent in medicine. **Informed consent** in medicine requires that the doctor explains potential risks to patients in order that the patients may consent to proposed procedures with full knowledge of the risks involved. Ravizza and Daruty (1984) consider informed consent in medicine and suggest an analogous situation for athletics:

> In an effort to develop the structure of a realistic and practical informed consent for athletics, full disclosure should be made to athletes in three basic areas:
>
> 1. The nature of the coach's philosophy or attitude related to coaching a particular sport;
>
> 2. Current information about the risks, complications, and benefits associated with the specific aspects of participation in that sport;
>
> 3. Recognition that feasible alternatives may exist to the coach's position in certain situations and the athlete is responsible for communicating reasons for a change in the team plan or individual strategy as it relates to training and performance. (p.78)

Regarding the first area, if the athlete is informed that the coach's philosophy involves screaming and yelling "to get the most out of" his or her athletes, then he or she can expect this behavior and, if unable to accept it, choose to play elsewhere. The second area, concerning risks and complications pertains particularly to the area of injuries (recall that whether to play injured athletes was one of the most frequently cited ethical issues shared by the coaches interviewed). If athletes are given all of the information concerning the risks of playing with their injury, they can make informed decisions, taking some of the pressure off the coach. "A truly informed disclosure has many advantages, not the least of which is a reduction of the coach's stress, as responsibility for the athlete's performance is placed upon both the athlete and the coach" (ibid.). The third area, concerning alternatives to the coach's position, requires an emphasis on communication between the coach and the athletes.

> The point here is that the coach and the athlete share a responsibility to communicate regularly. Flexibility is the nature of competitive situations, but most coaches are unwilling to allow last-minute changes in a tried and tested game plan unless there is a good reason. We have argued that the essence of informed consent in athletics is the coach's responsibility to ensure that there are no surprises during the season; however, the corollary is that athletes cannot expect last-minute flexibility in the absence of a regular ongoing communication with the coach. This continuing communication builds a bond between athlete and coach that ultimately results in mutual respect. (ibid., 79-80)

Respect for the coach requires not only ongoing communication, but also the recognition that the coach is knowledgeable about his or her sport. The notion of informed consent ushers in one final issue, the importance of being *an* authority and not just *in* authority. "Being in authority is to be placed in a socially sanctioned role, which carries with it certain rights and responsibilities.... Someone who is *an* authority is someone who is an expert in some area of knowledge or skill" (Hamm 1989, 121). Thus, a coach is in a position of authority, "a socially sanctioned role," but he or she also needs to be *an* authority in the sense of having the requisite knowledge and skill necessary to provide the information the athlete needs to make informed decisions in the playing of his or her sport.

When autonomy is understood as "self-sufficiency," it is no wonder that some coaches view the granting of autonomy to their athletes as fatal to the athletic enterprise. However, if autonomy is understood as "self-rule," with the athlete acting as "helmsperson," the coach then plays a fundamental role as "information provider." The analogous situation of "informed consent" in medicine allows for a large degree of input from the coach while still respecting the autonomy of the athlete. This situation of course assumes that the coach has the requisite knowledge to be an authority regarding the sport he or she coaches, rather than just being in a position of authority. When a coach, who is an authority, seeks informed consent from his or her athletes, the athletes will find themselves in a position where they can grow, not only as athletes, but as autonomous individuals.

Conclusion

Similar to the discussion in the previous chapter concerning athletes and ethical issues, it is important to hear the coaches' words concerning the ethical issues they encounter and how they resolved them. Ethical issues that the coaches interviewed referred to include: playing an injured player, playing a player who has missed practice, encouraging players to intentionally harm opponents, pushing the rules, pushing athletes, and considering an intimate relationship with an athlete. Where the athletes had been very particular in citing reasons for why they resolved ethical issues in the way they did, the coaches were less specific. The reasons the coaches gave for making the decisions they made were based on a consideration of their morals/values/ ethical beliefs as well as what was in the best interest of the individual athlete. Values such as fairness and respect for others would be subsumed under the coaches' morals/values/ethical beliefs.

When considering how the coaches resolved the ethical issues they encountered, there appeared to be a few gender differences. The female coaches spoke less of basing their decisions on core values and more on the context of specific situations. This difference may be a reflection of what has been referred to as gender theory, resulting in a more "relational" sense of self in women. Gender theory may also explain the differences the female and male coaches exhibited regarding their attitudes toward how much autonomy athletes should be given concerning ethical decisions. When coaches conceive of autonomy as self-sufficiency, they may deny their athletes any degree of autonomy. However, if coaches conceive of autonomy as self-rule, the athlete would make autonomous decisions recognizing the coach as an external influence. The self-rule conception of autonomy is similar to the informed consent situation in medicine where the patient makes an autonomous decision after being informed of the risks of the proposed procedure. This situation is analogous to the coach-athlete relationship where the coach provides information to the athlete but still respects the autonomy of the athlete regarding ethical decisions.

CHAPTER REVIEW

Key Concepts

- ethical issues
- moral/values/ethical beliefs
- concern for the individual
- fairness
- respect for others
- gender differences
- gender theory
- autonomy
- self-sufficiency
- self-rule
- coach-athlete relationship
- informed consent

Review Questions

1. What were the six ethical issues encountered by the coaches interviewed for this chapter?
2. What did the coaches cite as their basis for resolving the ethical issues they encountered?
3. What were the differences between the athletes' and coaches' perceptions and resolutions of ethical issues?
4. What were the different positions the coaches took concerning how much autonomy an athlete should be given?
5. What is gender theory, and how might this theory explain the way male and female coaches perceive the degree of autonomy that should be granted to athletes?
6. What is the difference between autonomy conceived as self-sufficiency and autonomy conceived as self-rule?
7. How would conceptions of autonomy as self-sufficiency and autonomy as self-rule translate into the coach-athlete relationship?
8. How does the notion of informed consent describe what should happen in the coach-athlete relationship?

7

When Is Cheating "Cheating," and What Makes a Good Sportsperson?

In a tennis match, the umpire calls player A's shot out, but player B knew the ball had landed on the line. Should player B acknowledge that the ball was miscalled?

During a basketball game, player A was about to go up for a basket. Player B knew that player A was not a good foul shooter, so player B fouled player A, forcing her to take a foul shot rather than completing the basket she had been going up for. Player B broke the "non-contact rule," but did player B "cheat" in fouling player A?

In the final inning of a baseball game, team A, who was up to bat, "stole signs" that the catcher had relayed to the pitcher resulting in a winning home run by team A. Was the game won fairly? Would one's opinion of the "fairness" of the game be affected if it was found out that the pitcher for team B had "doctored" the ball throughout the game?

Cyclists A and B have a large lead in a cross-country bike race. Cyclist A rounds a corner to find B on the side of the road with a broken bicycle part. Cyclist A has a spare part that would make it possible for cyclist B to get back in the race. Should cyclist A help his closest competitor?

To answer the questions raised by the preceding scenarios, we have to examine the value of following the rules of a game, and whether there are instances of rule breaking that should not be considered "cheating." The issue of fairness arises when one considers rule breaking; thus, we have to examine the value of fair play. Finally, does "playing fair" make one a good sportsperson, or are there other conditions required for sportspersonship? These are the questions to be addressed in this chapter. Key concepts utilized in this chapter include: the **incompatibility thesis, ethos of games, prices** or **sanction, unfair advantage, intention** and **intention to deceive, psychological conditions, striving together, freeloading, lack of respect, sport** and **athletics, supererogatory acts, athlete as person, necessary competitor**, and **virtuous mean**.

When Is Cheating "Cheating"?

As discussed in the first chapter, a condition for something to be considered a sport was that the activity involved the following of institutionalized rules. Many philosophers (Tuxill and Wigmore 1995; Arnold 1997; Pearson 1973; Delattre 1975) propose that, if players break the rules of the game, they are not actually playing the game: "Competing, winning, and losing in athletics are intelligible only within the framework of rules which define a specific competitive sport. A person may cheat at a game or compete at it, but it is logically impossible for him to do both. To cheat is to cease to compete" (Delattre 1975, 136).

There seems to be something counterintuitive to the notion that cheaters are not playing the game (this notion has been referred to as the "incompatibility thesis" by sport philosophers). The **incompatibility thesis** suggests that a player cannot be playing the game if he or she resorts to cheating, since a condition for playing a game is following rules. Lehman (1981) provides a counter-example to the incompatibility thesis by looking at Gaylord Perry's history of throwing "doctored" baseballs. Lehman asks, "Does anyone seriously want to say that no baseball game is ever played when Perry pitches?" (p.42). Lehman suggests that incompatibility advocates suppose a certain "romanticized social context" that demands absolute adherence to rules and ignores the customs surrounding the game (p.45). It is the customs surrounding games that have made some sport philosophers rethink the notion of "cheating."

D'Agostino (1981) was one of the first philosophers of sport to refer to the **ethos of games**: "[A]ny particular game has an ethos as well as a set of formal rules. The ethos of a game refers to those conventions determining how the formal rules of that game are applied in concrete circumstances" (p.7). D'Agostino cites the example of the ethos surrounding basketball. Basketball is a "non-contact" sport, but any game of basketball is filled with players who accidentally or deliberately make contact with each other. Only some of these observed incidents actually result in the invocation of penalties "because the players and game officials have, in effect, conspired to ignore certain of the rules of basketball, at least in certain situations, in order to promote certain interests, which they share, for instance, with team owners and spectators–e.g., to make the game more exciting" (p.14). D'Agostino is quick to point out that, although certain kinds of rule-breaking moves are regularly ignored, there is still an unofficial system of conventions that prevent a game from degenerating into anarchy. Thus, behaviors that deviate from the formal rules interpreted in terms of the set of implicit conventions are penalized. The ethos of a game provides the basis for distinguishing three sets of behavior: (1) behavior that is permissible (i.e., behavior in accordance with the formal rules of a game or behavior that violates the formal rules but, according to the ethos of the game, does not require the invocation of penalties); (2) behavior that is impermissible but acceptable (i.e., behavior that violates the rules of the game in such a way that, according to the ethos of that game, requires the invocation of penalties; and (3) unacceptable behavior (i.e., behavior that violates the rules of the game in a way that, according to the ethos of that game, disqualifies its perpetuator as a player of that game) (p.15).

The existence of penalties for behavior that D'Agostino refers to as "impermissible but acceptable" has sometimes been cited as evidence that not all rule breaking is "cheating." However, as Pearson (1973) points out, "[t]he obvious rebuttal to this position is that penalties for breaking the law are contained within the law books, but no sensible person concludes, therefore, that all acts are within the law" (p.117). Simon (1991) reiterates this rebuttal when he states: "[W]e surely would not say that murder is allowed by law simply because penalties for murder are prescribed by law" (p.48). Although the existence of penalties should not automatically condone penalty-invoking behavior, Simon does question the analogy between sport penalties and criminal sanctions. "A jail sentence for a crime should not be thought of as the price the law charges for a particular act, such as a felony. That would make the felony a *permissible* option for those criminals who are willing to bear the cost of a jail sentence if caught" (ibid.). Rather than a price for committing a felony, Simon points out that the jail sentence is a punishment. Simon distinguishes between penalties that should be thought of as **prices** paid for certain behaviors (e.g., a golfer taking an extra stroke when invoking the "unplayable lie" rule) and penalties that should be viewed as **sanctions** for prohibited behavior (e.g., banning a player from competition because he or she took a banned substance). Simon notes that it is sometimes difficult to tell whether a penalty should be regarded as a price or a sanction (pp.48-49).

The "fuzziness" involved in distinguishing price or sanction penalties is also evident in the distinction Feezell (1988) makes between the ethos of baseball and the ethos of golf. Feezell suggests that rule-breaking behaviors such as "stealing signs" or "doctoring" the ball in baseball should be considered part of the ethos of baseball but rule-breaking behaviors such as a golfer rubbing the front face of his driver with Vaseline or carrying more than the allowable fourteen clubs in his or her bag should be considered cheating. He suggests that the golfing examples should be regarded as cheating because the "cheating" golfer is attempting to gain an **unfair advantage** since the other golfers will be competing under conditions that are unjustifiably dissimilar to the cheater's. Since Feezell proposes that "stealing signs" and "doctoring" the ball in baseball should not be considered "cheating," one could only assume that Feezell considers the dissimilarities of the conditions of the two baseball teams to be justified by the ethos of baseball.

Rather than claim that the ethos of a game condones rule-breaking behavior in one sport but not another, it might be more prudent to return to Simon's (1991) discussion of penalties and look at the notion of fairness. "The intuitive idea here is that if a pricing penalty is fair in sports, violation of the rule should invoke a penalty that is fair compensation" (p.49). If pricing penalties are fair compensation for rule breaking, that is, the penalty "rights" the advantage gained by rule breaking, and if officials are ensuring the invocation of these penalties, then certain instances of rule breaking would not upset the "fairness" of a game. Leaman (1995) reiterates the need for officials to maintain fairness:

> The existence of an authority in games enshrines cheating in the structure of the game; the authority is there to ensure that cheating does not interfere with the principle of fairness in a game. He is there to regulate cheating so that it does not benefit one side more than the other except where one side is more skillful at cheating than the other, and to see that the amount of cheating which takes place is not so great as to change the general form of a particular game. (p.197)

The suggestion that officials "enshrine cheating in the structure of the game" seems somewhat counterintuitive. However, the problem may lie, not in the existence of officials regulating rule-breaking behavior by invoking pricing penalties, but rather in the reference to such behavior as "cheating." Perhaps not all rule breaking should be considered "cheating."

Leaman (1995), in attempting to define cheating, quotes Luschen's (1976) definition: "Cheating in sport is the act through which the manifestly or latently agreed upon conditions for winning such a contest are changed in favor of one side" (p.67). According to Luschen, cheating occurs when the agreed upon conditions are changed so that there is an **unfair advantage** for one of the teams. Leaman notes a problem with this definition in that it does not take into account any consideration of intention. By **intention**, we mean the purposeful nature of changing the agreed upon conditions. Leaman then considers McIntosh's (1979) distinction between intending to deceive, which McIntosh calls cheating, and breaking the rules without having that intention. However, Leaman (1995) points out that McIntosh's definition does not cover those cases where the rules are broken without any intention to deceive. An **intention to deceive** would involve the attempt to "get away with" the rule breaking, that is, to avoid getting caught.

> A player may commit a professional or tactical foul in front of the referee or umpire because he considers that it is better to break the rules and suffer the penalty rather than not commit the foul at all. Of course, such a player would *prefer* the offense to be unobserved, but cannot reasonably expect it in those

> circumstances to be over-looked. It is not obvious whether this sort of case is an example of cheating or not. (p.194)

Leaman (1995) also notes a difficulty in Luschen's (1976) definition of cheating as the changing of "manifestly or latently agreed upon conditions for winning such a contest" (p.67). Do the "latently agreed upon conditions" include **psychological conditions**; that is, conditions not covered by the rules but conditions that affect one's ability to concentrate on the game at hand? Leaman gives the example of a tennis player who knows that his opposition is put off when he coughs, does up his shoe laces, and so on:

> It might well be argued that A is cheating since the sorts of skill and strategy which are acceptable in a game involve being better at the motions of the game than one's opponent and successfully exploiting his weaknesses and one's own strengths. Such weaknesses and strengths should be limited to the moves of the game and not to the defects in psychological make-up which are not directly related to the moves of the game. (p.194)

Behavior that does not break rules but which "throws a player off" should not be considered an instance of cheating but rather bad sportspersonship. This situation will be discussed further in the section "What Makes a Good Sportsperson?".

Having considered instances of rule breaking that are not intended to deceive and that carry with them a price, for example, a foul shot for intentionally fouling a basketball opponent, a two-minute penalty for intentionally tripping a hockey opponent, and so forth, should we conclude that such instances are not "cheating" but rather are options that are available to all players (thus eliminating the "unfair" criticism)? Even extending the "rules" to include the ethos of the game, there still seems to be something counterintuitive to condoning intentional rule breaking. Fraleigh, in an article entitled "Why the Good Foul is Not Good" (1982), states that "[a]greeing to play basketball does not necessarily mean also agreeing to perform the 'good' foul, but it necessarily entails the meaning of performing acts of dribbling, shooting, passing, and so on" (p.42). Becoming clear on what is logically entailed in playing a particular game may help us to determine not only which behaviors should be considered "cheating" but also help us answer the question of what is wrong with cheating.

What Is Wrong with "Cheating"?

Some philosophers of sport have suggested that cheating is valuable in that it makes the game more exciting. "In so far as the contest is one of wits as well as one of skill and strategy, it can be exciting to compete with and against someone who uses his wits to try and cheat and it can be exciting for an audience to observe such intelligent behavior" (Leaman 1995, 196). Tamburrini (2000) adds:

> [S]ome cases of rule-breaking are sometimes "game-enriching", in the sense of enhancing the challenge and excitement of the competition, without necessarily affecting the skills or the flow of the game negatively. Take, for example, deterrent interventions in football [soccer]. Tougher play style will probably increase the heat of the game.... The same applies to diving [faking a foul]. A goal scored by a simulated penalty no doubt adds to the excitement of the game, as it compels the wronged team to play offensively to even the score.... Diving, no doubt, obliges defending players to play in a more cautious manner. Thus, indirectly, it rewards offensive football styles. Dribbling skills will flourish, more goals will be scored, all this adding to the enjoyment of the public. (pp.24-25)

Common to the preceding quotations is the notion that cheating makes the game more exciting and enjoyable *for the audience.* However, this raises an important question: "What is the purpose of sport?" In Chapter 1, the nature of sport was described as involving *com-petitio,* **striving together**, in the pursuit of excellence. This *com-petitio* is similar to Simon's (1991) conception of sport as a "test of skill, a mutual quest for excellence by the participants" (p.50).

> This, of course, is not to deny that sports serve other purposes in our society, such as provision of entertainment or the opportunities for professionals to secure financial gains. But these other purposes are parasitic in that what *ought* to be entertaining about our sports, and what makes them sometimes worth paying to see, is the test of excellence they provide. Gladiatorial contests or the throwing of the politically or religiously unpopular to the lions also *may* be entertaining to some people. Whether they *ought* to be entertained by such behavior is another issue. (ibid.)

If sport involves the striving together in the pursuit of excellence, the problem with cheating is a breakdown in the "striving together." When players break the rules, they are assuming that the majority of the other players will not be breaking the rules. If too many players break the rules, the game would degenerate into anarchy. Even something as supposedly innocuous as intentional fouling in basketball would become a problem if everyone fouled players going up for baskets; the game would become one continuous series of foul shots. A series of foul shots would no longer allow for the utilization (and testing) of basketball skills (other than shooting for baskets), for example, dribbling, passing, and so forth. So if a basketball game is to involve the testing of all the skills involved in basketball, intentional fouling has to be kept in check. As basketball is currently played, not everyone fouls players going up for baskets. Thus, those players who *do* practice intentional fouling are relying on other players *not to foul*; they take an exception to the rule they want the majority of others to follow.

> Thus, cheaters make arbitrary exceptions of themselves to gain advantages and in effect treat others as mere means to their own well-being. Cheaters fail to respect their opponents as persons, as agents with purposes of their own, by violating the public system of rules that others may reasonably expect to govern the activity in question. (Simon 1991, 40)

When cheaters make arbitrary exceptions of themselves, two things happen: they create an unfair situation for others, and they do not treat their opponents with respect.

Regarding the unfair situation created by cheating, it is helpful to recognize what it means to "strive together" in sports. When we compete with others, we co-operate in agreeing to play whatever sport we are involved in (and sports are, by definition, rule-governed activities). As Loland (1998) points out,

> [i]t is wrong to benefit from the co-operation of others without doing our fair share. When we voluntarily engage in a rule-governed practice, we enter a more or less tacit social contract in which a moral obligation arises: keep the formal playing rules of the game! Here, then, we have the core justification of the fairness ideal (p.85).

Wigmore and Tuxill, in their article "A Consideration of the Concept of Fair Play" (1995), refer to the situation of not doing one's fair share as "freeloading." **Freeloading** occurs when "cheating players" benefit from the fact that the other players are not cheating; that is, the cheaters are "freeloading" off the other players who are playing by the rules, and it is necessary that a majority of the players play by the rules if the game is to take place. Although some "cheating makes sport more exciting" advocates deny that cheating creates an unfair advantage because cheating is open to everyone (see Tamburrini 2000), cheating is only beneficial if the majority of players do not cheat. This situation requires that some players (those who do not cheat) take more than their fair share of abiding by the rules. Thus, "fair play" cannot happen if even one player cheats.

In creating an unfair situation for others, cheaters show a lack of respect for their opponents. A **lack of respect** is also evident in the Kantian sense in that cheaters treat their opponents as means, not ends (Wigmore and Tuxill 1995). When players "strive together" in the pursuit of excellence, they treat each other as ends, challenging each other to become the best volleyball, basketball, hockey, or other sport player they can become. When players cheat, their focus has moved from pursuing excellence to winning. In their drive to win, cheaters use their opponents as a means to their win; for example, by intentionally fouling a basketball player going for a basket, the player committing the foul does not let her opponent excel at her shooting. Rather, the person committing the foul values her desire for stopping the shooter's potential basket (thereby increasing her chance of winning) more than valuing the shooter's chance to demonstrate her skill within the rule-governed framework of the game. How far players should go in respecting their opponents as ends leads us to the question of what makes a good sportsperson.

What Makes a Good Sportsperson?

In examining the necessary conditions for someone to be considered a good sportsperson, the minimum condition would have to be someone who played fairly; that is, someone who followed the rules of the game. As Keating (1964) points out, "never in search of ways to evade the rules, the sportsman acts only from unquestionable moral right" (p.30). In determining how the sportsperson should act, Keating looks at the goal of sport: "[T]o the extent that the conduct and attitudes of the participants contribute to the attainment of the goal of sport, to that extent they can be properly characterized as sportmanlike" (p.29). Keating distinguishes between sport and athletics, and proposes that only the goals of sport require sportspersonlike behavior. Keating views **sport** as more of a recreational activity and **athletics** as more of a serious competition. According to Keating,

> sport is a kind of diversion which has for its direct and immediate end fun, pleasure, and delight and which is dominated by a spirit of moderation and generosity. Athletics, on the other hand, is essentially a competitive activity, which has for its end victory in the contest and which is characterized by a spirit of dedication, sacrifice, and intensity. (p.28).

Thus, Keating suggests that the maxim for sportspersonlike conduct that would contribute to the good of sport is "Always conduct yourself in such a manner that you will increase rather than detract from the pleasure to be found in the activity, both your own and that of your fellow participants" (pp.29-30). Keating's distinction between the goals of sport and athletics makes the sportsperson maxim of generosity inapplicable to athletics. According to Keating, the dedication, sacrifice, and intensity of athletics requires fairness, but no more. "Once, however, the necessary steps have been taken to make the contest a true test of respective abilities, the athlete's sole objective is to demonstrate marked superiority. Any suggestion that fair play obliges him to maintain equality in the contest ignores the very nature of athletics" (p.34).

The notion that sportspersonship in sport (as opposed to athletics) involves more than playing fair is similar to the thesis that sportspersonship involves supererogatory actions. **Supererogatory acts** are acts which, as Hare (1981) puts it, are "praiseworthy but not obligatory" (p.198). Thus, an athlete should be praised for performing such an act (e.g., stopping to give a spare part to a competitor in a cycle race whose bike has broken down), but the athlete should not be condemned if he or she does not perform the act. Arnold (1983) makes a distinction between supererogatory acts that are performed from a force of duty and those that are prompted by emotions of care and concern. "When acts in sport go beyond that which is expected of players generally and are done only out of concern for another's good and for no other reason, they are not only altruistic, but exemplify the best traditions of sportsmanship" (p.69).

Acts that go beyond playing fair, such as stopping to help a fallen competitor, should not be considered supererogatory but such acts should be expected of any athlete. The decision to help or not to help a fallen athlete (or one whose equipment needs repair) can be viewed on two levels. First, there is the **athlete as person**, a person who deserves the basic respect that all people deserve. Thus, if an athlete is in a position to help another athlete, that athlete should help another person who happens to be a fellow athlete. The other level from which one could view the decision to help a fallen athlete involves looking at the athlete in need of help as a **necessary competitor**. That is, if sporting competitions are viewed in the light of *com-petitio*, striving together in the pursuit of sporting excellence, then an athlete should want his or her competitors to be in top form in order to "push" him or herself to the height of excellence.

This situation is exemplified in an example cited by Arnold (1983): "An actual case is provided by Meta Antenan, who although leading in a long jump competition against her great German rival, asked of the presiding jury that her opponent have a longer rest period than is provided by the rules, because of her having just taken part in another event" (pp.67-68). Giving her rival adequate time to recuperate from a previous event provided Meta Antenan with the highest level of competition with whom she could "strive together" to push herself to excellence. Although Meta Antenan lost the competition by 1 centimeter, having given her opponent more rest time allowed for a situation that was a truer challenge for Meta Antenan's abilities. She was then challenged to try harder, thus pushing her on toward excellence. Thus, performing so-called "supererogatory" acts demonstrates respect not only for the athlete as person, but also respect for the goal of competitive sport, that is, to strive together in the pursuit of sporting excellence.

Tying the goal of sport into the notion of sportspersonship would appear to bring us back to Keating's work in which he made a distinction between sport and athletics–the goals of sport requiring supererogatory actions not required by the goal of athletics, which required only playing fair. Keating's radical distinction is an example of polarized thinking. Rather than advocating a rigid and precise distinction between play and athletics, Feezell (1986) suggests that "we must be content with a fuzzy picture of the fusion of these activities, a picture in which edges are blurred and complexity of attitudes is retained" (p.9). Feezell looks toward Aristotle's description of **virtuous mean** as a way of making sense of the notion of sportspersonship: "Now it [virtue] is a mean between two vices, that which depends on excess and that which depends on defect; and again it is a mean because the vices respectively fall short of or exceed what is right in both passions and actions, while virtue both finds and chooses that which is intermediate." (Aristotle 1941a, 959). Feezell quotes the oft-cited example of a person exhibiting the virtue of courage–the person who is neither fearful enough to be called a coward but not so confident as to be called foolhardy. Feezell (1986) applies this mean to sport: "Sportsmanship is a mean between excessive seriousness, which misunderstands the importance of the play-spirit, and an excessive sense of playfulness, which might be called frivolity and which misunderstands the importance of victory and achievement when play is competitive" (p.10).

Feezell's conception of sportspersonship can now be connected with the example of helping a fallen athlete, discussed earlier. A fallen athlete (or one who needs equipment to continue) deserves to be helped just as any person qua person deserves help. Seeing an athlete but not a person would be an example of taking sport too seriously. The other level of helping a fallen athlete, that of helping a fellow competitor who will help you to strive together in the pursuit of sporting excellence, is an example of recognizing the importance of victory and achievement. The victory is important as a gauge to one's progress, and whether an athlete wins or loses, a sense of achievement can be felt. Thus, helping a fallen (or in-need-of-equipment) athlete should not be considered supererogatory but should be an action expected of all athletes who respect people and who respect sport.

Before concluding, it is important to acknowledge that not all athletes do respect people and sport, at least not enough to sacrifice winning. Feezell (1986) suggests that "many, if not most, examples of bad sportsmanship arise from an excessive seriousness that negates the play-spirit because of an exaggerated emphasis on the value of victory" (p.10). As mentioned in the section on cheating, when cheaters create an unfair situation for others, they show a lack of respect for their opponents–opponents are treated as means, not ends. The same thing happens when opponents are treated in an unsportspersonlike manner. If we want to restore the proper end to sport, that is, find the mean that values but does not exaggerate victory, we need to treat opponents as ends by not cheating and by exhibiting good sportspersonship.

Cheating or Poor Sportspersonship?

Having examined the concepts of cheating and sportspersonship, we are now in a position to review the scenarios in the introduction of this chapter. The first scenario, the miscalled tennis shot, involves the breaking of the rule that, if a ball lands on the line, it should be considered in play. However, this rule was broken unintentionally, that is, the umpire miscalled the shot. Even if the player who saw the ball land on the line does not correct the call, she should not be considered a "cheat" since she did not make the call. However, she could be considered a poor sportsperson in that she is not respecting her opponent's skill in making the shot. An additional issue that should be considered here involves the role of the official. If the umpire's calls are to be respected, is the player disrespecting the role of the umpire by questioning his call? Perhaps a distinction could be made between calls that would benefit the player questioning the call, and calls that would benefit the player's opponent; this would avoid the situation in which players would be continuously questioning calls to their own advantage. The umpire should not feel his role is being disrespected if a player is questioning calls that would put the player at a disadvantage, since any disrespect the official might feel would be balanced by the player showing respect for her opponent.

The basketball scenario has been referred to throughout the chapter. To reiterate, even something as seemingly innocuous as the intentional foul in basketball should be considered cheating. For a basketball game to include skills other than shooting, the majority of the players have to refrain from continuously fouling their opponents. This situation results in the non-cheaters shouldering more than their fair share of "rule following." Thus, intentional fouling should be considered "cheating" and should be discouraged.

The baseball scenario involves two different issues. The first issue involved one team "stealing signs," resulting in a winning home run. The question was asked as to the "fairness" of the win. Since "stealing signs" is not a formal rule, we may not be able to say the win was "unfair" (the team whose signs were "stolen" was not shouldering more than its fair share of "rule following"). However, we could say that the win was "unsportspersonlike"; that is, the "stealing" team did not respect their opponents as ends–as players seeking to excel in their baseball skills (the particular skills to be used being determined by the signal between the catcher and the pitcher). Regarding the "doctoring" of the ball, this would definitely be an example of rule breaking. Once again, the team whose pitcher did not "doctor" the ball would be carrying a greater share of "rule following." If it was the case that both teams were breaking the rules concerning the "doctoring" of balls, we might want to say that there was no unfair advantage, but regarding the game as an institution, batting skills would have to change and this would require a change in the way the game is played.

Conclusion

The purpose of this chapter was to determine what constituted cheating and what was required to be a good sportsperson. The counterintuitiveness of the incompatibility thesis was partially explained by taking into account the ethos of games. When considering intentional rule breaking, it is important to view resulting penalties as a price rather than as a sanction. When committing an intentional foul, the player has decided that the advantage gained from fouling the opposition is worth the price of the penalty. The intentional foul appears to be a less obvious example of "cheating" than an instance of rule breaking with the intent to deceive. An example of this situation would be the taking of banned performance-enhancing substances. However, even if there was no intent to deceive, for example, the intentional foul, and even if the option to foul opponents is open to everyone (thus eliminating the concern that cheating creates an unfair advantage), fouling an opponent requires that some players do not foul (to keep the game from changing into a single skill activity) and thus, the non-fouling players are required to shoulder more than their fair share of "rule following." This situation is referred to as freeloading. Not only are cheaters not shouldering their fair share of the rule following required to maintain the integrity of the game, these cheaters are showing a lack of respect for their opponents.

Sportspersonship requires respect for athletes as persons as well as necessary competitors. Although some acts (beyond playing fairly) are typically considered supererogatory, for example, giving a fellow cyclist a spare part for his or her bike, such acts should be expected of athletes; firstly, because such acts show respect for the athlete as a person, and secondly, because such acts show respect for the athlete as a necessary competitor, as someone with whom you are striving together in the pursuit of excellence. The situation of respecting your opponent is also important when respecting the psychological conditions affecting one's opponent. When athletes shoulder their fair share of the rule following as well as show respect for their opponents as people and competitors, the virtuous mean of sport, as a not-too-serious, but not frivolous, valued human experience can be achieved.

CHAPTER REVIEW

Key Concepts

- incompatibility thesis
- ethos of games
- prices or sanction
- unfair advantage
- intention and intention to deceive
- psychological conditions
- striving together
- freeloading
- lack of respect
- sport and athletics
- supererogatory acts
- athlete as person
- necessary competitor
- virtuous mean

Review Questions

1. What is the "incompatibility thesis," and how does it relate to cheating?
2. What is the "ethos of a game," and how does it relate to cheating?
3. What is the difference between price and sanction, and how does this difference relate to penalties?
4. What role does intention and deception play in cheating?
5. What is "freeloading," and how does this concept explain what is wrong with cheating?
6. How does cheating and poor sportspersonship demonstrate a lack of respect?
7. What are "supererogatory acts," and how should these acts relate to good sportspersonship?
8. What is Aristotle's "virtuous mean," and how might this concept make sense of the notion of sportspersonship?

8

To Dope or Not to Dope?

Some of us are almost forced into taking substances just to remain competitive and I guess it is up to your will whether or not to succumb to that. (Elite-level athlete)

"To dope or not to dope?" is a question that most athletes will face at some point during their careers. This decision is not only a concern for elite athletes. The temptation to "bulk up" is a concern for the recreational weightlifter as well as those participating in many sports at all levels. Before looking at specific arguments for and against taking performance-enhancing substances, it is important first to ask the fundamental question of why athletes are involved in sport.

There would appear to be many reasons why people participate in sport: as a way to meet people, as a means to staying active, as a chance to "let off steam," or as an opportunity to test their abilities against people with similar skills. The focus of this chapter will be on the latter reason, since the question of taking performance-enhancing substances would seem most relevant to this reason for participating in sport. When athletes participate in sports to test their abilities, they may have one of two goals: to improve their skills or to win the competition. These goals might not be perceived as exclusive. However, one of these two goals will always dominate the other. If the athletes' goal is to improve their skills, they will value a loss (though they would prefer a win) because they will have the opportunity to see where they can improve their skills. A good example of athletes with this attitude are those who would not want to play against a competitor with an obviously lower skill level since, although they may be guaranteed a win, they will not have the opportunity to improve their own skill level. On the other hand, if their goal in competing is to win, they will avoid competitors who will likely "whip" them, or they may take on the challenge but may "push the rules" when possible in order to give themselves an advantage.

What do these two different goals for participating in sport have to do with the question of whether or not athletes should take performance-enhancing substances? Well, if winning is the most important goal for their participation in sport, than athletes may think that taking performance-enhancing substances is worth any of the risks involved. What are some of the risks involved in taking performance-enhancing drugs? What are the ethical issues involved in taking performance-enhancing drugs? In this chapter we will address these questions by looking at what philosophers and athletes have to say about the use of performance-enhancing substances. Eight Canadian elite-level athletes were interviewed concerning their thoughts on the use of performance-enhancing substances. Key concepts utilized in answering the question "To dope or not to dope?" include: **health risks, autonomy, paternalism, legal risks, coercion, unfairness, unnaturalness, supplementation** and **exploitation, practice, internal goods, external goods, athletic meritocracy, mutually acceptable challenge**, and **lack of respect**.

Health and Legal Risks

Some performance-enhancing substances pose a potential threat to the athlete's health. "While claims about possible bad consequences of steroid use are controversial, the American College of Sports Medicine warns against serious side effects. These are believed to include liver damage, atherosclerosis, hypertension, personality changes, a lowered sperm count in males, and masculinization in females" (Simon 1984, 6). One of the reasons that a firm decision cannot be made regarding the **health risks** of using some performance-enhancing substances, particularly steroids, is that research has not been conducted on subjects taking the levels of steroids ingested by athletes. "[S]tudies in laboratories cannot mimic the doses that many athletes take. Some athletes take dosages of *more than 100 times* their body's own replacement level. No such studies are ethically permissible today in American laboratories due to public hostility concerning the perceived dangers" (Holowchak 2000, 41). Some philosophers may see this lack of research as a reason to lift the ban on performance-enhancing substances. "[R]ather than sustaining the prohibition, the present objection [health risks] speaks for allowing doping, combined with medical supervision and followed up by research on its eventual effects. If lack of knowledge is the problem, abolishing the prohibition is no doubt a good strategy to know what the risks of doping are" (Tamburrini 2000, 42). There seems to be something intuitively wrong in allowing doping for the reason of researching the possible negative effects of performance-enhancing substances. So, although the "jury is still out" concerning the health risks of performance-enhancing substances, the fact that there could be significant health risks should give athletes pause when deciding whether they should dope or not dope.

Proponents of the use of performance-enhancing substances would not consider the supposed health risks to be that serious. It might be argued that, in some sports, the very risk of competing is higher than the risks involved in taking certain performance-enhancing substances. One of the athletes interviewed for this chapter stated: "But if it [taking performance-enhancing substances] was that much of a concern for me health wise, I wouldn't be weightlifting, because it is a tough sport." Philosophers have also pointed out the inconsistency between prohibiting performance-enhancing substances based on their potential health risk while accepting the health risks inherent in many sports. "We cannot plausibly argue that we prohibit professional football players from using steroids or amphetamines because of concern for their health, when the sport itself permanently disables a high proportion of participants" (Fost 1986, 6). W.M. Brown (2001) cites authorities who note that scarcely more than a dozen deaths can be attributed to drugs and sport (with most of these resulting from recreational, not performance-enhancing, drugs) while deaths and serious injuries due to the sports themselves number in the hundreds in sports such as football, boxing, mountain climbing, and so forth.

Just as a liberal society allows people to choose to participate in dangerous sports such as football, boxing, or mountain climbing, proponents of doping would argue that so too should society allow athletes to choose whether to take potentially dangerous performance-enhancing substances. This argument relies on the notion of **autonomy**; that is, the right of an individual to make a free, informed choice. J.S. Mill ([1859] 1985) argues that the right to make autonomous choices is absolute, as long as those decisions do not harm others.

> The sole purpose for which power can be rightfully exercised over any member of a civilized community, against his will, is to prevent harm to others. His own good, either physical or moral, is not a sufficient warrant.... In the part which merely concerns himself, his independence is, of right, absolute. Over himself, over his own body and mind, the individual is sovereign. (pp.68-69)

To interfere with a person's will is to act paternalistically. **Paternalism** is not always negative. Gerald Dworkin (1983) defines "soft paternalism" as "the view that (1) paternalism is sometimes justified, and (2) it is a necessary condition for such justification that the person for whom we are acting paternalistically is in some way not competent" (p.107). A person would be considered not competent if his or her actions were not fully voluntary. "The soft paternalist argues that limitation of one's liberty is justified when one's behavior or actions are not fully voluntary because they are not fully informed, or because one is not fully competent or is in some relevant way coerced" (Brown 1984, 15). It could be posited that many athletes are not fully informed about the health risks of performance-enhancing substances, and thus they would not be acting in a fully voluntary manner when choosing to take these substances. Some philosophers (Dixon 2001b; Tamburrini

2000) suggest that rather than banning performance-enhancing substances based on athletes' lack of knowledge regarding them, the solution would be to take steps to correct this lack of knowledge, for example, through warnings such as those put on cigarette packages, or through attendance at obligatory information meetings. One of the athletes interviewed agreed that health risks would not be an issue if athletes acquired accurate information: "[T]he health risk would never be an issue as far as taking performance-enhancing substances because I think that you can do them all intelligently. You can learn enough and do it properly."

Cases where people are fully informed and are acting voluntarily but society still feels justified in restricting personal liberty are instances of hard paternalism. Examples of such cases would be mandatory seat-belt laws or the prohibition against recreational drugs. Philosophers of sport have argued that performance-enhancing substances are not comparable to mandatory seat-belt laws or illegal recreational drugs. Claudio Tamburrini (2000) points out that vehicle drivers are numerous so to abolish mandatory seat-belts would result in an intolerable increase and severity of accident-related injuries. Legalizing recreational drugs could also result in an intolerable situation where too many people indulged in the practice with devastating effects on their social life.

> So both safety-belt regulations and the proscription of recreational drugs can be justified on grounds of the *aggregate* social harm they are expected to prevent. This, however, is not the case with the ban on doping. Professional elite athletes are by definition few. The aggregate social harm that might follow from their doping use would therefore not be sufficiently large to justify the ban. (Tamburrini 2000, 44).

Nicholas Dixon (2001b) also suggests that hard paternalism does not work regarding performance-enhancing substances. He calls the most plausible form of hard paternalism "pre-emptive" paternalism. This form of paternalism allows restrictions on people's freedom when allowing them to act would result in a loss of future autonomy. Dixon points out that pre-emptive paternalism provides a cogent rationale for prohibiting recreational drugs such as crack and heroin "because, while the initial decision to take the drug might be fully autonomous, users' voluntary control of their decision to continue using the drug–and thus their autonomy–will likely erode over time" (p.9). Dixon, however, notes that drugs such as crack and heroin differ from performance-enhancing substances such as steroids in that crack and heroin will impair a person's ability to control his or her desires and his or her capacity for rational deliberation. While steroids may result in liver damage, atherosclerosis, hypertension, and so on, a person taking steroids still has the ability to control his or her desires even though the harms caused by the steroids will impair his or her ability *to act* on his or her autonomous decisions. This distinction between not being able to make autonomous decisions and not being able to act upon decisions made is significant enough to conclude that hard paternalism is justified regarding drugs such as crack and heroin but not performance-enhancing substances such as steroids.

Having considered the health risks involved in taking performance-enhancing substances, one can conclude that, even though there may be serious risks (although the "jury is still out" on the severity of such risks), such risks may be no greater than other health-related risks we *do* allow in sport, for example, injury and even death in high-risk sports such as football and mountain climbing. Since we live in a liberal society that values personal freedom, there would have to be very good reasons for restricting athletes' freedom regarding their choice to dope or not to dope. Having considered paternalistic arguments for restricting the use of peformance-enhancing substances due to their potential health risks and having found them wanting, we now turn to other reasons for choosing not to use performance-enhancing substances.

A reason for not doping that arose during the interviews with the athletes involved their concern about "getting caught"; that is, they did not want to risk **legal ramifications**. In the words of the athletes: "The only risk for sure that I think that you have to worry about is the risk of getting caught," and "I have since stopped [taking performance-enhancing substances] and not for health reasons, which is frightening, but because my training partner tested positive," and "I am not willing to take that risk because I don't want to test positive, it is not because I am worried about my kidneys." Many performance-enhancing substances are banned by sport-governing bodies. Thus, if athletes take the banned substances, they risk the chance of being caught and suffering fairly severe penalties. However, even if doping were not illegal, there are still moral questions concerning the use of performance-enhancing substances. Two significant moral issues that arise involve fairness and coercion. If some athletes are using performance-enhancing substances and others are not using them, there is the issue of whether the competition between "dopers" and "non-dopers" is a fair contest. Also, if a majority of athletes are using performance-enhancing substances, some athletes may feel they must also dope if they want to remain competitive. This situation might be viewed as a "coercive" one.

Coercive, Unfair, and Unnatural

As mentioned in the previous section, proponents of the use of performance-enhancing substances advocate that athletes should be free to choose whether or not to take these substances. The soft paternalist counter-argues that society can justify limiting one's liberty when one's actions are not fully voluntary. Actions may not be fully voluntary if the "actor" is not fully informed or if he or she "is in some relevant way coerced" (Brown 1984, 15). The issue of **coercion** arose in the interviews with the athletes: "The reality of it is that if I want to be competitive against countries that are funding their athletes, promoting a healthy system–whatever that means ... I guess we can't define that–then for us to even be close, I need to do whatever I can." So a significant ethical question regarding performance-enhancing substances concerns the issue of whether athletes who would rather not dope feel "coerced" into taking performance-enhancing substances in order to remain competitive.

Philosophers of sport have examined the issue of coercion. Robert Simon (1984) argues that

> [w]hile the competitive pressures to use performance-enhancing drugs undoubtedly are real, it is far from clear that they are unfair or improperly imposed. Suppose, for example, that some athletes embark on an especially heavy program of weight training. Are they coercing other athletes into training just as hard in order to compete? If not, why are those athletes who use steroids "coercing" others into going along? (p.9)

M. Andrew Holowchak (2000) argues that the difference between weight training programs and steroid use is the danger inherent in steroid use: "[S]teroids place regard for enhancement of athletic performance above regard for the health of athletes themselves.... There is no such reasonable suspicion concerning heavy weights. Athletes do get hurt while training with heavy weights, but, done cautiously, such training is more helpful than hurtful" (p.40). The notion that competitors should not have to engage in dangerous practices to compete with each other is criticized by Tamburrini (2000):

> In the realm of professional ethics, it is widely accepted that benefits should be distributed in relation to efforts and risks undertaken. An ambitious war correspondent puts her life at risk to obtain interesting news or the most impressive picture. If she succeeds, she will be rewarded. By so doing, she is, albeit indirectly, challenging her colleagues to do the same, if they want to achieve a similar success. Should we prohibit war correspondents from coming too near the battle line, to avoid submitting other war correspondents from coming too near to the battle line, to avoid submitting other war correspondents to such pressure? The suggestion seems to me preposterous. (p.45)

Even if the charge of coercion is perceived to be too strong, Dixon (2001b) examines the revised argument that performance-enhancing substances harm other athletes by forcing them into a position where they must choose between excelling in their sport or avoiding the risks of doping.

> [W]hile presenting rival athletes with this choice [between excelling in their sport or avoiding the risks of doping] undoubtedly harms their interests, it hardly constitutes an impermissible harm: a wrong. Any concerted effort to excel in our careers imposes competitive pressures on rivals who may have to make sacrifices if they wish to surpass our achievements. Even when these sacrifices are significant, as in the case of Tamburrini's war correspondent, we are not acting wrongly. In an athletic community that lifts the ban on PEDs [performance-enhancing drugs], then, when an athlete uses them her rivals are not wronged by the fact that they too will have to use them in order to compete successfully at the highest level. (pp.8-9)

Norman Fost (1986) also points out that confronting the choice of whether to take performance-enhancing substances should not be considered "coercion": "Athletes confronting the choice of whether to use steroids face an opportunity to be better than they are, admittedly at some risk, but with no loss of property, health, or basic rights if they refuse.... Imagine a candidate for professional football who argues he is being coerced into risking knee injury" (p.7).

If the argument based on coercion (including the revised version examined by Dixon) fails to convince proponents of doping that athletes are "wronged" by other athletes taking performance-enhancing substances, perhaps the "wrong" lies elsewhere–with the notion that doping creates an unfair playing field. When referring to the doping situation as **unfair**, it should be clarified that we are referring to something "deeper" than cheating. The very act of cheating creates an unfair situation. As stated in Chapter 7, when an athlete cheats, the situation requires that some players (those who do not cheat) take more than their fair share of abiding by the rules. When some athletes use banned performance-enhancing substances, they are relying on the other athletes not to be taking these substances, thus giving the "users" an unfair advantage over those athletes respecting the ban.

However, even if there were no ban on performance-enhancing substances, would there still be an issue of fairness? The athletes interviewed for this chapter felt that there was still an issue of fairness concerning performance-enhancing substances: "There will always be a point about fair/unfair. It would come down to money and it would come down to the countries that are currently practicing more substance use and availability to their athletes" and "Nothing will ever be fair is what it comes down to.... [I]t is going to be better drugs, they have better chemists working to produce better anabolics and better creatines and whatever."

Philosophers have also examined the issue of fairness regarding performance-enhancing substances. Roger Gardner (1989) makes a distinction between an advantage over an opponent and an *unfair* advantage. Two issues arise from this distinction:

> First, it would appear that it is not the advantage per se that we object to, because gaining a competitive edge in skill or strategy is an essential feature of sport. Instead, what we object to is the way in which the athlete acquires the advantage.... The second point is that in order to distinguish between acceptable and unacceptable advantages in sport, it appears that we need simply to determine whether the advantage is fair or unfair. (p.61)

However, there would seem to be examples of unfair advantages that one would consider acceptable. Gardner gives the examples of countries such as Austria and Switzerland having an unfair advantage over America when it comes to winter sports, or American athletes having an unfair advantage over Third World athletes because of better facilities and sophisticated training techniques. Gardner proposes that it is not whether the advantage is unfair that is the issue, but rather how the advantage was gained. He gives the example of Chicago Cubs pitcher Bruce Sutter, the first pitcher to develop an effective split-finger fastball (a pitch that makes a sudden downward movement as it approaches the plate as a result of the way the ball is held). At the same time, Gaylord Perry, a pitcher for the San Diego Padres, was suspected of applying a foreign substance to the ball to achieve the same effect that Sutter had with his split-finger pitch. What would make Sutter's advantage acceptable but not Perry's? "Sutter's use of a split-finger fastball is evaluated as a fair and ethical way to gain an (unfair) advantage over the hitter. Perry's use of a spitball is evaluated as an unfair and unethical way to gain the same advantage" (p.62).

Relating the issue of fairness to the way an athlete gains an advantage using performance-enhancing substances, Gardner (1989) considers the possibility of unrestricted doping. Since there could still be inequality due to some athletes having greater access because of financial ability or a nation's technological advancement, equal access might be proposed as a requirement for permitting performance-enhancing substances. However, Gardner points out that there are many things athletes do not have equal access to, and such situations are not considered unacceptable, for example, good coaches, modern training facilities, knowledgeable physiologists, and so forth. Also, even if all athletes had access to performance-enhancing substances, some might still choose not to use them (for health reasons perhaps). If this were the case, advantages gained by users would appear to be permissible. For athletes who did avail themselves of the equal access to performance-enhancing substances, there is still the inequality that exists as a result of bodies reacting differently to such substances. However, as Gardner points out, there are many innate inequalities in athletes that enable some to benefit more than others, for example, every athlete has a unique response to available training stimuli, diets, and so on. "Gaining an advantage through inequalities in innate capabilities is unavoidable and it hardly seems unethical; nor from a practical standpoint do such discrepancies seem to be distinguishable" (p.64).

Thus, Gardner concludes that athletes gaining an advantage through greater access, choice, or better physiological response to performance-enhancing substances does not seem to create an unacceptable situation in sport. He then tries another angle by attempting to distinguish gaining an advantage through the use of doping as opposed to gaining a similar advantage through acceptable modes of enhancement. He gives the example of blood doping versus training at high altitudes. Both processes result in increased blood volume and hemoglobin count. What is it about blood doping that is unacceptable while high-altitude training is acceptable? Gardner (1989) suggests that the difference is that blood doping involves a supplemented substance. However, he is quick to point out that there are many legal substances used by athletes to gain an advantage over opponents, such as amino acids, protein powders, vitamins, and so forth. Attempting to distinguish between "good" and "bad" substances will lead us into a discussion of the "natural," which will be examined at the end of this section.

Another attempt to distinguish between good and bad substances could involve determining whether the substance offered a "shortcut" to the desired end, for example, high-altitude training requires long hours of hard work while a blood transfusion requires no training effort. However, Gardner (1989) points out that the amount and intensity of effort required to become an elite athlete varies greatly between athletes. "But because it may be 'easier' for some, we do not then claim that they have unethically gained any ensuing competitive advantage" (p.67). A final distinction offered by Gardner attempts to view the acquired capabilities as external to the athlete–viewing the endurance promoted by blood doping to be analogous to using the subway during the New York City marathon. But as Gardner is quick to point out, how do the capabilities and accompanying advantages resulting from running shoes or legal substances differ from the "external" capabilities acquired through blood doping?

Through pointing out the inconsistencies in attempting to distinguish between good and bad substances or methods of acquisition, Gardner (1989) concludes that justifying doping prohibitions on the basis of unfairness is problematic. As Gardner points out, some athletes are more suitably "genetically endowed" than their competitors, and there is already unequal access to the best coaches, facilities, equipment, and so forth; thus athletes already start in an unfair position. In fact, one could go so far as to say that the use of performance-enhancing substances might help level the playing field for those athletes who are at a disadvantage genetically or training and/or coach-wise. Tamburrini (2000) adds the issue of sponsorship into the "unfair mix." He suggests that it is ironic that the International Olympic Committee abandoned amateurism but maintains doping bans.

> Sponsorship creates, no doubt, a situation of inequality in competitive conditions: those who get a succulent contract with a powerful company end up in a better position than non-sponsored athletes.... If sports organizations really cared about equal conditions of competition, rather than banning performance-enhancing methods, what seems to be needed is a selective doping policy. Non-sponsored athletes might be allowed to dope, while those supported by commercial firms would not. Surely this measure would contribute to levelling out all participants' chances of winning much more efficiently than would banning doping. (pp.50, 51)

Although the proposal to allow selective doping policies to "level out" the playing field might seem a little extreme, such a proposal emphasizes the fact that allowing doping does not introduce unfairness, since the playing field is already unfair to begin with.

The arguments based on unfairness and coercion are concerned with the moral issues of equality and freedom. Another argument to consider is based more on a metaphysical distinction; this is the argument based on the **unnaturalness** of performance-enhancing substances. The athletes interviewed for this chapter admitted to taking substances that they considered "unnatural" but they all thought that the ideal would involve taking only "natural" substances: "Whatever you can do naturally I think is a bonus," and "If I had some sort of drug that increases the amount of glycogen in the muscles and then the more pasta you ate, the more energy you could store, I would have a problem with that because now you are kind of working outside of what is natural for you," and "Anything your body can naturally take in and use whatever it needs–I am kind of okay with it." Although the athletes seemed clear on what was natural and what was not (e.g., "I take Centrum [multi-vitamins] twice a day.... Let's say I get a 120 ml, then I just get rid of whatever extra–but I wouldn't say that I am taking a natural substance. I consider that artificial"), philosophers have pointed out that the distinction between "natural" and "unnatural" is not easy to make, and even when one can make a distinction, the "natural" is not always an unqualified "good."

Tamburrini (2000) and Brown (2001) note that blood doping or taking steroids involves natural substances (steroids being derived from the male hormone testosterone). If it is the amount taken that is considered unnatural, one would have to question why the International Olympic Committee allows carbohydrate diets and extremely demanding training methods (Tamburrini 2000, 53). If the "unnaturalness" lies in the manufacturing process used in making steroids or the medical technologies used in blood doping, one would have to discount much of what is accepted as part of the athlete's regimen, for example, foods and vitamins (Brown 2001, 147). Fost (1986) cites an interesting example concerning athletes' diets:

> Consider a special diet, developed by a nutritional scientist, proven to enhance performance. Would we suggest that victories aided by such a diet were corrupt, or that athletes who used such information to enhance their performance were immoral? Would it matter whether the diet used "artificial" food, made in factories and packaged in cans, or "natural" foods, eaten fresh from the farm, with or without chemical fertilizers? Would we establish testing procedures to ensure no athlete used such a diet? The difference between this kind of chemical assistance and drugs is unclear. (p.7)

Clifton Perry (1983) attempts to clarify the difference between food and drugs by making a distinction between supplementing as opposed to exploiting an athlete's natural abilities. **Supplementing** one's natural abilities would involve adding something to one's natural abilities that would result in a performance partially attributable to the supplementation. In **exploiting** one's natural abilities, one's natural abilities are utilized to achieve a certain level of performance.

> High altitude training, carbohydrate loading, interval training, etc. would appear to all to be appropriate examples of securing a particular performance level through exploitation. In such cases, enhanced performances are secured not by compensating or supplementing the body but by having the body adjust to changes in environmental factors. Taking an auto in a boat race, placing heavy weights in one's boxing glove, etc., all appear to be examples of achieving a specific performance level through supplementation. (p.41)

Tamburrini (2000) is critical of Perry's distinction between exploiting or supplementing one's natural abilities, for it cannot account for easy, intuitive cases of performance-enhancing techniques. "For instance, specifically designed running-shoes and smooth track-surfaces do not only help to exploit the athlete's physical capacity, but supplement it also. Were we to adopt this criterion, we practically would have to condemn all kind of technical equipment" (p.53). It appears that the distinction between exploiting or supplementing natural abilities is as difficult to maintain as the distinction between "natural" and "unnatural" performance-enhancing substances.

If the arguments that performance-enhancing substances are unnatural, that athletes taking performance-enhancing substances coerce other athletes into doing the same, or that doping creates an unfair playing field fail to provide adequate justification for prohibiting doping in sport, are we left with no choice but to lift doping bans? There is another approach one can take in attempting to justify the prohibition of performance-enhancing substances, and it is to this approach we now turn.

Why Play Sport?

If the arguments against taking performance-enhancing substances can be countered by those advocating that athletes should be able to use these substances, why should athletes refrain from doping? To argue this case, one must return to the question asked at the beginning of the chapter–why do athletes play sports? If they play simply to win, it will be difficult to convince them not to use performance-enhancing substances. However, if athletes participate in sports to improve their skills, there is a good reason not to take the risks involved with doping because performance-enhancing substances do not improve skill levels. These thoughts are echoed in the words of the athletes: "Drug taking is going to be okay for people who are in the sport to win, wouldn't it be? If your goal, what sport is to you, is to beat everyone else, then drugs–well, that is part of it, isn't it? If your goal is to become the best that you can be without sacrificing this sense of integrity–then it is not okay," and "A lot of these drugs are to give you the physical edge, but only time, practice and repetition, and doing it over, and over, and over again, will develop the skill," and "I want to represent Canada. To do that in this realm now you have to be the best and that means whatever. And granted, drugs will make you stronger and quicker and won't necessarily establish your skill, but once you have established the skill, it is those other things that make you a better athlete," and "My biggest promotion of sport is that if I can't do it on my own, then why am I doing it?"

The question concerning performance-enhancing substances and the goals of sport has been addressed by philosophers of sport. One approach taken by some philosophers (Brown 1990, 2001; Schneider and Butcher 1993-94, 2000) is to view sports as a practice with internal and external goods. The notion of a **practice** is borrowed from Alasdair MacIntyre (1984):

> By a "practice" I am going to mean any coherent and complex form of socially established cooperative human activity through which goods internal to that form of activity are realized in the course of trying to achieve those standards of excellence which are appropriate to, and partially definitive of, that form of activity, with the result that human powers to achieve excellence, and human conceptions of the ends and goods involved are systematically extended. (p.187)

Angela Schneider and Robert Butcher (1993-94) point out that sports lend themselves to the "practice" account since they are socially constructed.

The notion of "goods internal to that form of activity" is also realized in sport. The **internal goods** of a practice include the joy of mastering the skills inherent to that practice.

> The internal goods of a practice act as their own rewards to practitioners and aficionados. For the player, the joy that comes with mastering a skill, with the perfect execution of a difficult play, or with the elation at the end of a well-played game are the rewards of the hard work, dedication, and commitment that went into building up those skills in the first place. These joys cannot be duplicated in any other way. (p.66)

Schneider, a former Olympic rower, cites the example of the internal goods available through rowing:

> The joy that comes from getting the stroke just right and being in harmony with the rest of the crew as the entire boat strokes at the same time cannot be exactly duplicated in any other sport. The beauty of a well-rowed boat is unique. So while one may get the external goods of money and fame from a variety of sources, one can only get the joy of a well-rowed boat from rowing. (Ibid.)

Another elite-level rower interviewed reiterates the internal good found in the "joy of a well-rowed boat": "Once you have obtained that skill, it is just a great feeling. No matter how many wins or losses you have, if you know that you have been working three times a day, six days a week just to get this one placement of the blade and you have done that–that's enough gratitude."

If the external goods become the goal of the athletes, then no argument from internal goals will be found to be convincing. **External goods** include extrinsic rewards such as gold medals, prestige, endorsements, and so forth. "If a person performs an action solely for the sake of extrinsic reward, there is no good reason to perform the action properly, or well, or even not to cheat. If the goal is the reward, then the action is just a means, a means that can be shortened or bypassed whenever possible" (Schneider and Butcher 1993-94, 71). This situation relates particularly well to doping. If the sole goal of an athlete is to win the gold medal, the exercise of his or her skills will not be as important as winning. Doping becomes an option since the exercise of skills is a means that could be bypassed through the taking of performance-enhancing substances. Schneider and Butcher (1993-94) point out that performance-enhancing substances may increase an athlete's strength and speed, but he or she will not improve his or her technique. Added strength and/or speed may increase an athlete's chances of winning, but this does not mean that he or she is the more skilled player.

Brown (2001) is critical of the internal/external distinction regarding doping and sport: "[I]t [internal/external distinction] divides motives and satisfactions too neatly, borrowing the metaphor of inside and outside to suggest that practices are like the bodies of the players themselves, inwardly pure and driven by their own dynamics, confronted by external forces of corruption and greed" (p.150). Brown argues that the internal/external distinction blurs at crucial places. The notion that internal goods involve sport-specific skills blurs when one considers skills that are carried over from one sport to another (e.g., skills for biathlon, triathlon, and decathlon), as well as skills that are carried over to practices other than sports (e.g., teamwork, co-operativeness, planning, etc.). Brown also criticizes the notion that winning is an external good: "[W]inning surely emerges as the final, overall configuration of the game itself, internal to the dynamics of the play, its culmination, not an externally imposed determination by those external to the activity" (p.151). Finally, Brown is critical of Schneider and Butcher's argument that performance-enhancing substances bypass the exercise of skills.

> [T]o the extent that performance drugs could enhance performance, they would contribute to the exercise of skills at a higher level where the challenges and satisfactions might be all the greater.... To this extent, sports recapitulate life and reflect a constant striving to win and enjoy, to compete and share in the competition of the game. In this sense, performance drugs may be as relevant to sports and their internal goods as any other way of enhancing one's performance. (p.152)

Because of the difficulties using the internal/external goods distinction, some philosophers have looked at the role of skill in sport without invoking the internal goods distinction. Dixon (2001b) examines the notion of **athletic meritocracy**. "In the ideal contest, on this view, victory is determined primarily by the qualities that are central to athletic excellence: skill, strategy and effort" (p.12). An issue that arises in Dixon's work is the influence of genetic endowment on an athlete's abilities. Athletic meritocracy would seem to require downplaying genetic abilities. However, Dixon points out that we do not eliminate advantages due to innate qualities as necessary for meritocracy in other fields, for example, we do not handicap applicants to law school who have a greater inherited intelligence.

> A more reasonable goal for athletic meritocracy is to accept the unavoidable influence of genetic gifts, while maximizing the role played by factors that *are* within athletes' control: practicing in order to convert their raw natural talents into skill, developing astute strategy, and working hard in both preparing for and competing in contests. The effect of allowing widespread use of PEDs [performance-enhancing drugs] would be to compound the "unearned" component of athletic success, by allowing both affluence and differential responses to PED use to influence the outcome of contests. (p.20).

Dixon argues that as the role of physique increases (which would happen with an increase in the use of performance-enhancing substances), the role of technique and finesse (i.e., skill) decreases. When this happens, contests become less interesting and may, in some cases, be barely recognizable as sport. Dixon gives an interesting example of a mythic contest called the "high reach," where contestants stand on tiptoe, trying to reach as high as they can up a wall. "The outcome would be almost solely determined by the physique of contestants.... The absence of any need for skill would rid the contest of any interest and disqualify it as a sport. Since PEDs push us in the direction of such grotesque events, we should not allow athletes to use them" (p.22). Although Dixon eventually concedes that it is difficult to make the distinction between performance-enhancing substances and other methods of performance enhancement, for example, long-handled golf putters that reduce the need for a steady hand and make it easier to sink putts, the reduction of skill in sports contests would risk diminishing public interest in sport, thus harming sport itself.

> Sport events would increasingly become tests of rivals' access to good pharmaceutical technology and knowledge and their bodies' ability to use these chemicals efficiently, while the role of skill is diminished. It's not that people aren't interested in science fairs; it's just that people expect sport to be a different kind of test, one in which technique and finesse are the major determinants of success. (p.28)

Another philosopher who argues that performance-enhancing substances change the nature of the competition is Robert Simon. "[T]he whole point of athletic competition is to test the athletic ability of persons, not the way bodies react to drugs" (Simon 1984, 11). The fact that spectators want to watch people and not robots compete supports the claim that performance is not everything. "[I]f all we are interested in is better and better performance, we could design robots to 'run' the hundred yards in 3 seconds or hit a golf ball 500 hundred yards when necessary. But it isn't just enhanced performance that we are after. In addition, we want athletic competition to be a test of persons" (ibid., p.12). Thus, the goal of athletic competitions is not just to lift heavier and heavier weights or run the mile faster and faster, but

> [r]ather, it is to do so in a particular way by meeting as a person the challenges set by opponents or by the qualities of an obstacle, such as a golf course. The good competitor does not see an opponent simply as a body to be beaten down but as another person whose acts constitute a mutually acceptable challenge and which calls for appropriate response. By making victory dependent on qualities of bodies, the ability to efficiently utilize a drug, which has nothing to do with athletic ability or our status as persons, the use of performance enhancers moves sports in a direction that makes it less and less an expression of our personhood. (Ibid., pp.87-88)

Simon's conception of competition as **a mutually acceptable challenge** (recall also the notion of *com-petitio* discussed in Chapter 3) has been criticized as involving a stipulative conception of sport. According to Brown (1984), "[t]here is ... no single conception of sports on which we need agree" (p.20). Schneider and Butcher (2000) also point out that "sport is socially constructed and there is no obvious reason why it could not be constructed to include doping" (p.196). Simon acknowledges this concern but emphasizes that the accepted paradigm of athletic competition should have moral force. When athletes take performance-enhancing substances "[i]t becomes more and more appropriate to see the opposition as things to be overcome–as mere means to be overcome in the name of victory–rather than as persons posing valuable challenges" (Simon 1984, 12). Seeing opponents as means rather than ends demonstrates a Kantian **lack of respect**. "So, insofar as the requirement that we respect each other as persons is ethically fundamental, the prevailing paradigm does enjoy a privileged perspective from the moral point of view" (ibid., p.13). Thus, if we want sports to remain a competition between people who are ends in themselves, not means to achieving the goal of winning, athletes should refrain from using performance-enhancing substances.

Conclusion

In answering the question of whether to dope or not to dope, athletes need to consider arguments for and against the taking of performance-enhancing substances. The health risks involved in taking some performance-enhancing substances raises the issue of autonomy and paternalism; that is, should informed adults be able to choose to dope even if doping carries potential health risks. There are also legal risks involved in taking banned substances. However, even if the bans were lifted, moral issues having to do with coercion and unfairness would still need to be addressed. Regarding the unnaturalness argument against taking performance-enhancing substances, a distinction has been made between supplementing and exploiting an athlete's natural ability. However, this distinction seems to be as "fuzzy" as the distinction between natural and unnatural substances. If the arguments concerning health and legal risks, coercion, unfairness, and the unnaturalness of performance-enhancing substances do not seem conclusive in supporting a drug ban, perhaps a more profitable approach involves considering the practice of sport, with an emphasis on the internal versus the external goods. A similar approach involves considering the qualities involved in athletic meritocracy and arguing that performance-enhancing substances do not affect the qualities by which we should judge an athlete's performance. Finally, if sport is perceived as a mutually acceptable challenge, athletes who dope show a lack of respect for their opponents; that is, they perceive their opponents as means to the end of winning rather than an end in themselves.

CHAPTER REVIEW

Key Concepts

- health risks
- autonomy
- paternalism
- legal risks
- coercion
- unfairness
- unnaturalness
- supplementation and exploitation
- practice
- internal goods
- external goods
- athletic meritocracy
- mutually acceptable challenge
- lack of respect

Review Questions

1. What are some of the counter-arguments against the health-risk reason for banning performance-enhancing substances?
2. How do the notions of autonomy and paternalism relate to the health-risk argument?
3. Are athletes "coerced" into taking performance-enhancing substances in order to compete with athletes who dope? Why or why not?
4. Is the unfair advantage gained through doping different from other advantages found in competitions? Why or why not?
5. What are some of the counter-arguments against the unnaturalness reason for banning performance-enhancing substances?
6. How do the notions of "practice" and "internal goods" relate to a justification for banning performance-enhancing substances?
7. What is meant by "athletic meritocracy," and how does this notion relate to doping?
8. How does the conception of competition as a mutually acceptable challenge have moral force, and how does this conception relate to the taking of performance-enhancing substances?

9

Violence in Sport: Just Part of the Game?

[W]ith less than a minute on the score-clock and Brashear already on the ice, McSorley jumped over the boards intending, he said later, to provoke another fight. But instead, in a grotesque lapse of character, McSorley skated up from behind and , with just 2.7 seconds left, clubbed Brashear in the right temple with a vicious two-handed slash of his stick. The Vancouver forward dropped backward like a felled tree. Making matters worse, his helmet slipped off just before impact, allowing his head to bounce sickeningly on the ice. McSorley was immediately besieged by several Canucks, while Brashear–unconscious, his body twitching ominously, blood seeping out of his nose–was treated by emergency medical staff and rushed away on a stretcher. (Deacon 2000, 45)

I just timed my hit. When I felt I could zero in on Riley's head at the same time the ball arrived in his hands, I moved.... Because of the momentum built up by the angles and speed of both Riley and myself, it was the best hit of my career. I heard Riley scream on impact and felt his body go limp. (Tatum and Kushner 1979, 18)

Boxers die from acute brain trauma, caused either by a blow (or blows) to the head or, sometimes, a heavy fall to the canvas. The brain is like so much jelly suspended in a bucket, and when you strike the bucket sharply, the brain inside accelerates, twists and bumps around. In a knockout, which is technically a concussion, the force of a punch, transmitted to the brainstem, causes the fighter to lose consciousness. A KO is considered an acute injury, but it's relatively mild compared to what happens if the jarred brain ruptures the blood vessels that surround it. Then a hematoma (a massive buildup of blood) occurs in the narrow space between the rigid skull and the soft brain. As it expands, the hematoma simply squeezes the brain to death. (Boyle and Ames 1983, 44)

The citations above are all examples of or the result of violent behavior. This behavior, a frequent occurrence in sport, is rarely questioned. However, as a civilized society, we must ask whether violence in sport can be justified. Just because violence has become so much a part of the fabric of sport, that is, the notion that "it's just part of the game," does not provide an adequate justification. In this chapter, three examples of sport will be considered and the role violent behavior plays in each. A distinction will be made between behavior that is intrinsic to a particular sport and behavior that is gratuitous to the internal goals of the sport. Distinctions will also be made between assertive, aggressive, and violent behavior. Perhaps some levels of behavior might be justified even while others are not. Having analyzed the role of violence in various sports as well as the levels of behavior leading to violence, we will be in a position to make recommendations concerning violence in sport. Other key concepts utilized in this chapter include: **anger release, motivational aspect, nature of the game, is-ought fallacy, constitutive rules, regultive rules, ethos of a game, level and pain of injury, glorified violence, social effects, attitude toward another self, aggressive instinct, honest violence, dangerous thrill, autonomy, paternalism, legitimate** and **illegitimate violence**, and **vulnerability principle**.

Hockey

Violence in hockey can take many forms, from slashing to fighting. As hockey critic Stan Fischler (1974) points out, "[v]iolence has been part of the woof and warp of hockey since the first game was played in Montreal on March 3, 1875" (p.4). Watson and MacLellan (1986), having reviewed judicial proceedings of the past eighty years, suggest that hockey has had a long history of extreme violence. Sociologists and psychologists have also studied violence in hockey, seeking explanations for violent behavior (Colburn 1985, 1986; Smith 1978a, 1979; Widmeyer and Birch 1984); possible deterrents for violence (Terry and Jackson 1985; Vaz 1979); effects of violence on spectators (Cullen 1974; DeNeui and Sachau 1996; Harrell 1981; Russell 1986); and the role played by the media (Smith 1978b, 1983). As well as academic treatments, popular literature has been written concerning hockey violence (Fischler 1974; Swift 1992, 1993), and a few provinces have conducted inquiries into violence at the amateur level (McMurty 1974; Gouvernement du Quebec 1977). One discipline that has not dedicated a significant amount of research into the area of hockey violence is that of philosophy. Although philosophers have a long history of studying ethics, and hockey would appear to provide many examples of ethical dilemmas, hockey has not been the subject of much philosophical research.

In an attempt to understand the violence in hockey, a number of university-level and midget fifteen-year-old) hockey players were interviewed concerning the fighting in their sport. The answers given were then analyzed from a philosophical perspective. Although the university hockey players spoke freely of the fighting and cheap shots involved in hockey, when they were asked to give examples of ethical issues in their sport, they were unable to think of any. When asked if fighting or cheap shots were ethical issues, they said, "No, they [are] just part of the game." When the midget players and their parents and coaches were interviewed, a number of reasons for fighting in hockey arose. The reason for fighting that was cited most frequently during the interviews was that fighting was a way to

release anger. One coach stated: "[I]t [fighting] gives them an opportunity to release some anger and there are a lot of kids on this team, in this league or level that will." A number of reasons were given for why players were angry. The most common reason for being angry was that the team was losing: "If they're [teammates] not winning and they know they are going to lose, it makes them angry so they fight," and "I find that with the kids, like if they are losing, they're getting really upset and they start taking really cheap shots," and "It gets harder and harder to walk away from it [fighting] towards the end of the game when you're really losing badly."

Another reason for fighting that arose in both the interviews with the university-level and midget hockey players concerned the **motivational aspect** of fighting. "Sometimes people get into a fight and that will get your players into the game and wanna play more," and "It [fighting] might get their team into the game a bit more when people see you fight, then they get pumped up." Closely related to motivating the team would be fighting in order to protect one's teammates.

> But we've had circumstances this year where we've sent guys off the bench to go out and fight other players on other teams just to kinda get a message across. So that may be… I mean, for me that's not really unethical. That's part of the game if the team's going after your best player, I mean, you have to do something to stop that. But for a person like yourself or a fan, you may think, "Well, he's sending him out to beat someone up! That can't be ethical." But from the player's perspective, I mean, you see that as part of the game. You don't want your best players getting injured and you have to take measures to stop that.

In conducting a philosophical analysis of the reasons hockey players gave for the fighting in their sport, it was interesting to note that the most common reason cited by the midget players was the need to release anger. A number of issues arise when considering the "anger release" reason for fighting. First, is fighting an appropriate means to release anger? Second, if the anger is a result of losing, perhaps we have to consider the significance placed on winning in our society. The appropriateness of fighting as a means to release anger may be more of a question for empirical psychology than philosophy; but the question must still be asked, if fighting does provide a release for anger, whether the release of anger on the part of the aggressor is worth the potential suffering of the recipient of the aggression. Regarding anger resulting from losing, a serious question that must be addressed concerns the significance placed on winning in our society. In Chapter 3 it was noted that society has moved away from the meaning of the root word of competition, *com-petitio*, to strive together, and replaced it with a "winning-at-all-costs" attitude. We cannot expect our young hockey players to view sports as a means to becoming better hockey players when society continuously pushes the importance of winning as opposed to self-improvement in the pursuit of excellence.

The motivational reason for fighting would also fall under the purview of sport psychology. However, even if fighting was perceived as having motivational potential, the question could again be asked concerning whether this motivational potential is worth the risk of people getting hurt. A far safer (and perhaps more effective in the long run) approach to motivating players would lie in a return to the root word of *com-petitio*, to strive together. If players saw their teammates as well as the opposition as people with whom they are "striving together" to improve their abilities as hockey players, they would view the opposing team itself as motivating. As mentioned in Chapter 3, social psychologists have noted the motivational factor involved in playing against opponents of similar skill level (Dakin and Arrowood 1981; Gastorf, Suls, and Lawhon 1978; Suls and Miller 1977). The closely related reason for fighting as a means to protect teammates takes on an almost "noble" air. However, what happens in this situation is that the virtue of loyalty (which is how one might interpret protecting one's teammates) comes into direct conflict with the virtue of beneficence. Deciding between conflicting virtues is a perennial problem. However, there is an alternative to having to choose between potentially hurting the opposition in order to be loyal to one's teammates. This alternative involves more calls by the referee. This recommendation, among others, will be addressed in the final section of this chapter.

The reason for fighting that was common to both the university-level hockey players as well as the midget players interviewed was that "it's just part of the **nature of the game**," part of what it means to play hockey. This justification for fighting raises a number of questions. First, what do we mean by the "nature of the game"? Second, is "the nature" of something an unqualified good? Finally, is there a distinction between the way something "is" and the way something "ought" to be, that is, the **is-ought fallacy**?

A number of philosophers of sport have examined the nature of play, sport, and games (see Chapter 1). However, no one has looked explicitly at what we mean by the "nature" of a particular sport, that is, in this case, hockey. The "nature" of a sport would include the rules, both constitutive and regulative (Rawls 1955; Searle 1995), and the ethos of the game (D'Agostino 1981). The **constitutive rules** include the rules that make up the game (e.g., the puck must be put in the opposing team's net to score a point) while the **regulative rules** include rules concerning how the game is played (e.g., a forward cannot hold onto the opposition's goalie while a teammate tries to score a goal). The **ethos of a game** includes the "unwritten rules." Fred D'Agostino (1981) gives the example in basketball where there is a regulative rule concerning not touching an opponent. However, many touches are left "uncalled" because, as D'Agostino points out, "the players and game officials have, in effect, conspired to ignore certain of the rules of basketball, at least in certain situations, in order to promote certain interests, which they share, for instance, with team owners and spectators–e.g., to make the game more exciting" (p.14).

The question to be asked is whether allowing fighting in hockey is one of those "unwritten" rules. An unwritten rule of not calling every contact in basketball is different from allowing fighting in hockey. Not calling every touch in basketball speeds up playing, allowing for more exercise of the skills of basketball. Fighting in hockey, on the other hand, slows down play and decreases the opportunity of exercising the skills of hockey. Thus, fighting violates the "written" rules of hockey, and to consider allowing fighting as an "unwritten" rule seems counter-productive to the development of hockey skills.

If someone refused to accept the above argument that fighting falls outside the "nature" of hockey, the response could still be made that just because *x* is part of the "nature" of *y* does not mean that *x* is an unqualified good. For example, just because breaking down someone's door is part of the nature of thievery, this does not make breaking down someone's door a good thing. Closely related to this objection is the "is" and "ought" distinction, that is, the is-ought fallacy. Just because something "is" a certain way (i.e., fighting is perceived to be a part of hockey) does not mean it "ought" to be that way (i.e., it is possible to play hockey with less fighting). That hockey can be played without fighting is obvious when we compare the way hockey is played in Europe with the way it is played in North America. The possibility of playing "fight-free" hockey is evident even in North America during playoff time. To the spectator who follows hockey throughout the season, there is an amazing drop in the number of fights during the playoffs compared to games in the regular season. An explanation for this situation could be the fact that there is more to lose during the playoffs, and players do not want to take the risk of playing short-handed if their team has to take a penalty for fighting. Thus, it can be seen that there are a number of serious objections to justifying fighting for the reason that it is part of the "nature of the game." Having considered some of the issues involved with fighting in hockey, we turn now to the role of violence in football and boxing.

Football

As mentioned in the previous section, fighting in hockey slows down play and decreases the opportunity of exercising the skills of hockey. This statement is intended to make a distinction between the skills of hockey and the action of fighting. Such a distinction makes it obvious that hockey can be played without fighting. Even if one agrees that fighting could be removed from hockey games, the fact is that some of the skills involved in hockey (apart from actions involved in fighting) could be considered by some to be violent. The most obvious of these legitimate skills would be the body check. The example of the body check in hockey could be utilized to argue that violent behavior is actually intrinsic to hockey, that is, part of the game, and not gratuitous behavior, that is, unrelated to the goals of the game. However, a better example of a sport where the game skills themselves could be considered inherently violent is American football. Michael Smith, in his book *Violence and Sport* (1988), notes that football is in the vanguard for "[r]oughing up and intimidating opponents as a legal tactic" (p.11). "Consider the 'hook,' a sort of on-field mugging, whereby a defensive back in the course of making a tackle flexes his biceps and tries to catch the receiver's head in the joint between the forearm and upper arm" (ibid.). Smith notes that the casualty rate in the National Football League is said to be 100 percent–at least one serious injury per player per season (ibid.).

If the very nature of football skills lends itself to violent behavior, the question arises concerning whether the skills and/or rules of football should be changed to minimize the injuries–injuries that affect every player each season. However, one may challenge whether the very nature of football skills *is* violent. As Robert Simon (1991) points out, "[f]ootball clearly is a contact sport requiring the use of bodily force against opponents. It does not follow, however, that football necessarily is violent.... In particular games or on particular teams, players may indeed act violently towards opponents, but it does not follow that football is a violent game" (p.66). Important distinctions between force and violence will be made in the following section.

Boxing

It would seem logically possible to change some of the skills and/or rules of football to minimize the potential for violent behavior. For example, the "hook" that was described in a previous paragraph was eventually outlawed. However, the sport that is a paradigmatic example of an activity that would not exist were it not for violent behavior is the sport of boxing. Boxing, by its very nature, is violent–the purpose of boxing is to injure your opponent. Philosophers of sport have examined the ethical issues involved in boxing. Two main questions have been addressed. First, can boxing be justified in a civilized society? Second, if autonomous adults choose to take the risks involved in boxing, can a liberal democratic society impinge upon the freedom of their members to choose such risks?

A number of arguments have been put forward in opposition to boxing. Paul Davis (1993-94) critiques four of these: the level and pain of injury, the glorification of violence, the social effects of boxing, and the objective of boxing and attitude to selves. Regarding the **level and pain of injury**, there is no doubt that boxing carries a high risk of pain and injury. The British Medical Association (1993) states that between 1945 and 1993, 361 deaths occurred in the ring worldwide. Nicholas Dixon (2001a) cites research that states that 64-87 percent of current and former boxers tested in studies done in the 1980s suffered from measurable brain damage (p.323). However, Davis responds that sports such as football and rugby rival boxing in regard to risk of injury (he also points out that non-contact sports such as gymnastics and car racing appear to fare even worse than boxing). Davis then proceeds with an even "deeper" response, suggesting that pain and injury are essential ingredients in human self-realization (pp.49, 50). This response will be expanded upon in an explication of the arguments in favor of boxing.

The objection that boxing **glorifies violence** is evident in Simon's (1991) example of an imaginary sport called "Mayhem." In this imaginary sport, two teams of consenting adults are placed in an arena with swords and spears, and they fight until only members of one team are left alive. The surviving players get to divide $10 million. Simon suggests that the indirect harm of such a sport is substantial. "Violence would be glorified and the value of human life inevitably would be cheapened. Such effects may not be inevitable, but the likelihood of eventual harm to others seems sufficient to justify a civilized society in banning Mayhem" (p .61). Davis (1993-94) responds that the analogy between Mayhem and boxing is not adequate. "Boxing, like Mayhem, is undertaken in a ring, but that is probably where the analogy ends. The stringent rules, the delimiting of time, the quality of medical supervision, and the skill of participants, serve to distinguish boxing from Mayhem and from all forms of untrammelled physical aggression" (p.51).

The objection concerning the **social effects** of boxing does not suggest that boxing promotes violence in general, but that boxing exacerbates social violence. Davis (1993-94) states that there is little factual support for this claim. "There is little warrant for asserting that a possible world that doesn't include boxing has less general violence than a world that includes boxing and is identical in all other respects" (p.51). Davis also questions whether, even if boxing does not essentially promote violence, boxing has contingent features that play a causal role in generating some violence. However, he suggests that we do not "believe that beer producers are a priori implicated in alcoholism, nor car manufacturers in road fatalities, nor candy makers in premature tooth decay" (ibid.).

The argument against boxing that Davis finds the most challenging is the concern over the objective of boxing and attitude toward selves. Although there is some controversy over what the exact objective of boxing is; that is, Simon (1991) asserts that "boxing has the goal of infliction of harm by one opponent on another at its core, and so makes violence central (p.64) while Lord Ross, who boxed for Edinburgh University, states that the objective of boxing is not to inflict harm but to "land blows" (Davis 1993-94, 52), the objective of boxing "means that the ring legitimizes an attitude towards another self that is forbidden in other sports and that is generally forbidden in the rest of life" (ibid.). This **attitude toward another self** is one of viciousness–a viciousness that is not legitimized in other aggressive contact sports such as football or rugby. Defenders of boxing might reply that "the viciousness appropriate in boxing is not viciousness towards self but towards the body of one's sporting opponent. All that is really required of boxers, psychologically and morally, is that they view their opponents as *opponents in a game*" (ibid., p.53). This defense would suggest that viewing opponents in boxing is no different than viewing opponents in football, tennis, chess, or Monopoly. However, this analogy linking boxing with other games appears troublesome for boxers themselves as noted in Davis's quotation by Pat Clinton concerning fighting his stablemate Drew Docherty: "We were both taught the rudiments of boxing by my late father, and Drew is like a brother to me. I would not fight against him for a million pounds" (ibid., p.55).

As well as examining arguments against boxing, Davis (1993-94) considers three arguments in favor of boxing: primeval aggression and catharsis, psychological violence and the moral high ground, and Radford's unbearable greyness of heaven. The first argument in favor of boxing is grounded on the anthropological hypothesis that the **instinct to aggression** is a feature of human psychology that, if denied, is likely to have harmful consequences. This argument, although powerful, begs the question. As Davis notes, "it does not follow from the premises about human nature that boxing is a morally sound management of aggression" (p.57).

The second argument in favor of boxing raises the issue that social life is filled with disguised forms of violence and that boxing manages this **violence honestly** and responsibly. However, like the second argument, this hypothesis begs the question. As Davis (1993-94) points out, "[t]he openness of boxing contrasts strikingly with the hypocrisy that smears psychological violence. But honesty does not secure moral tenability. The moral character of boxing is a question that remains open" (p.58).

The final argument in favor of boxing relies on Colin Radford's thesis that

> man's essential nature lies in the actual world, as a creatively danger-seeking, risk-taking, pain-experiencing creature. A condition bereft of danger, risk, and pain would lack essential ingredients of human self-realization. Boxing is an activity that provides those invigorating and precious dangers, risks, and pains. Therefore, boxing is vindicated (Davis 1993-94, 59).

Davis finds this argument the most compelling of the three he examines. However, Davis notes that, just because boxing is a **thrillingly dangerous** activity, it does not follow that boxing is morally tenable. "From the premise that the good life contains a measure of invigorating and dangerous self-exposure, it does not follow that all invigorating and dangerous self-exposure is morally supportable.... It could not be alleged that the life of a Hitler, a Stalin, or a serial murderer, is one of fat contentment" (ibid., p.60).

Having examined the possibility of justifying boxing, we now turn to the second question raised by philosophers of sport; that is, if **autonomous** adults choose to take the risks involved in boxing, can a liberal democratic society impinge upon the freedom of their members to choose such risks? Dixon (2001a) proposes two substantial **paternalistic** (i.e., interfering with a person's will) arguments for restricting boxing: "first, the need to protect boxers from serious losses of future autonomy due to irreversible brain damage, which is all the more urgent because, second, many boxers' decisions to enter the profession in the first place are of questionable autonomy because of de facto coercion resulting from their socioeconomic disadvantages" (p.343). Dixon notes the high incidence of brain damage in boxers and suggests that brain damage is the most direct way to reduce a person's autonomy. He then points out that "boxers face a considerably higher probability of autonomy-reducing injuries than do automobile drivers and motorcycle riders, whom we already protect with paternalistic laws" (ibid., p.332). The fact that many boxers come from disadvantaged backgrounds lends support to Dixon's second argument that, because of seeing boxing as the only means of escaping their situation, boxers are not really making a "free" choice when entering the boxing ring.

Having examined boxing, where violence would seems to be intrinsic to the very nature of the sport; football, where football skills appear to lend themselves to violent behavior; and hockey, where fighting seems gratuitous to the actual skills of the sport, it would seem prudent to look more closely at what we mean by violence, aggression, and assertion, as well as legitimate and illegitimate uses of these different levels of behavior.

Assertive, Aggressive, and Violent Behavior–Legitimate or Illegitimate?

Jim Parry, in an article entitled "Violence and Aggression in Contemporary Sport" (1998), provides a conceptual analysis of the terms *assertion*, *aggression*, and *violence*. In describing assertion, Parry refers to an inborn capacity where "there is the sense of affirming or insisting upon one's right; protecting or vindicating oneself; maintaining or defending a cause" (p.207). Aggression differs from assertion in that it involves force. According to Parry, "aggression is vigorous (trying to gain an advantage by sheer force); offensive (in the sport context; battling for the ball); and proactive (striking first)" (ibid.). Just as one can be assertive without being aggressive (by not using force), one can be aggressive without being violent. As Parry points out, violence "is centrally to do with intentional hurt or injury to others, as well as attempts to harm, recklessness as to harm, and negligence" (ibid.).

Parry's conception of violence as "intentionally hurting or harming another" would definitely place a sport such as boxing into a "violent category." Because of the negative connotations of the term *violent*, some people prefer to make a distinction between **legitimate** and **illegitimate violence**. Parry (1998) notes that "violence may be justifiable (in war, or revolution, or terrorism; or in boxing, where 'violence' within bounds is legitimate). Illegitimate violence must be characterized as the attempt to harm by the use of illegitimate force" (p.209). The use of legitimate violence in sport seems to be accepted by the general populace as well as social scientists. For example, "[p]layer violence in sport is of two types. There is normative violence where it is a part of the game to aggress against the opponent. Examples of normative violence are bodychecking in hockey, blocking and tackling in football, and legitimately sliding hard into a fielder in baseball" (Schneider and Eitzen 1983, 1). However, an important distinction should be made between the situation where a player gets hurt as a result of a body check and the situation where the player body checking is doing so with an intent to injure.

The distinction between assertion, aggression, and violence would appear to be very helpful in making sense of the skills and behaviors practiced in the sports under discussion. Body checking in hockey and tackling in football are skills intrinsic to these sports and are definitely examples of aggressive behavior; they are forceful, vigorous, offensive, and proactive. If these skills are performed for the purpose of getting the puck or stopping the ball, they would appear to be examples of aggressive behavior that are an essential (and acceptable) part of the game. However, if the hockey player body checks with the intention of hurting the opponent (even if it means the player will, as a result, gain control of the puck) or if the football player tackles an opponent with the intention of hurting him (stopping the play but perhaps also taking him out of the game), then these behaviors have become violent and should not be condoned.

Making distinctions based on the intention of the player theoretically makes it easier to determine whether a behavior is violent or simply aggressive. However, it is not always easy to determine a player's intention. An aggressive play might result in an opponent being injured, even though the injury was not intended by the aggressive player. Referees will obviously have to make judgment calls in determining whether a player was behaving violently instead of just acting aggressively. Although there will be difficult calls (which is part of the territory of officiating games), there are many examples where a behavior is clearly violent. Whenever a player is body checked or tackled who is not in possession of the puck or ball (and the body check or tackle is not being made for strategic purposes), a violent act has occurred.

When a distinction is made between aggressive and violent acts, it would appear that the distinction between legitimate and illegitimate violence could be abandoned. That is, all violent acts would be considered "illegitimate" while many acts that some people consider to be "legitimate" violence, for example, body checking and tackling, would be considered aggressive acts that could turn violent depending upon the intention of the player. This distinction between a body check used to gain control of the puck as opposed to injuring the opponent helps us make sense of fighting in hockey. Starting a fight in hockey is usually intended to harm an opponent. Although, as mentioned above, players may start a fight to motivate their team or protect their teammates, these ends are only accomplished as a result of hurting an opponent. Thus, fighting in hockey is violent, not simply aggressive behavior and, as such, should not be condoned.

If fighting in hockey is considered to be violent and not simply an aggressive skill necessary for the game, where does this leave boxing? Is it possible to box without intending to injure your opponent? Although some people may argue that the objective of boxing is not to inflict harm but to "land blows" (recall Lord Ross's comment in the previous section), this situation would apply (if at all) only to amateur and not professional boxing.

> The objective of amateur boxing is the scoring of points. Knockdowns are not scored more highly than other scoring blows. (To score, a blow must connect with the target area of the opponent, must be of sufficient force, and must be

> delivered with the striking area of the glove, which is designated in white.) Knockouts are not described as an objective. (Schneider and Butcher 2001, 360)

Although the objective of amateur boxing may be to score points, the fastest way to a win is a knockout or a referee-stopped fight. Both of these situations require that one's opponent is injured to the point of not be able to get up or to the point where the referee thinks the downed player is not fit to continue fighting. These strategies then, require one to intentionally harm one's opponent–a paradigmatic example of violence. The possibility of "redeeming" boxing will be explored in the following section.

Recommendations Concerning Violence in Sport

Having examined issues related to violence in hockey, football, and boxing, recommendations will now be made in an attempt to improve the situation concerning violence in sport. In the section on hockey, a distinction was made between hockey skills such as body checking (which are aggressive in nature but have an appropriate role to play in relation to the goals of the game) and fighting (which would appear to be at odds with the skills intrinsic to the game of hockey, since time spent fighting takes time away from the use of the skills internal to the game of hockey). It was mentioned that one of the reasons hockey players gave for fighting was that they were angry about losing. It was suggested that society should place less emphasis on winning and more emphasis on *com-petitio*, striving together in the pursuit of excellence. Edmund Vaz (1977) stresses that there is nothing wrong with winning but we must emphasis "winning according to the game rules" (p.32). Vaz (1979) proposes the following scheme that would allocate points both for success and for conformity to normative game rules:

> (a) The maximum number of points in the game is allocated to the team that wins the game if it violates no rules or fewer rules than the losing team.
>
> (b) The least number of points is allocated to the team that loses the game, and violates more rules than the winning team.
>
> (c) However, points are allocated to the losing team if it violates fewer rules than the winning team.
>
> (d) In case of a tie game, the team with the lesser number of infractions receives more points than the other team.
>
> (e) A fifth outcome is a tie game in which each team has committed an equal number of infractions. (p.88)

Vaz's scheme requires a change concerning the reinforcement structure involved in hockey. This is important if we want to discourage fighting. As

Terry and Jackson (1985) point out, "[i]n order to keep a check on aggression, the reinforcement structure of a sport should be such that rule violations result in punishments that have greater deterrent value than any potential advantages" (p.35).

A reason that is frequently given against changing the structure of hockey in order to discourage fighting is that fans would no longer be interested in the game. For example, veteran hockey promoter Conn Smythe was confronted with a group complaining about the amount of violence perpetuated by the Toronto Maple Leafs. "'Yes,' snapped Smythe, 'we've got to stamp out this sort of thing or people are going to keep on buying tickets!'" (Fischler 1974, 11). However, the justification for fighting based on public demand may have a very local flavor. When Wayne Gretzky moved to California from Canada, he realized that the taken-for-granted truths of the hockey subculture did not necessarily transcend national borders: "We always talk about the people who come to the games to see the fighting, and I was one of the ones who believed that.... I wonder if they've ever done an analysis on how many people *don't* come just because of fighting. People who don't want their kids to see it" (Dryden and MacGregor 1989, 181-182). Although such an "analysis" would require an empirical study, it seems a logical possibility that there are people who are *turned away* from hockey because of the fighting. Gruneau and Whitson (1993) suggest that

> [Gretzky] is talking about a different audience, some of whom have drifted away from the game because of the extent to which force can dominate skill, and most of whom will never have been part of the hockey subculture. He is talking, ultimately, about the larger audiences for general sports entertainment who could fill rinks in non-traditional centres and, even more important, could make hockey on television worth more to the U.S. networks and cable companies. (pp.186-187)

Although an empirical study would be required to determine how many people are attracted to fighting in hockey versus how many people are turned off from the sport because of it, it would appear premature to justify fighting based on public demand. However, even if it was determined that more people wanted to watch fighting than people who did not, the question could (and should) be asked, just because it is the case that the public wants to see fighting, should it be the case? This is a clear example of the is-ought fallacy. This same situation will arise when looking at recommendations for changing boxing.

Before considering boxing, it would be helpful to consider changes to football that parallel the situation in hockey. It was mentioned previously that some of the skills in hockey, for example, body checking, are aggressive in nature but do not have to be violent (the behavior would be considered violent only if the player intended to harm the opposing player). This situation would appear to parallel the case in football where many of the skills, for example, blocking and tackling, require aggressive, but not necessarily violent, behavior. Because the player at the receiving end of the block or tackle might be injured, even if that was not the intention of the player making the block or tackle, Simon (1991) proposes what he calls the "**vulnerability principle**, or VP": "According to the VP, for the use of force against an opponent in an athletic contest to be ethically defensible, the opponent must be in a position and condition such that a strategic response is possible and it is unlikely injury will ensue" (pp.66-67). Thus, a tackle that is defensible against a professional running back would not be defensible if made against an out-of-shape older businessman who hasn't played in years. Simon suggests that the VP may represent a useful first step in the direction of drawing the line between defensible and indefensible uses of force in contact sports. "Perhaps football can be criticized because violence is too prevalent in the sport or because the use of force creates too much risk for the players, but it does not seem that football by its very nature must be violent" (p.67).

Although the nature of football does not seem to be intrinsically violent, such a claim does not apply to boxing as it is practiced today. At the end of the previous section, the question was asked if any changes could be made to boxing to "redeem" the sport from its intrinsically violent nature. Some philosophers of sport have proposed such changes. Schneider and Butcher (2001) struggle with the tension between the barbaricness of boxing and the place of choice in a liberal democratic society. Their compromise proposal is to ban boxing for children under the age of eighteen (since the state does have a role in protecting the interests of those who are not yet in a position to give their consent). Although adults would be free to box, Schneider and Butcher propose that all direct and indirect support for boxing should be withdrawn, that is, boxing should not be featured in national and international, for example, Olympic, competitions.

Dixon (2001) also struggles with the role of the state in banning boxing and thus proposes a compromise where, because of the possibility that boxers experiencing brain damage may lose their ability to act autonomously, a complete ban on blows to the head should be instituted. A step further than the ban on the head proposed by Dixon would involve making boxing more like fencing. The analogy would appear to be an apt one. Both boxing and fencing have their roots in deadly activities, where people were killed from punches or stab wounds. However, the sport of fencing has retained the skills of accuracy and agility once required to kill a foe, yet the sport has few injuries, since fencing skills can be practiced using blunt foils on padded chest pads. Why would it not work to have heavily padded outfits with electronic pads that could calculate the force of a punch? In this way, the skills of accuracy and agility once used in deadly combat could still be practiced with relatively few injuries. Such a change to the sport of boxing might lead to the demise of professional boxing. As Dixon (2001a) points out,

> the many fans who are currently drawn to boxing by the prospect of seeing bloody fighters become groggy and drop to the canvas after repeated blows to the head would most likely lose interest if boxing became a relatively safe sport in which knockouts are rare and skill and strategy, rather than the infliction of injuries, are the major determinants of victory. And boxing purists who continue to like, and even prefer, this safer form of boxing would probably be too rare for professional boxing to continue to be a profitable business. The likely result of eliminating blows to the head, then, is the withering away of professional boxing, which depends on attracting large numbers of spectators to pay fighters and their handlers. (p.343)

The fact that market forces rather than government intervention would lead to the demise of professional boxing saves such a proposal from the criticism that directly banning all boxing would involve too much impingement on the rights of members of a liberal democratic society. However, the disappearance of the goal of intentionally harming one's opponent in today's boxing rings would seem fitting not only for a liberal democratic society, but for a civilized society.

Conclusion

When examining violence in sport, it is important to distinguish between behavior that is intrinsic to a particular sport and behavior that is gratuitous to the goals of that sport. Violence in hockey would appear to be gratuitous. Hockey players interviewed for this chapter said they engaged in fights to release anger, to motivate teammates, and because fighting was part of hockey, that is, the nature of the game. The nature of the game would include the constitutive and regulative rules as well as the ethos of the game. It would appear that fighting breaks not only the written but also the unwritten rules of the game in that fighting takes time away from the utilization of the skills intrinsic to the game of hockey. In football, violence does not appear to be as gratuitous as it is in hockey. Although both hockey and football involve legitimate aggressive behavior, the gratuitous violence, that is, intentionally trying to hurt the opponent, found in hockey does not appear to be as prominent in football. The sport where violence is paradigmatic is boxing. Some philosophers have suggested that the arguments against boxing (the level and pain of injury, the glorified violence, the social effects, and the violent attitude toward another self) outweigh the arguments for boxing (aggressive instinct, honest violence, and the dangerous thrill). Some philosophers have proposed paternalistic arguments, citing that boxers have the potential to lose their autonomy as a result of brain injuries. The vulnerability principle has been proposed, where the use of force is only defensible if it is unlikely that injury will ensue. Following such a principle would change much of the violent behavior witnessed in hockey, football, and boxing; changing the "is" to an "ought" regarding violence in sport.

CHAPTER REVIEW

Key Concepts

- anger release
- motivational aspect
- nature of the game
- is-ought fallacy
- constitutive rules
- regulative rules
- ethos of a game
- level and pain of injury
- glorified violence
- social effects
- attitude toward another self
- aggressive instinct
- honest violence
- dangerous thrill
- autonomy
- paternalism
- legitimate and illegitimate violence
- vulnerability principle

Review Questions

1. What were the reasons the hockey players cited for the fighting that occurs in their sport?
2. How does the "nature of the game" justification and the "is-ought" fallacy apply to fighting in hockey?
3. In which of the sports of hockey, football, and boxing is the violent behavior gratuitous or intrinsic to the sport?
4. Describe the three arguments in favor of and the three arguments against boxing as examined by Davis.
5. Describe the two paternalistic arguments for restricting boxing as proposed by Dixon.
6. What are the distinctions made between assertive, aggressive, and violent behavior? Give examples from hockey, football, and boxing that demonstrate these different concepts.
7. What is the gist behind Vaz's recommendations concerning violence in hockey?
8. What are the recommendations for changing boxing as proposed by Scheider and Butcher, and Dixon?

10

Should Girls and Boys Play Together?

Heather Mercer was an all-state kicker who helped lead her high-school football team to a state championship. Several coaches who worked with Mercer regarded her skills as competitive to those of any kicker playing at the collegiate Division One level. After graduation, she attended Duke University where she was a walk- on player on the school's football team. Because she was female, however, she was not treated like most of the walk-ons. The coaches gave her a private try-out, and she was only allowed to practice with the other walk-on kickers (all of whom were male) even though the other walk-on kickers were allowed to practice with the full team. She was not issued a uniform, nor was she allowed to dress for games. Despite this discrimination, she was still able to demonstrate her remarkable skills. In the team's spring intrasquad match, Mercer kicked the twenty-eight-yard winning field goal for her team, and the coach told her she had made the Duke University team. Nonetheless, the discrimination continued the following year. Even though she was a member of the team, the coach told her she would be a distraction to the other players if she were allowed to dress in uniform and stand on the sideline. The coach later told her she had no place on the team. (Crouse 2000, 1655)

[The] West Valley Girls' Softball (WVGS) was a longstanding, thirty-year-old league of more than 400 girls ranging in age from five to eighteen. What WVGS lacked throughout its existence was a permanent home field. For years, WVGS had tried to obtain access to a home field, but each time the City of Los Angeles said that the local fields had already been taken by baseball little leagues. Indeed, for decades, three boys' baseball little leagues had enjoyed long-term permits to choice fields in city parks or city-owned land in the West San Fernando Valley. Because the field permit system essentially granted a perpetual permit renewal to existing programs, "newcomers"—even thirty-year-old applicants like WVGS—were out of luck. The girls' softball league was effectively excluded from the permit system by this "grandfather" clause that favored the boys' leagues.

Confronted with this problem, WVGS went to great lengths to seek alternative space for a home field in its community. Attempts by WVGS staff and parents to negotiate with city, park, and school officials were unsuccessful. Consequently, year after year, the WVGS girls were relegated to temporary fields that were grossly inferior to the pristine, well-equipped facilities enjoyed by the local baseball leagues. Finally, WVGS enlisted the aid of the ACLU-SC to file Baca v. City of Los Angeles, a class action complaint against the city alleging discrimination on the basis of gender. (Cordoba 2001, 139-140)

The excerpts presented above are obvious examples of discrimination based on sex; that is, females being denied equal positions on sports teams because of their sex, and females being denied equal access to resources and/or facilities because of their sex. Although these situations appear to be blatantly unfair, the notion of sex discrimination in sport is readily accepted in today's society. To make sense of these situations, it is important to clarify what is meant by sex discrimination in sport. If arguments against such discrimination were accepted, the options to rectify the situation would include: immediate integration of male and females in sport, some integrated and some segregated sports, and finally, some segregation as an interim measure while more "female-friendly" sport was developed. If rectifying the discrimination issue is to be realized in our society, legal action will have to be implemented. Legal action already taken in the United States and Canada will be acknowledged in the final section of the chapter. Key concepts utilized in answering the question of whether boys and girls should play together include: **separate sports and/or teams, weight classes, violent response, feeling discouraged, unique value, scarce benefits, sex not being relevant, basic benefits, grouping by ability, developing a variety of new sports, masculine$_d$, interim solution, feminine$_d$, one-way crossover approach, quota approach, components approach, separate-and-mixed approach, assimilation, gender equity position, Title IX**, and **Women in Sport: A Sport Canada Policy**.

Forms of Sex Discrimination

When sexual discrimination exists in sport, such discrimination can be understood in two forms: (1) sport involves sexual discrimination when sports are divided into men's sports and/or teams and women sports and/or teams, and (2) sexual discrimination exists when men's sports receive more funding, media coverage, public support, and so forth than women's sports. If the first form of discrimination did not exist, the second form would not likely exist. However, if one decides that it makes sense to have **separate sports and/or teams** for men and women, it does not follow that men's sports should receive more attention and support than women's sports. Each of these forms of discrimination will be examined in turn.

Sport has traditionally been perceived as a male terrain. As Tony Mason (1993) points out, there was powerful opposition to the participation of women in the Olympics:

> Although they officially competed for the first time in 1908, there was no athletics programme for women until 1928 and then there were only five events–the 100 and 800 metres, the long jump, the discus and the 400 metre hurdles. Moreover, some female competitors collapsed after the 800 meters,

> thereby enabling male and female critics of women's sport to underline feminine fragility. As late as 1949 the President of the International Olympic Committee, Avery Brundage, said: "I think women's events should be confined to those appropriate for women–swimming, tennis, figure skating and fencing, but certainly not shot-putting." (pp.74-75)

The notion that women should be confined to participating in events that are "appropriate for women" still exists today. When women *do* participate in traditional "male sports," for example, hockey, basketball, baseball, they have their own leagues. Other than mixed doubles in tennis and equestrian events, there are very few sports where men and women play together. This situation epitomizes discrimination based on sex. Is there any justification for this discrimination?

Immediate Integration?

Tånnsjø (2000) examines and critiques some of the arguments supporting sexual discrimination in sport, after stating his own position:

> The reasons for giving up sexual discrimination within sports, and for allowing individuals of both sexes to compete with each other, is simple. In sports it is crucial that the best person wins. Then sexual differences are simply irrelevant. If a female athlete can perform better than a male athlete, this female athlete should be allowed to compete with, and beat, the male athlete. If she cannot beat a certain male athlete, so be it. If the competition was fair, she should be able to face the fact that he was more talented. It is really as simple as that. Sexual discrimination within sports does not have any better rationale than sexual discrimination in any other fields of our lives. (p.101)

To demonstrate that sexual discrimination does not have much of a rationale, Tånnsjø (2000) examines four arguments typically given in favor of sexual discrimination. First, he looks at the argument that sexual discrimination in some sports is no different than using **weight classes** in sports such as boxing and wrestling. Tånnsjø is in favor of weight classes (and suggests weight classes for running and height classes for basketball, and so forth). He suggests that such classes are of immediate relevance to the capacity to perform well within the sport; that is, one's weight will have a direct effect on one's boxing performance. Sex, on the other hand, is only indirectly relevant to the outcome of a fair competition; that is, females might be lighter than males statistically but it should be the weight, not the sex, that is relevant. "It [sex] is relevant in the sense that it predisposes, statistically, for more or less of a certain characteristic, crucial to performing well in a certain sport. But then, if we should discriminate at all, we should discriminate in terms of this characteristic itself and not in terms of sex" (p.103). Since sex characteristics are statistical rather than universal, there will be some women (albeit, not many) who will outperform men, and it would be discriminatory to prohibit these women from competing against particular men on the ground that women in general do not perform well against men in general.

The second argument in favor of sexual discrimination discussed by Tånnsjø (2000) suggests that if women and men compete, and women defeat men, this will trigger a **violent response** from these men. Tånnsjø thinks that aggressive responses should be a matter of concern, but there is another way of responding to the phenomenon of male aggressiveness against women. "This could be done if the rules of the game in question were changed. Aggressive assault on competitors could be punished more severely than it is in many sports currently. One physical assault could mean a red card–and the aggressive male competitor would be out" (p.104). Tånnsjø also thinks that when a man is upset about being defeated by a women, personal prejudices and biases are exposed, and this is a positive thing.

The third argument favoring sexual discrimination is the flip side of the second argument. Just as there is a possibility of a man having an aggressive response if defeated by a woman, there is the possibility of a woman **feeling discouraged** when defeated by a man. Tånnsjø (2000) stresses that the situation would be discouraging if it was *impossible* for women to defeat men. However, if the problem lies not in sexual differences but in socially constructed gender differences, the situation could be perceived, not as one of inevitable disappointment, but rather as a challenge to abolish gender biases in sport. Tånnsjø suggests that adding weight and height categories and punishing aggressive competitors would help eliminate some of the gender-biased obstacles. However, he does acknowledge that there may still be some sports where the elite is made up of men exclusively. Although this situation would be disappointing for women, Tånnsjø suggests that this kind of disappointment should be accepted as a natural part of life. He gives the analogy of black athletes performing better on average than Caucasians. "This is disappointing to white people, of course, but is no reason to introduce racial discrimination within sports. But if this is not a reason to introduce racial discrimination in sports, then we should not retain sexual discrimination either" (p.107)

The fourth argument supporting sexual discrimination discussed by Tånnsjø (2000) has to do with the **unique value** represented by female sports. Giving up sexual discrimination would mean giving up valuable existing sports. Although Tånnsjø (2000) thinks there may be unique female qualities, for example, "inventiveness, sensibility, cooperation, strategy, playfulness, wit, and so forth," a better way to accommodate these unique qualities than retaining sexual discrimination is to introduce these qualities into *all* sorts of sport. He suggests that introducing these qualities will provide a "moderating" affect on many existing sports:

> The object of the moderation, that which ought to be moderated, is arrogant outbursts of (male) aggressiveness and (mere) strength.... [W]hen we introduce more moderation into sports, in order to save sports from going extinct, we abolish the rationale behind sexual discrimination in sports, and we deepen the inherent value of sports as a cultural phenomenon. (pp.110, 111)

Tånnsjø's (2000) position concerning the elimination of sexual discrimination in separating men and women's sports and/or teams has been criticized as being too utopian; unrealistic and unattainable in the real world.

> The proposal contained in Tånnsjø's chapter is dangerous, because it masquerades as a genuine proposal for changing sport as it is currently practiced, whereas it is really a utopian fantasy, first of a society–and then of sport–transformed. If the world were a radically different place, then yes, the vision of sport where discrimination is based on ability not on gender (or weight or size, for that matter) would be good. (Schneider 2000, 136)

The world we live in has a history of sport being dominated by men. Thus, women have not had the opportunity to develop and practice skills needed in the sports that currently exist. For many philosophers of sport, eliminating the first form of sexual discrimination and not creating separate men's and women's sports and/or teams would put women at even more of a disadvantage and would result in even fewer women being involved in sport.

> To integrate sports fully before women have been given full opportunity to develop in the traditionally male sports would be disastrous and would serve initially to reinforce the stereotypes and prejudices and worse, would yield fewer opportunities and would discourage women from participating in the activities at all. The hope is that there will come a time when the best athletes, male and female, compete together, but that time has not yet been reached. Thus, a policy of separate but equal is still necessary. The question is: Is separate but equal ever equal? (Boxill 1993-94, 28)

Although many philosophers of sport do not think doing away with the first form of sexual discrimination is possible in today's world, they emphasize that this does not mean that the second form of sexual discrimination discussed earlier, that is, allowing men's sports and/or teams to receive more funding, media coverage, public support, and so forth than women's sports and/or teams, has to follow. How can society change the way sports are played in an attempt to eliminate this second form of discrimination? A number of philosophers have addressed this question. Philosophers of sport who favor separate men's and women's sports and/or teams seem to take two positions on the discrimination-assimilation continuum. One group argues that, in some contexts, men and women should play separate sports while the other group feels that assimilation is a worthy goal in the long run but an interim stage of discrimination and/or assimilation is required to reach that goal. Each position will be considered in turn.

Some Segregation?

Philosophers who see some separate men's and women's sports as an end goal typically feel that the costs of competing with men are too great–for women and for the enterprise of sport. Jane English, in her seminal article "Sex Equality in Sports" (1978), argues that women have a justifiable demand for what she calls the **scarce benefits** of sport, that is, media coverage, prize money, and so on. Because women are statistically at a physiological disadvantage compared to men, English presents three options (opting for the third one) for treating women fairly. The first option would involve integrating sports where **sex is not relevant** to performance, for example, dressage, riflery and car racing, and having separate competition groups for sports where sex is relevant, that is, similar to weight classes in boxing. "If we apply the boxing model, several conclusions about this practice follow. Women should be allowed to 'move up' and compete against men if they wish" (p.272). An objection to the use of groupings by sex is that it discriminates against those males whose level of performance is similar to the females. "For example, if we have a girls' football team in our high school, is it unfair to prohibit a 120-pound boy who cannot make the boys' team from trying out for the girls' team?" (ibid.).

A second method used to give the disadvantaged equal access to what English (1978) refers to as the **basic benefits** of sport, that is, health, self-respect gained by doing one's best, and so on, involves **grouping individuals by ability** alone, for example, second and third string games, B-leagues, and so forth. "Groupings by age, sex, or weight are often just attempts to approximate ability groupings in a convenient and quick way. When convenience is the intent, it must not be rigidly imposed to keep talented girls off the first string" (p.273). A problem with grouping by ability is that such groupings sometimes lead to disrespect for those playing in the lower ability groups. "The problems arise when losers are scorned or discouraged from playing, and winning becomes the end rather than the means to basic benefits" (p.274).

A third method for treating women fairly is suggested (and preferred) by English (1978). She notes that although women are physiologically at a disadvantage to men in some areas, they are at an advantage in others. "The hip structure that slows running gives a lower center of gravity [hence, an advantage on the balance beam]. Fat provides insulation and an energy source for running fifty-mile races" (p.275). English's approach to treating women fairly in sport is to **develop a variety of sports** in which a variety of physical types can excel. She emphasizes that most of our major sports are fairly recent inventions. Things could have been different if it had been women, not men, inventing our sports.

> But if women had been the historically dominant sex, our concept of Sport would no doubt have evolved differently. Competitions emphasizing flexibility, balance, strength, timing, and small size might dominate Sunday afternoon television and offer salaries in the six figures. Men could be clamoring for equal press coverage of their champions. (p.276)

Another philosopher who argues for the creation of **new sports** is Betsy Postow. Postow (1980) distinguishes between different senses of "masculine" sports and she uses the term **masculine**$_d$ to refers to a sport that "due to biological factors, most men are significantly better at it than most women, and the best athletes in it are men" (p.53). Postow argues that women should withdraw their support from masculine sports and rather promote activities in which women have a natural advantage over men.

> The number and prestige of sports in which men have a natural statistical superiority to women, together with the virtual absence of sports in which women are naturally superior, help perpetuate an image of general female inferiority which we have a moral reason to undermine. An obvious way to undermine it is to increase the number and prestige of sports in which women have a natural statistical superiority to men or at least are not naturally inferior. (p.54)

As well as arguing for the creation of new sports that emphasize qualities statistically found in females, both English and Postow make distinctions between various levels of sport. English (1978) argues that the basic benefits of sport, for example, health and fun, should be available to everyone and thus participatory sports should not be based upon having the ability to play the sport well. "The primary emphasis would be on participation, with a wealth of local teams and activities available to all, based on groupings by ability. Only where style of play is very different would groupings by weight, age or sex be recommended" (p.276). The scarce benefits of sport, for example, prizes and media coverage, cannot be received by everyone, but English proposes that half of these should be shared with women. Thus, she argues for the development of new sports in which women can excel. Postow (1980) also advocates that the basic benefits of sport should be shared by all (at least regarding school sports), not just those with "suitable physiques."

> A way to grant fully everyone's *prima facie* claim (even those with unsuitable physiques) to an equal right to the benefits of participating in the school sports which she or he most enjoys, and still to grant fully everyone's *prima facie* claim to equal formal freedom to compete, would be to sever the connection between winning a place on a team and being granted access to moderately

> scarce athletic resources. In team sports, either enough teams could be available at every ability level to accommodate everyone who wanted to play and who was willing to turn out for practice (with scarce athletic resources simply spread as thinly as necessary to go around), or there could be at least one team for each ability level, with membership in the teams determined by some form of lottery that equalized the probability of being on a team for everyone who wanted to play and was willing to turn out for practice. (pp.55-56)

Postow makes a distinction between sports played in school and professional sports. Regarding professional sports, Postow (1980) agrees with English that "there may appear to be a special reason for maintaining single-sex teams in masculine$_d$ sports.

Interim Solution?

Making distinctions between different levels of sport is an approach used by some philosophers wishing to find an **interim solution** to the inequality that currently exists between men's and women's sports and/or teams, with the long-term goal of removing sexual discrimination in both forms, that is, no preference for men's sports and/or teams because men's and women's sports and/or teams would be assimilated. Mary Anne Warren (1983) argues that

> [t]he problem of how to eliminate sex segregation without sacrificing equal opportunity for women would be optimally solved ... by offering an equal number of male- and female-favoring sports, with sex-blind competition for places on the most skilled teams (etc.), but opportunities for even the least athletically able students to participate in the sport of their choice. In such a system, women would no doubt still be scarce on the highest ranked teams in some masculine$_d$ sports, but men would be equally underrepresented in the various **"feminine$_d$"** sports [sports where women have a biological advantage]. Since the feminine$_d$ sports would receive equal status and resources, the generally inferior performance of women in masculine$_d$ sports would lend no support to the myth of general female inferiority, athletic or otherwise. (p.27)

Warren (1983) admits that such a solution could not be implemented immediately since a full range of feminine$_d$ sports has yet to be developed and there are still economic, social, and political obstacles that have to be overcome regarding the equal acceptance of feminine$_d$ sports with the well-established masculine$_d$ sports. Thus, she proposes a number of strategies that could achieve some degree of integration without sacrificing equal opportunity. These strategies will be considered in turn.

The first strategy proposed by Warren (1983) involves what she calls the **one-way crossover approach**. With this approach, separate teams are provided for males and females, and females are permitted to try out for the males' teams but not vice versa. Although this approach would be easy and inexpensive to implement, Warren notes two serious drawbacks. The first is that it is blatantly unfair to males. However, if males were permitted to try out for the females' teams, there would be a preponderance of males on both teams. The other problem with such an approach is that the best female players will be siphoned away, and this situation could be demoralizing for the players who remained.

The second strategy Warren (1983) discusses is known as the **quota approach** where each team consists of 50 percent males and 50 percent females. With this approach, women would only compete with other women for positions on the team (and men with men). However, practice and play would be fully integrated. Warren perceives the quota approach to be very promising, and she responds to three major objections. The first objection is that the quota system provides half as many teams and half as many positions as the "separate but equal" alternative. Warren points out that this objection is irrelevant since a school can support two integrated teams as easily as two segregated teams. A more serious objection is that the quota system is inconsistent with the principle of merit for determining team membership. Thus, males who might have made the team, but didn't because of the quota system, might feel resentment toward the females who were not as skilled as they were but who still made the team. Warren suggests that such resentment could be defused (somewhat) by expanding the total number of opportunities in conjunction with the introduction of sex quotas. A third objection to the quota approach is that the stronger members of the team (usually males) will resent the weaker members of the team (usually females). Warren suggests that this concern would be most relevant to masculine$_d$ sports such as football, where size and strength are overwhelmingly important. In the case of less extremely masculine$_d$ sports, the quota system would still seem feasible since, in this case, the difference in effectiveness between males and females would be not greater than between the best and worst male players.

Warren (1983) refers to the third strategy she proposes as the **components approach**. With this approach, each school fields a composite team composed of a male and female sub-team. Although the sub-teams play separate games, their combined scores would determine the outcome of the match. Warren points out that the primary drawback of the components approach is that the success or failure of each team is dependent upon the other, not upon the basis of athletic excellence. Warren suggests that the force of this objection could be lessened if the two sub-teams functioned as a co-operative unit, for example, by practicing together, exchanging members, and so on. "The encouragement of such intrateam cooperation would have to be a major goal of the components approach, which might otherwise share most of the drawbacks of simple segregation" (p.30).

The fourth strategy proposed by Warren (1983) is the **separate-and-mixed approach**. With this system, each sport has three teams: the first team consisting of the best players, regardless of sex; and the second-level teams being segregated. Warren notes two drawbacks with this approach. First, most of the members of the first team will be males. Second, males will have almost twice as many opportunities to play as females. "It is probably fairer to exceptional female athletes than is strict segregation, and fairer to males who can't make the first team than the one-way crossover option; but it does little to eliminate the male hegemony in masculine$_d$ sports" (p.31). Warren responds to this criticism by arguing that if there are at least twice as many males as females who want to participate (especially in masculine$_d$ sports), then it is not unjust to provide males with almost twice as many opportunities to participate. However, this system *would* be unfair if the reason females do not want to participate is because only the very best female athletes make the first team and the second-level team receives considerably less reward and recognition.

Warren (1983) concludes her exploration of interim integration strategies by pointing out that "[t]here can be no *fully* just way of settling the integration/segregation issue as long as most widely supported and heavily subsidized school sports inherently favor the average male over the average female physique" (p.31). When equal support to sports that favor female qualities is provided, and when enough teams or competition classes in each sport to allow everyone who is interested and able to participate are available, Warren argues that society could do away with both forms of sexual discrimination, that is, no preference for men's sports and/or teams because men's and women's sports and/or teams would be assimilated. "Given these changes, we could safely adopt a policy of strict sex-blindness in determining team membership without jeopardizing equality of opportunity for either sex" (p.32).

Another philosopher whose end goal is also **assimilation** of men's and women's sports and/or teams is Claudio Tamburrini. Like Warren, Tamburrini (2000) does not think total assimilation is possible at the present time. He proposes a two-step strategy that he calls the **gender equity position,** which involves

> (a) the immediate abolition of sex segregation in all sport disciplines in which women are superior or equal to men; and (b) maintaining sex divisions in those disciplines in which female athletes perform at an inferior level than

> their male colleagues–at least temporarily, until current performance gaps between men and women are reduced or, when possible, overcome. (p.106)

Tamburrini proposes that the current performance gap between men and women would be narrowed if sex integration began in childhood. Physiologists have shown that there are no significant physiological differences between boys and girls in elementary school.

> Thus, we can expect that girls, if given equal initial opportunities, will be able to reach the same competitive level as boys. Properly encouraged during their adolescence, and with shared responsibility of child caring in middle age, there is no reason either to fear that women will not be able to keep that high standard throughout their whole life. (pp.145-146)

Tamburrini argues that early participation in sport, carried on throughout a woman's life, creating role models for future women, will lead to radical questioning of the physiological differences between the sexes. "Physical strength is not the exclusive patrimony of masculinity. Sex integration in professional sports might become a powerful instrument for modeling women warriors who, like modern Amazons, could take up competition with men on equal terms, and beat them in their own domains" (p.147).

The possibility that women could one day "beat men in their own domain" receives support from some writers in the medical field who suggest that the differences between the sexes is no greater than the differences within the sexes. "[W]hile there are very significant sex-related differences between males and females, it should be borne in mind that there are undoubtedly greater differences between the third and ninety-seventh percentile in each sex than there are between the average female and the average male in terms of physical performance" (Shaffer 1979, 23).

Some of the variation within sexes is not necessarily biological. K. Dyer (1982) points out that there are social and environmental factors that result in physical differences.

> In Britain, for example, the difference between men in the highest socio-economic class and those in the lowest is about ten centimetres in height and between ten and fifteen kilograms in weight. These differences are about the same as the average differences between men and women in the same class. In other words, some at least of the average sex difference may be due to the same things producing the class differences–and few would suggest that they are primarily biological. (p.91)

Dyer (1982) also cites an example of a sex difference that is usually assumed to be biological. This difference concerns the blood hemoglobin concentration levels in men and women. Dyer suggests that this difference is partly due to the lower level of iron in women's diets as well as the amount women lose through menstrual loss. He cites a study done in Japan, where it was found that about 10 percent of female athletes in various college sporting clubs were anaemic. These women were given iron preparations for two months, and the number of red blood cells and the amount of hemoglobin improved in all of them. These female athletes all improved their performances, especially the high jumpers and middle-distance runners. "What, one wonders, would be the result of surveying all women athletes and treating them this way?" (p.92).

Tamburrini and Warren seek the long-term goal of removing the first form of sex discrimination, that is, the segregation of men's and women's sports and/or teams, but they both recognize that interim steps must be taken before full integration is possible. Warren (1983) proposes a number of possible strategies, including the one-way cross over, the quota approach, the components approach, and the separate-and-mixed approach, that could be used to achieve some degree of integration without sacrificing equal opportunity. Tamburrini (2000) advocates the immediate integration of all sport disciplines in which women are superior or equal to men and the integration of all sports in childhood with the goal of narrowing the performance gap that currently exists between men and women. English and Postow do not think the "performance gap" between men and women can ever be narrowed and thus, they advocate maintaining the first form of sex discrimination. English (1978) and Postow (1980) also both propose the development of new sports that emphasize feminine qualities. Postow (1980) goes so far as to suggest that women withdraw their support from sports that emphasize masculine qualities.

At the end of the segregation-integration continuum, opposite those of English and Postow, lies Tånnjsø's radical proposal. Tånnsjø proposes that maintaining sexual discrimination in sport has no better rationale than any other area of our lives. He argues that, as long as the competition is fair, the most talented player should win. Tånnsjø does not appear to take into account the second form of sex discrimination, that is, the unequal funding, public support, and so forth that men's sports and/or teams have received historically. Since he does not consider the fact that women are starting behind men as a result of this historical discrepancy, he proposes that the first form of sex discrimination can be abolished immediately. Whether these historical conditions can be overcome, or whether the performance gap is truly insurmountable, is what distinguishes the English/ Postow position from the Tamburrini/Warren position.

Whether the performance gap between men and women can be overcome (particularly in masculine$_d$ sports) invokes the debate between biology and socialization. It would appear that if there are biological differences that create an insurmountable gap between men and women regarding masculine$_d$ sports, these cannot be determined until negative socialization factors have been eliminated. That is, until we integrate sports and/or teams in childhood (as suggested by Tamburrini), we will not know if masculine$_d$ sport qualities *can* be acquired by females if they are given the opportunity to play the sports that help develop these qualities. If it happens that masculine$_d$ sports qualities cannot be acquired by women even with the second form of sex discrimination having been removed since childhood, then it would become necessary to adopt the English/Postow position and keep sex segregation for elite levels as well as develop sports that emphasize feminine qualities.

Legal Action

In the previous section, the conclusion reached was that society should try to eliminate the second form of discrimination, that is, the unequal funding, public support, and so forth that men's sports and/or teams have received historically. If this second form of discrimination was eliminated starting in childhood, the thesis was put forth that masculine$_d$ sports qualities could be acquired by women and the first form of sex discrimination, that is, the segregation of men's and women's sports and/or teams, could also be eliminated. However, if eliminating the second form of sex discrimination does not result in the acquisition of masculine$_d$ sports qualities by women, then elite sport should remain segregated and new sports should be developed that emphasize feminine qualities. The arguments for and against sex discrimination were philosophical in nature, resting on the moral issue of equality. However, the translation of these philosophical positions into the real world will require not only moral support, but legal support.

In 1972, the United States Congress passed **Title IX** of the Educational Amendments, which declared, "No person in the United States shall, on the basis of sex, be excluded from participation in, be denied the benefits of, or be subjected to discrimination under any educational program or activity receiving federal financial assistance." From the time of its passing, there have been court cases where school athletic programs claimed they did not have to concur with Title IX because they did not directly receive money from the federal government. In 1992, the U.S. Supreme Court ruled that, if schools intentionally violated Title IX, women involved in these athletic programs could sue for damages. "This ruling is likely to make a positive impact on efforts to establish gender equity in sports, although it will come only through court cases" (Coakley 1994, 210).

In Canada, in 1986, federal and provincial programs published **Women in Sport: A Sport Canada Policy**. "It not only set the official goal of equality of opportunity for women at all levels of sport but it also called for a specific action-oriented program to achieve this goal. Thus Canada became the only Western country to have an official policy on women in sports" (Coakley 1994, 210). However, just because a country has an "official policy" on women and sport, it does not necessarily follow that the policy will be adhered to. Participants in all levels of sport, for example, athletes, parents, coaches, administrators, and so forth, have to be convinced that the moral issue of equality makes it worth adhering to the relevant government Acts and/or policies. Because sport has so long been a male-dominated domain, the issue of sex discrimination has seldom been questioned. The intent of this chapter has been to examine the different forms of sex discrimination and to suggest strategies for responding to sex discrimination in sport.

Conclusion

Sex discrimination in sport can take the form of separate sports and/or teams for men and women and/or the unequal provision of funding, media coverage, and so on for men's as opposed to women's sports and/or teams. Philosophers, in responding to these forms of discrimination, have suggested a few options for rectifying the situation. One of these options involves the immediate integration of men and women's sports and/or teams. Tånnjsø examines and critiques four arguments in favor of sexual discrimination. The first argument suggests that sex differences are similar to weight differences and so sex discrimination should be as acceptable as weight classes. Tånnjsø makes a distinction between differences that are immediately as opposed to indirectly relevant to one's sport performance. Other arguments examined and critiqued by Tånnjsø include the possibility of a violent response by men if they are defeated by women, women feeling discouraged if they are continuously defeated by men, the unique value represented by female sport. As a result of his critique of sexual discrimination arguments, Tånnjsø proposes immediate integration. However, his proposal has been criticized as being utopian. Other philosophers have proposed the option of retaining some segregation between male and females involved in sport. English distinguishes between scarce and basic benefits and argues that women should have equal access to both kinds of benefits. To ensure equal access, English suggests three options for various levels of sport: integration when sex is not relevant, grouping individuals by ability, and developing a variety of new sports. Postow agrees with English that new sports should be developed since both philosophers do not feel women will be able to succeed in masculine$_d$ sports.

Some philosophers are not happy with maintaining sex discrimination but realize that segregated sports and/or teams are required as an interim solution. Warren argues that until feminine$_d$ sports are as established as masculine$_d$ sports, strategies will be required to give women equal opportunity to excel in sport. These strategies include the one-way crossover approach, quota approach, components approach, and separate-and-mixed approach. The hope of Warren and Tamburrini would be that eventually men and women's sports will be assimilated. However, this will only happen when a gender equity position helps bridge the current performance gaps between men and women. Whatever option is chosen to deal with sex discrimination, legal action such as the passing of Title IX in the United States and Women in Sport: A Sport Canada Policy will be required to translate philosophical positions into real world policies.

CHAPTER REVIEW

Key Concepts

- separate sports and/or teams
- weight classes
- violent response
- feeling discouraged
- unique value
- scarce benefits
- sex not being relevant
- basic benefits
- grouping by ability
- developing a variety of new sports
- masculine$_d$
- interim solution
- feminine$_d$
- one-way crossover approach
- quota approach
- components approach
- separate-and-mixed approach
- assimilation
- gender equity position
- Title IX
- Women in Sport: A Sport Canada Policy

Review Questions

1. What are the two forms of sexual discrimination discussed in this chapter?
2. Describe the four arguments in favor of sexual discrimination examined by Tånnjsø.
3. Describe the distinction made by English between basic and scarce benefits of sport and the methods she proposes for enabling men and women equal access to both types of benefits.
4. What does Postow mean by "masculine$_d$" sports, and how does she propose women should respond to these sports?
5. Describe the four interim strategies for achieving integration as proposed by Warren.
6. Describe Tamburrini's "gender equity position."
7. What do writers in the medical field suggest regarding the differences between the sexes?
8. What is Title IX and Women in Sport: A Sport Canada Policy, and how do they relate to the issue of equality?

11

The Coach-Athlete Relationship: How Close Is Too Close?

Be clear about and avoid abusing relationships (e.g., with athletes, assistants, officials, administrators, board members) and avoid other situations that might present a conflict of interest or reduce the ability to be objective and unbiased in the determination of what might be in the best interests of athletes. (Canadian Professional Coaches Association's Coaching Code of Ethics, 10)

The sport context is one that is conducive to the development of relationships between coaches and athletes. Coaches and their athletes spend enormous amounts of time together (much more than teachers and their students–another context where personal relationships often develop). Not only do athletes spend many hours on many days of the week working with their coaches, they frequently travel out of town together to attend competitions. With the amount of time coaches and athletes spend together, it is no wonder that relationships that span the continuum from friends to lovers often develop.

In this chapter, the negative and positive aspects of friendly and intimate coach-athlete relationships will be examined. The question will also be raised concerning whether it is even possible for coaches and athletes not to be friends, considering the amount of time they spend together, and whether being friends is necessary for the sports goals they are trying to achieve. Since little philosophical work has been conducted in the sport area concerning personal relationships between coaches and athletes, the literature pertaining to professor-student relationships will be utilized.[1] As mentioned previously, the professor-student relationship would seem analogous to the coach-athlete relationship except that coaches and athletes typically spend even more time together than professors and students and so personal relationships seem even more likely to occur in the sports context. Key concepts utilized in this chapter include: **the relationship continuum, intimate relationships, power differential, autonomy, sexual harassment, conflict of interest, deep friendship, social convention, goodness friendship, pleasure friendship, utility friendship**, and **policy implications**.

The Relationship Continuum

At one end of the **continuum**, we have coaches and athletes relating to each other in the role of coach and athlete. In a following section, the very possibility (or desirability) of coaches and athletes maintaining strict coach-athlete roles without becoming friends will be examined. At the other end of the continuum, we have coaches and athletes who have formed sexual and/or romantic relationships. Between these ends of the continuum are varying degrees of "friendship"–coaches and athletes who share personal aspects of their lives with each other and/or who spend time with each other outside the sporting context. At any point beyond the strict coach-athlete role end of the continuum, there is the danger that the athlete might not want to be too friendly with his or her coach. This situation will be considered along with the possibility of the mutually intimate situation.

When Coaches and Athletes Are Intimate

When considering the **intimate** end of the continuum, Dixon's (1996) distinction between relationships that are sexual without the involvement of intimate romantic feelings, and those that are romantic without any sexual intimacy will be utilized. Both kinds of relationships will be included at this end of the continuum. The positive and negative aspects of these intimate relationships as well as the possibility of unwanted sexual advances will be considered.

In the studies conducted for Chapters 5 and 6, a number of coaches who have married their athletes, or who married their coach (when they themselves were athletes) were interviewed. When asked about the positive aspects of this situation, the overwhelming answer was "he [or she] understands my passion for the sport." Although this positive aspect is significant (considering the number of relationships that break up because "he or she didn't understand me"), this aspect has to be weighed against the potential dangers that exist when coaches become intimate with their athletes.

There are two main "danger" areas when coaches have romantic and/or sexual relationships with their athletes: (1) the power differential, and (2) the conflict of interest. Although all relationships involve **power differentials** in the sense that one partner may have expertise in one area, for example, home finances, while the other has expertise in another area, for example, cooking, the situation of coach to athlete (or teacher to student, or doctor to patient) involves a power differential that is not confined to an *area* of expertise but rather to a *position* of expertise. A position carries with it "power" that extends beyond the area of expertise. That is, the coach's position gives him or her the power to cut a player, to demand extra training sessions, to play or not to play a player in a particular game, and so on. The problem with this kind of "all-encompassing" power is that the relationship cannot possibly be equal. In a non-position power differential, for example, the lover who cooks and the lover who balances the check book, it is possible (and desirable) for there to be an overall equality of power.

The main problem with an unequal balance of power (as evident in the position of coach to athlete) is the possibility of true consent on the part of the athlete. Can an athlete make an **autonomous** choice, that is, a free informed choice, to become involved in an intimate relationship with his or her coach when the coach has the power to cut him or her from the team, add extra training sessions, play or not play him or her, and so on? Thus, a player may fear repercussions if he or she does not accept the coach's advances. This situation can quickly lead to **sexual harassment** if the player feels that he or she cannot say "no" to the coach and the coach continues to pursue the athlete.

Although there is no question that sexual harassment is morally wrong, there still remains the possibility that the athlete *does* want to pursue an intimate relationship with the coach. However, as Hitchcock and Baumgarten (1986) note, concerning the professor-student context (which is analogous to the coach-athlete situation), the strongest argument against intimate relationships between professors and students is an epistemological one–the professor will need to judge that the student who is his potential sexual partner is in fact able to consent. Given the difficulty of ascertaining whether the student really does give full voluntary consent, and the fact that the professor judging the capabilities of his would-be lover will not be a disinterested party, Hitchcock and Baumgarten argue that, except in rare cases, intimate faculty-student relationships are morally inappropriate (p.259).

Since there may be "rare cases" where the athlete has truly consented to his or her coach's advances, the power differential danger may not be conclusive. However, as Dixon (1996) argues regarding professor-student relationships, the potential **conflict of interest** is a more conclusive objection against coach-athlete relationships. As Dixon points out, a conflict of interest exists even when the favoring of the intimate partner is not done consciously. "Unlike explicit sex-for-grades offers, in which the awarding of unfair grades is deliberate, in the case of consensual relationships the unfairness in grades and other benefits is likely to result from *unconscious bias* in favor of the intimate partner" (p.526). Regarding the coach-athlete situation, there is a high probability that a coach will unconsciously give the intimate partner more attention, more playing time, and so on. In the words of a coach who married one of his athletes: "Sentiment is the product of our more intimate relationship, therefore it makes you operate, feel and think differently, in other words, I would think twice for my athlete-wife than for any other athlete" (Jowett and Meek 2000, 162). There may be instances where the coach is aware that others might perceive that he or she is favoring the intimate partner and thus go out of his or her way not to give the intimate partner as much attention, playing time, and so on as the other athletes.[2] Either way, the athlete with whom the coach is having the intimate relationship is being treated unfairly.

Besides the athlete involved in the intimate relationship, the other athletes on the team are treated unfairly by the coach, even if this is done unconsciously. Dixon (1996) makes an important point when he states that (concerning the professor-student relationship) "the conflict-of-interest argument is based in part on preventing harm to *third parties*, as well as the intrinsic injustice of giving undeservedly high grades, and is thus less controversial than paternalistic restrictions designed to prevent students from harming *themselves* by making inautonomous decisions" (p.528). When a coach gives the intimate partner extra attention, playing time, and so on, the other athletes are not treated fairly in that *they* are not given the same sort of attention, and so on. If, in the case where a coach goes out of his or her way to avoid giving the intimate partner attention, playing time, and so on, the other athletes suffer in that their teammate is not given the attention he or she needs to be the best player possible, and thus, the best possible contributor to the team.

Before concluding a discussion concerning intimate relationships between coaches and athletes, there are two additional issues that must be addressed: (1) what if it is the athlete who initiates the relationship, and (2) what if the coach is not the coach of the intimate partner but they are involved in the same sport? Concerning who initiates the relationship, it would appear that, if it is the athlete, the coach does not have to worry about whether the athlete is making an autonomous choice. However, while student-initiated romances are less likely than professor-initiated ones to be exploitive of the student, Zalk (1990) argues that, once the relationship is underway, the origin of the romance will not remove all moral concerns (pp.152-153). For example, even if the athlete initiated the relationship, if things turn sour, the athlete might be hesitant to break things off because of the power the coach holds as a result of his or her position as coach.

The second issue concerning the situation where the coach is not the coach of the intimate partner but they are involved in the same sport was brought to my attention by a coach who was concerned about coaches dating other coaches' athletes when the sporting community in question is fairly small.[3] My response to this situation would be that as long as the coach will not have any professional responsibilities for that athlete, there really is no position-of-power issues or conflict-of-interest issues that would make the relationship questionable. However, in a small sport community, coaches would have to make sure that there would not be occasion where the coach would be put in a position of having professional responsibilities, for example, having to assist the coach who is coaching his or her intimate athlete, and thus putting him or herself in a conflict-of-interest position.

When Coaches and Athletes Are Friends

Having examined the intimate end of the coach-athlete continuum, we now consider the degrees of friendship that can exist between coaches and their athletes. As mentioned previously in this chapter, there are varying degrees of friendship that can exist between coaches and athletes–coaches and athletes who share personal aspects of their lives with each other and/or spend time with each other outside the sporting context, for example, going out for meals together, and those coaches and athletes who are simply "friendly" with each other. All types of friendship between coaches and their athletes will experience the benefit of a shared passion, that is, the sport that has brought them together. However, like intimate relationships, there are dangers inherent in the "friends" portion of the continuum. Thomas's (1987) conception of **deep friendship** will be utilized for the more intense end of the continuum. There are two main issues that arise when considering deep friendship between coaches and their athletes: (1) can "unequals" (regarding the power differential discussed earlier when examining intimate relationships) be friends, and (2) does the same conflict of interest that exists between intimates exist between friends?

Regarding the question of whether "unequals" can be friends, it is helpful to examine what it means to be a "friend." As far back as Aristotle, philosophers have noted the importance of equality between friends. Thomas (1987) suggests that one of the salient features of friendship is that "[n]either party to the relationship is under the authority of the other" (p.217). Another way that Thomas looks at friendship is in relation to the degree of structure involved in the interaction. He considers social interaction to lie on a continuum with regard to being structured, for example, at the highly structured end would lie interaction between heads of states that would involve highly ritualized behavior and at the other end would lie deep friendships and romantic lovers–"the only two forms of interpersonal relationships where the involved parties interact with one another intensely and frequently, but yet, aside from the rules of morality, the nature of the interaction is not defined by this or that set of social rules" (p.219). The coach-athlete relationship lies somewhere along Thomas's continuum in that this relationship, unlike "deep friends and lovers," *is* governed by certain social conventions.

The **social conventions** governing coach-athlete relationships could be seen to be analogous to the social conventions governing parent-child relationships. Psychologists Neal and Tutko (1975) concur with this analogy when they suggest that, "although the relationship between coach and player changes over time and under different circumstances, basically it is a relationship like that of the parent and child" (p.143). Although philosophers have debated to what extent parents can be "friends" with their children, Kupfer (1990) makes an important point when he argues that the parent-child relationship lacks the equality required by friendship. The inequality that prevents friendships between parents and their children is inequality in autonomy.

> Ideal friendship requires equal autonomy in the relationship for several reasons. Without it, there will be unequal influence and power. One friend will be making more of the decisions or having more impact on the decisions at which they mutually arrive.... The more autonomous friend may be reluctant to confide deeply out of lack of respect for the other friend's judgment or doubts about her willingness to respond with independent convictions. (p.16)

Kupfer argues that the reason children (even grown children) cannot be as autonomous as their parents within the relationship is that the parents developed into adults independently of their children but the parents have shaped who their children are. Although coaches may not have had the same influence in "shaping" their athletes as the athletes' parents have had, sport theorists have pointed out that the degree of influence coaches have on their athletes is enormous (Gough 1997). Part of the "shaping" that occurs with parents and their children (as well as coaches and their athletes) has to do with what Thomas (1987) refers to as the right of the parents to determine the good of their children:

> Understandable though this may be, since children rarely have the wherewithal to determine their own good, the fact remains that children initially experience their parents as individuals who are entitled to determine the good for their children, and thus as individuals who are entitled to make authoritative assessment of the behavior of their children. (p.222)

The same situation exists between the coach and his or her athlete. The coach and athlete entered the coach-athlete relationship based on the ability of the coach to determine what was good for the athlete concerning their sport. This authoritative role of the coach would not disappear if the coach and athlete became friends. As Thomas (1987) points out,

> in examining our lives with another, it is of the utmost importance that we be able to do so without there being any sense, on the part of either party, that the hearer is entitled to make authoritative assessments of the speaker's life and is entitled to the speaker's deference with respect to those assessments.... These considerations speak to the importance of deep friendships being between equals. (p.222)

Because of the unequal situation brought about by the authoritative role of the coach compared to the less autonomous role of the athlete, the coach and athlete cannot be "deep friends." However, there may be a different form of friendship possible and this will be explored in the following section.

Concerning the issue of whether the same conflict of interest that exists between intimates exists between friends, the answer would be affirmative. The argument Markie (1990) gives against professor-student friendships would also apply to coach-athlete friendships:

> If engaging in an activity is likely to limit severely our ability to honor one of our moral obligations, then we have a prima facie moral obligation not to engage in that activity. Establishing and maintaining a friendship with one or more students is likely to limit severely a professor's ability to honor his or her moral obligations. Hence, each professor has a prima facie moral obligation not to engage in such friendships. (p.141)

According to Markie, the moral obligation that would not be honored if a professor had a friendship with one or more students in his or her class would include the duty to give all students in the class equal consideration in instruction, advising, and evaluation. This situation would seem to aptly parallel the situation of a coach and his or her athletes. If a coach was friends with one or more of his or her athletes, the other athletes would not be treated equally in that, as mentioned in the section on intimate relationships, there is a high probability that a coach will unconsciously give his or her friend more attention, more playing time, and so on.

The objection could be made that although there is a high probability of preferential treatment for the athlete who is a friend of the coach, the coach can carefully monitor his or her behavior to ensure that this unequal treatment does not happen. However, as Markie (1990) points out regarding professors and their students, we would be expecting an ability on the part of the professor (as well as the coach) that we do not expect of other professionals, for example, we require even the most respected jurists to excuse themselves from hearing cases that involve the interest of a friend, we require letters of support for promotion and tenure to be solicited from professors who are not friends of the candidate, and so on (p.144).

Another objection that could be made concerning professors and students that also applies to the coaches and athletes is the objection that professors who give extra attention to their friends do nothing improper as long as they give the other students an appropriate level. Blum (1980) suggests that "[a] teacher is permitted to give more attention to some students than to others (not merely on pedagogical grounds), as long as he gives full and adequate attention to all" (p.48). Markie's response to this objection would seem very fitting for the sports context. Markie (1990) points out that "[o]ur students are competing for class rank, honors, and job opportunities, and we are running the competition.... Whether the competition is fair is determined not just by how much preparation–instruction and advice–each student gets, but by how much each gets relative to each other" (pp.145-146). This situation would clearly apply to the world of sport where athletes end up competing against each other for sport scholarships, places on the national team, and so on.

In summary, if coaches cannot treat their friends impartially, and this would seem to be what is implied in a deep friendship, that is, "[i]t is only when two individuals allow their feelings about each other to influence how they treat each other that a friendship can exist" (Jollimore 2000, 72), then coaches should not be deep friends with their athletes. However, there may be a type of friendship that *is* acceptable for the coach-athlete situation, and we turn now to an exploration of this possibility.

When Coaches Are Coaches and Athletes Are Athletes

There are two questions to be asked regarding the "opposite of intimate" end of the continuum: (1) is it possible for coaches and athletes to maintain strict coach-athlete roles, and (2) is it even desirable, given their shared sporting goals, for coaches and athletes not to be friends? The benefits of coaches being coaches and athletes being athletes (if it is possible to maintain these roles without becoming friends) is that the power differential between the two roles is acknowledged, no conflict of interest arises, and there is no potential for harassment or abuse. On the surface, these benefits appear to be worth working toward a strict role relationship between coaches and athletes. But is this possible and/or desirable?

The perceived dangers of a strict coach-athlete role relationship is that it would be so cold and formal that coaches would not be able to coach effectively. Markie (1990) looks at this objection in the professor-student context:

> Professors who act toward their students in a warm and friendly manner and are sensitive to their student's needs and concerns must be interested in information about them, but they need not be willing to share personal information about themselves. They must value and give special consideration to each student's welfare, but they can value each student's welfare because it

is the welfare of one of their students rather than because it is that student's welfare in particular. (p.139)

It would seem then, according to Markie, that it is possible to maintain the roles of coach and athlete, even acting friendly toward each other, but not becoming friends. A critical point of Markie's position is that the professor (or coach) must be interested in information about the student (or athlete) but not share personal information about him or herself. This one-way sharing of information would appear to fit in with the unequal power differential discussed earlier in the chapter. However, is this one-way sharing of information conducive to the shared goals of the coach and athlete?

Annis, in his article "The Meaning, Value, and Duties of Friendship" (1987), suggests that there is an epistemic aspect to friendship, "a sharing of information about one's experiences, beliefs, values and so on; friendship requires getting to know the person" (p.349). Sharing information would seem to be a critical factor in the coach-athlete relationship. In an empirical study involving coach-athlete married couples, Jowett and Meek (2000) reported that, for the coaches, "knowing the athlete enabled them 'to strike the athlete's right chords' at the right moment resulting in efficient and effective procedures during training and competitions" (p.169). Although the dangers inherent in coach-athlete intimate relationships were discussed earlier, the benefits of the coach knowing his or her athlete cannot be overemphasized, for example, knowing the athlete's abilities, knowing how far the athlete can be "pushed," and so on. But a coach would not necessarily have to have a personal relationship with his or her athlete in order to gain this knowledge. According to Markie (1990), a coach could have knowledge of his or her athlete but refrain from sharing personal knowledge about him or herself, thus avoiding the mutual sharing required of friendships.

However, in order for the coach and athlete to achieve their shared goals concerning their sport, the athlete must also "know" his or her coach. One of the coaches in the Jowett and Meek (2000) study pointed out that "[i]t is important for the athlete to understand the coach.... [I]t is the coach who tries to help and aims for the best of the athlete... [I]f there is no understanding that they both try to achieve literally the same things, then the relationship cannot go ahead" (p.167). Ravizza and Daruty (1988), in discussing the limits of the coach's exercise of authority over the adult athlete, suggest that principles of informed consent could be used to clarify the limits of a coach's authority. They propose that full disclosure should be made to the athlete concerning the nature of the coach's philosophy or attitude related to coaching a particular sport (p.225). With coaches sharing their philosophies and attitudes with their athletes, the athletes will be better able to anticipate what will be involved in training and competing with their coach, and there will be a much better chance that the coach and athlete will be working together toward their shared goals.

If sharing of information between coaches and athletes is necessary for the coach and athlete to achieve their shared sporting goals, how do they share information but avoid becoming friends? It would be fruitful to look again at what it means to be a friend. Aristotle suggests that there are three forms of friendship: "Whether there is one species of friendship or more than one.... The kinds of friendship may perhaps be cleared up if we first come to know the object of love. For not everything seems to be loved but only the lovable, and this is good, pleasant, or useful (1941a, 1059). Scholars have characterized these types of friends as goodness friends, pleasure friends, and utility friends (O'Connor 1990; White 1990; Koehn 19984). In a **goodness friendship**, the bond is based on the friends' characters. "Each partner loves the other for what makes her the person she is, with her particular attitudes, aspirations and dispositions" (White 1990, 83). **Pleasure friends** enjoy one another's company, and the bond between them is simply their mutual pleasure seeking. **Utility friends** love each other because each is useful or advantageous to the other.

In order for coaches and athletes to share the information needed to achieve their mutual sporting goals, they should develop utility friendships. Utility friendships are viewed by some scholars as friendships only in a minimal sense, only by analogy to goodness friendships (Koehn 1998, 1756). Aristotle himself says that "good men will be friends for their own sake, i.e. in virtue of their goodness. These [goodness friends], then, are friends without qualification; the others [pleasure and utility friends] are friends incidentally and through a resemblance to these" (Aristotle 1941a, 1063). Although utility friends are not as valuable as goodness friends, the coach-athlete friendship is not meant to be as valuable as other forms of friendship (otherwise we would run into the conflict of interest issues raised earlier in the chapter). Although utility friendship may be a minimal form of friendship, it will serve the purpose of both coach and athlete in their shared sporting goals.

Besides the utility of achieving shared sporting goals, the utility friendship between coach and athlete might also be viewed as having a few other benefits. Koehn, in an article entitled "Can and Should Businesses Be Friends with One Another and with Their Stakeholders" (1998), makes the interesting suggestion that virtue can be developed and exercised in utility relationships in a couple of ways. She uses the analogy of the parent-child relationship to show how the child uses the parent, but only up to a point.

Parents have their own interests and do not always coming running when the child cries, and thus the child learns through this utility relation that the world is not just there for him or her. Koehn then applies the same point to commercial relations of utility. Commercial relationships expose us to other people, for example, product managers, bank tellers, and so on to whom we have to listen and sometimes negotiate. "[F]riendships of utility play an important role in teaching basic social skills, in building community, and in preparing people for more challenging friendships" (p.1758).

Another benefit from utility relationships that applies to the sporting world as well as the business world has to do with the expectation that, although a utility friendship is based on utility, utility friends tacitly expect the friendship to continue when they enter it. Koehn (1998) gives the example of a customer expecting to return to a particular business in the future. Because of this relationship, the business should not think of itself merely as selling goods to customers but rather as providing long-term satisfaction. Conversely, the customer is obligated not to return goods if they have met their needs–"getting something for nothing" would destroy the friendship of utility (p.1758). This sort of respect between customer and business is also required by the coach-athlete utility relationship, and the development of this respect is necessary for future goodness friendships.

Thus, the development of utility friendships between coaches and athletes would make it possible for them to share the information needed to achieve their shared sporting goals. As well, a side benefit of these utility friendships is that they have the potential to promote the development of the more valuable goodness friendships. As mentioned earlier, utility friendships require a respect between the "utility" friends. In the business-customer relationship, this respect plays itself out when the business provides the best service possible to the customer, respects warranties, and so on, and in return, the customer does not bring back goods after they have met their needs, the customer returns to the business in the future, and so forth. In the coach-athlete relationship, this respect plays itself out when the coach shares his or her philosophy and attitudes toward coaching and the shared sporting goals with his or her athletes, and in return, the athlete agrees to respect the coach's training approach, practice schedules, and so on. Learning to respect utility friends is a precursor to respecting goodness friends.

Although goodness friendships are a more valuable form of friendship than utility friendships, it often seems that the familiarity that accompanies goodness friends can sometimes override the respect that should occur in these friendships. For example, because of the deep friendship we share with our spouse or best friend, during a conflict we might say things to them that we would never dream of saying to the local grocer or bank teller. Having utility friendships in our lives gives us the opportunity to practice respecting these friends, and this situation should be reflected upon when we engage in our goodness friendships. The fact that utility friendships are a minimal form of friendship and not as valuable as goodness friendships is not problematic because these utility friendships are not meant to replace goodness friendships–athletes should be encouraged to develop deep friendships outside their sport. Maintaining a separation between deep friendships outside one's sport and utility friendships within one's sport is important for avoiding the dangers of sport-related deep friendships discussed earlier in the chapter.

Conclusion

Having examined the continuum of relationships from utility friendships to intimate relationships with deep friendships in between, it is important to consider the consequences of this discussion for policy implications concerning coach-athlete relationships. In other words, we need to answer the question of how close is too close. Intimate relationships and deep friendships between coaches and athletes share the benefits of the partners understanding each other as well as experiencing the shared passion of their sport. However, these benefits do not outweigh the dangers of the power differential created by the coach's position of authority. This power differential affects intimate partners in that one can never be sure if the athlete is truly consenting to the relationship. Regarding deep friendships, the coach will have more autonomy than the friend who has been shaped, in part, by their relationship with the coach. This unequal autonomy will result in the more autonomous coach making more decisions, having more impact, and being reluctant to confide in the less autonomous athlete.

Although the power differential is reason enough for suggesting that an intimate or even deep friendship between coach and athlete is "too close," the argument that conclusively closes the door on intimate and deep friendships between coach and athlete is the conflict of interest argument. Whether the athlete in question is an intimate partner or close friend of the coach, there is a high probability that the coach will unconsciously give the athlete more attention, more playing time, and so on. This creates a situation of unequal treatment between the athlete involved in the relationship and the other athletes on the team.

With the dangers outweighing the benefits of intimate or even deep friendships between coach and athlete, the implications for sport-governing bodies is clear, but difficult. With the amount of time athletes spend with their coaches, along with the shared passion they have for their sport, deep friendships and intimate relationships are sure to develop. The implication of the preceding discussion would require the athlete or the coach to leave that particular sporting context, for example, the athlete would have to find another coach or the coach another team. Although this situation will be difficult (especially if the sporting community in question is small, thus requiring a possible change in location), the integrity of the coach, athlete and particular sport organization is at stake. For the sake of all involved, it is important that **policy** is set in order to rectify situations where the coach-athlete relationship has become too close.

Although it has been proposed in this chapter that sport organizations should prohibit intimate relationships or deep friendships between their coaches and athletes, this does not mean that coaches and athletes should not develop some form of friendship. The type of friendship proposed in this chapter is Aristotle's utility friendship. Not only would a utility friendship help the athlete and coach share the information needed to achieve their shared sporting goals, but such a friendship could also act as a training ground for the more valuable goodness friendships–which athletes should be encouraged to develop outside their sport.

Notes

1. I would like to thank Nicholas Dixon for his guidance regarding the literature concerning professor-student relationships.
2. I must thank Barbara Desjardins (a handball coach who married her former coach and then decided to find another coach) for this example.
3. Thanks to Heather McFarlane for this example.
4. Koehn and White refer to goodness friends as character friends, and utility friends as advantage friends.

CHAPTER REVIEW

Key Concepts

- relationship continuum
- intimate relationships
- power differential
- autonomy
- sexual harassment
- conflict of interest
- deep friendship
- social convention
- goodness friendship
- pleasure friendship
- utility friendship
- policy implications

Review Questions

1. What are the various positions on the relationship continuum as described in this chapter?
2. What is the positive side of an intimate and/or close friendship between a coach and his or her athlete?
3. Describe the two main "danger" areas when coaches have romantic and/or sexual relationships with their athletes.
4. What is meant by "inequality in autonomy," and how does this relate to potential friendships between athletes and their coaches?
5. What are the perceived dangers of a strict coach-athlete role relationship?
6. What are Aristotle's forms of friendship, and which form would be most appropriate for the coach-athlete relationship?
7. What are some of the side benefits of utility friendships?
8. What sort of policy should sport organizations establish concerning coach-athlete relationships?

12

Can Sport Be "Art"?

I want to show them a race that is so beautiful *that people will remember it forever* [emphasis added]. (Deford 2001, 67)

[Runner Jim Ryan]'s graceful *and fast and can churn out killing 400-meter repeats until the sun drops past the flat, distant horizon* [emphasis added] (Layden 2001, 51)

Thrashers rookie wings Ilya Kovalchuk, 18, and Dany Heathy, 20, are ... poetry on ice [emphasis added]. (Farber 2001, 56)

That is so "beautiful," "graceful," or "poetry on ice" are common utterances heard at sporting competitions. Talk of beauty and grace in reference to sport is not new. The philosophy of sport literature includes numerous articles that connect aesthetics and/or art with sport (Best 1978; Hyland 1990, 1991; Kaelin 1968; Kupfer 1975, 1983; Roberts 1986, 1995). Most of the scholars who have written in this area take it for granted that there is a connection between aesthetics and sport. Their work typically "fleshes out" what this connection entails. Although there are some commonalities between aesthetics and sports (e.g., emphasis on form, visions of beauty, and so on), the contrasts outweigh the commonalities. However, delineating the distinctions between aesthetics and/or art and sport should not be perceived as a negative move. Rather, such a project highlights what is fundamental and significant to aesthetic activity as separate from what is fundamental and significant to sport. Some perspectives on aesthetics will be considered, followed by an examination of what it is about sport that tempts us to refer to such activity as aesthetic. Key concepts utilized in this chapter include: **analytic, postmodern, aesthetic response, aesthetic qualities, sensuous understanding, aesthetic** and **artistic, form** and **content, aesthetic** and **purposive sports, flow, engaging** and **expressing**, and **intrinsic value**.

Aesthetics and/or Art

The realm of aesthetics is one that encompasses a variety of perspectives, from analytic to postmodern thought. An **analytic** perspective would involve looking for necessary and sufficient conditions for something to be referred to as aesthetic. A **postmodern** perspective involves, among other things, a suspicion of the very possibility of value judgments (which would, needless to say, include aesthetic judgments). One of the first analytic philosophers to advance a serious analysis of aesthetic response was Urmson (1957). He proposed that the criterion for distinguishing an **aesthetic response** from other kinds of responses lay in the kind of reasons given for the response. He gives the example of someone gaining satisfaction from a play. If the playhouse is full, and the person watching the play has financed it, the satisfaction would probably be economic. If the person watching the play feels that the play will have an improving effect on the audience, the satisfaction could be considered moral (pp.75-76). An aesthetic response, on the other hand, would involve a response to the form and content of the play. Hospers (1982) argues that the whole concept of aesthetic experience is confused and that it is extremely difficult to distinguish aesthetic experience from moral, religious, intellectual, or sexual experience. Price (1979) argues that the "question 'What makes an experience aesthetic?' asks not what makes the awareness in an aesthetic experience aesthetic since that cannot be a question, but what makes the object in an aesthetic experience an aesthetic object" (p.142). Focus on the aesthetic object is evident in the work of Mitias (1986), who argues against Hosper's view that the concept of an aesthetic experience is untenable. Mitias defines an aesthetic experience via the **aesthetic qualities** possessed by an object, that is, features of the work that evoke the aesthetic experience, such as color, line, symmetry, and so on:

> [O]n the basis of my experience and the testimony of art critics and philosophers I can, however, say that though rich in its scope, appeal, and depth the aesthetic quality appears to have a general identity in all the arts, and art works: regardless of its habitat–a poem, a novel, a statue, a dance, a building, a symphony or a film–aesthetic quality belongs to the art works as a potentiality, i.e., as a human aspect that can be actualized as meaning in the aesthetic experience. (p.53)

The notion of aesthetic quality involving potentiality for meaning is reiterated in the work of Abbs (1989c). Contrary to the conception of "art for art's sake," Abbs advocates art for meaning's sake (p.209). By "art for meaning's sake," Abbs is referring to the potential for people to derive meaning from encounters with art. Abbs (1989b) refers to the aesthetic as "*a particular form of sensuous understanding*, a mode of apprehending through the senses the patterned import of human experience" (p.1). The apprehension of the sensuous as it pertains to experiences of the senses is a necessary condition for having an aesthetic experience (Bergmann Drewe 1996a, 58). However, such perceptive experiences, be they visual, oral, tactile, and so forth, are not sufficient for an aesthetic experience to occur. Also needed for an aesthetic experience is the involvement of feelings on the part of the participant. This involvement of feelings is part of the sensuous in the definition of aesthetic as sensuous understanding. It is interesting to note the linguistic connections between sensation and feeling. Abbs (1989a) provides some illuminating illustrations:

> "To keep in touch" is both to keep in contact and to remain close in feeling. To *touch* an object is to have a perceptual experience; *to be touched* by an event is to be emotionally moved by it. To have a *tactile* experience is to have a sensation in the finger-tips; to show *tact* is to exhibit an awareness of the feelings of others" (p.3).

Both the employment of the senses and the experiencing of feelings are necessary for an aesthetic experience to occur. The final condition necessary for an aesthetic experience involves understanding, that is, Abb's **sensuous understanding**. The apprehension through the senses (including feeling) makes it possible to attain sensuous understanding of the human experience. How is this possible? The art historian Gombrich (1969) proposes some possible answers. Gombrich traces the history of representative painting by analyzing image making. He suggests that artists "make" not "match" images: "What [artists] had to learn before they could create an illusion of reality was not to 'copy what they saw' but to manipulate those ambiguous cues on which we have to rely in stationary vision till their image was indistinguishable from reality" (p.29). Thus, "[w]hat a painter inquires into is not the nature of the physical world but the nature of our reactions to it" (p.49).

It is not only the artist's reaction to the physical world that is the basis of artistic inquiry, but also the reaction of the audience. In reference to Renaissance art, Gombrich (1969) states that "[i]t is clear that an entirely new idea of art is taking shape here. It is an art in which the painter's skill in suggesting must be matched by the public's skill in taking hints.... The willing beholder responds to the artist's suggestion because he enjoys the transformation that occurs in front of his eyes" (pp.195, 202). It is the acquaintance with a "transformed" world that can lead to an enriched understanding of the human experience. As Hurthouse (1992) so aptly put it, "[Artists] can also reveal how they think, consciously or unconsciously, about things by what they represent and the ways in which they do it. This can make us think differently, and, again because of the way in which 'interpretation' and 'reception' are interdependent, this may lead us to see differently" (p.277). A good example of "seeing the world differently" concerns the area of moral truths in works of art. As Sorell (1992) suggests,

> it is possible to hold that through works such as novels we enlarge the range of people we can empathize with, the range of situations we can imaginatively project ourselves into, and therefore the perspectives from which we can assess

> the rightness of actions or ways of life that we otherwise would never have thought twice about. (p.307)

Another way of looking at an artist's transformation of the world and the enriched understanding gained by the audience as a result of apprehending the artist's work is to view the process as a communication of an artist's "discovery." Keller (1974) gives the example of an artist painting a picture of a mountain:

> The purpose of the picture of the mountain is communication. It is an attempt on the part of the artist to get something across–a discovery of his own. Nor is he just communicating what he feels about the mountain; he expresses something which we all feel about it–without our having been conscious of it prior to the emergence of his work of art. (p.89)

In using the term *communication* to describe what is happening between the artist and the audience, one must be careful not to think of communication in purely discursive terms. Maquet (1986) makes a distinction between receivers of linguistic messages and beholders of art:

> Receivers of linguistic messages–the readers of this page, for instance–apprehend meanings embodied in the words, sentences, and texts by the sender–the writer of this book, for instance–ideally without adding anything to them.... Beholders, on the contrary, invest the visual object with meanings related, in part, to their past experiences. Because of this rooting in individual experiences, symbolic meanings attributed to the same object by different beholders are bound to be different. However, this symbolic variety is limited. (p.157)

The variety of aesthetic responses is limited for a couple of reasons. One, which Maquet (1986) points out, is that the commonalities in our experiences are many (ibid.). Another limiting factor concerns the artist's intention. Maquet states: "[A] beholder's interpretation of a visual work is valid for the beholder if it has the quality of compelling evidence" (ibid.). Compelling evidence would include the recognition of the formal features the artist has chosen to express the experience he or she is expressing. A more detailed exploration of aesthetic form and content arises in an examination of the distinction between the aesthetic and the artistic.

A criticism that may be raised concerning the previous discussion is that the **aesthetic** and the **artistic** have been conflated. A response to this criticism requires a closer look at potentially competing conceptions of the aesthetic. Best (1978) distinguishes the aesthetic from the artistic by suggesting that the "aesthetic applies, for instance, to sunsets, birdsong and mountain ranges, whereas the artistic tends to be limited, at least in its central uses, to artifacts or performances intentionally created by man" (p.113). According to Best, "the arts are characteristically concerned with contemporary moral, social, political and emotional issues. Yet this is not true of the aesthetic" (p.115). Best's definitions of the aesthetic and artistic might appear to be in conflict with Abbs's (1989b) definition of the aesthetic as "sensuous understanding" (p.1), for upon first glance, sunsets do not seem to have much to contribute to an understanding of the human experience. However, a closer look at the sunset experience is in order here. At times, when confronted with a beautiful sunset, a person simply enjoys the colors, the shapes of the clouds, the changing of colors and shapes. This person is enjoying the "form" of the sunset. If, on the other hand, the perception of the colors and shapes creates a context for the observer to reflect upon something of the human experience, such as humankind's minute position in the cosmos [or Shusterman (1998) suggests the potential of "a sunset experience involving complex interpretation or 'a sense of foreboding, insecurity, even of danger' (say, before some anticipated terrors in the night)" (p.52)], the conditions are ripe for an aesthetic experience. Thus, nature can provide aesthetic experiences, but more than perception of form is necessary if one is to experience nature (or works of art) aesthetically.

In arguing that more than "form" is required for an aesthetic response to occur, one must elaborate on what is entailed by aesthetic form and content. Although some aestheticians have tried to separate **form**, that is, "how" something is expressed, and **content**, that is, "what" is being expressed, and extol form as the aspect that gives art value [Bell (1958) would be the most staunch proponent of this view], Bailin (1993) argues that form and content cannot be separated:

> Rather than being separate components which are simply added together to come up with a work, form and content are more like aspects of the same thing. The terms are abstractions which are helpful in discussing facets of works of art, but this need not imply that they are elements which can in reality be separated.... Any attempt to extract a content and express it in another form is necessarily inadequate since it will no longer be the same content. Similarly, there cannot be form in isolation. A form must be a form of something, and it is difficult to imagine how one could isolate the form of a work in order to attend to it alone. (p.36)

Acknowledging the importance of content *and* form is important in dealing with the criticism concerning the suggestion that the sunset example opens up too many experiences as being potentially "aesthetic" in nature. For example, someone could counter that contemplating a hair falling from his or her head could be a context for thinking about life and death. However, one could argue that a hair falling from one's head does not have a particular emphasis on form, that is, "how" the hair falls or what the hair looks like is not essential for provoking thoughts of life and death. This is not the case with the sunset. It is the sunset that fills the entire sky with intense colors and shapes and that seems to lend itself to reflection upon the immensity and intensity of nature and thus, perhaps, humankind's minuteness in comparison.

Having considered the possibility of aesthetic responses to nature, we return now to the artistic. A criticism that may be raised is that advocating "art for meaning's sake" applies only to certain kinds of art, that is, representational art, particular art forms, and so on. Cordner (1988), among others, questions the possibility of "meaning" in nonrepresentational art: "It just seems mistaken, because too intellectualist, to hold that abstract paintings express a conception of life-issues. And how could a piece of music express a conception of poverty, or war, or loyalty, or death, or honor? Architecture, and possibly dance, also seem unfitted to express conceptions of life-issues" (p.37). Cordner appears to be mistaken. Part of the problem lies in his use of the term *life-issues.* In fairness to Cordner, however, he has adopted this term from Best, whose position Cordner is criticizing. Best (1978) suggests that "any art form, properly so-called, must at least allow for the possibility of the expression of a conception of life-issues such as contemporary moral, social and political problems" (p.117). Rather than using the term *life-issues,* which connotes particular issues, usually issues involving a negative aspect of the human experience such as poverty, violence, and so on, the term *human experience* would be more appropriate. To suggest that all art expresses something of the human experience would allow for the expression of negative and positive aspects of the human experience, including humankind's appreciation of form. Dancers may not always express particular issues through dance, but when they are moving for the sake of movement, they are expressing thoughts pertaining to the joy of pure movement (Bergmann Drewe 1996a, 42). Conceiving of art as expressing something of the human experience would seem to *allow* for Cordner's description of what happens when one engages with portraits. Cordner (1998) suggests that "[t]he force of the portrait lies not in its presenting us with a face on which it then makes a comment or about which it then expresses a conception, but in the vividness and fullness with which it realizes or makes manifest certain life-values" (p.38). Are these "life-values" not part of the human experience? Thus, Cordner's example *supports* the proposition that artists are always expressing something of the human experience through their work.

Regarding the variety of art forms, all art forms have the potential to be responded to aesthetically. Meynell (1986) compares and contrasts different art forms by first suggesting features common to all art forms and then considering how the emphasis varies according to the specific art form under discussion:

> Each type of art is a matter of *manipulation of a medium* (a) to provide a *structure* (b) which is a means to satisfaction through *exercise and enlargement of consciousness.* While representation is certainly not the only means by which such an end may be secured, it is at least characteristic of literature and the visual arts that they exercise and enlarge consciousness through representation (c); and that such representation is more deeply satisfying when it involves some kind of reference to what is of central importance in human life (d). (p.45)

Regarding the specific artistic forms of literature, Meynell specifies the features deemed to be valuable:

> When examining the criticism of novels, plays, and other works of literature, such works are deemed to be of value in proportion to (i) their illustration and demonstration of what is of central importance for human life; (ii) the originality of their use of language and their treatment of plot, character, situation, and so on; (iii) their just representation of people, things and circumstances; and (iv) their overall unity in variety of substance and effect. It will be seen that these features correspond respectively to (d), (a), (c) and (b) above. (ibid.)

Regarding works of visual art, Meynell suggests that they "are found to be of value in proportion to (as well, presumably, as their exploitation of their medium as such) (i) their enhancement of perception and imagination (often through representation); (ii) their emotional significance; (iii) their unity in variety–which correspond to (c), (d), and (b)" (ibid.). Finally, regarding works of music, Meynell suggests that their value "is found to be a matter of (i) its exploitation of the medium of sound as such; (ii) the clarity and intensity of its depiction of emotion and mood; (iii) its unity in variety–which correspond to (a), (d) and (b)" (pp.45-46).

While Meynell (1986) considers the art forms of literature, visual art, and music, Dimondstein (1974) performs a similar analysis, but she includes dance in her discussion:

> Each art form has its own distinguishing characteristics, provides a unique image, and uses particular media. How, then, can we give the arts a sense of unity as well as recognize their distinctiveness? To do so is to consider them in their broadest context, as parameters of space-time-force through which the functions of the arts are expressed. As parameters, they may have various values, yet each in its own way is necessary in creating and determining the aesthetic effects of any particular form. They cannot, then, be conceived as technical elements, but as the connective tissue underlying the expression of ideas and feelings. (pp.30-31)

Dimondstein gives examples of how the same feature is expressed in different art forms: "When we speak of an energetic line or a strong color relationship in painting, of tension between the volumes or contours in a sculpture, of the power of a movement in dance or the intensity of an image in poetry, we are expressing a sense of vitality" (p.32).

Although the preceding discussion gives the impression that there are agreed-upon aesthetic features common to all art forms, one must be careful not to jump to the conclusion that one can come to understand these features apart from the works of which they are constitutive (Bergmann Drewe 1996a, 37). Redfern (1991) makes this point when she insists that "aesthetic concepts (that is, concepts functioning aesthetically) are not grasped intellectually and then applied over a variety of instances: appreciation of works even within the same art form requires judgment (in that sense which involves perception and thought in felt experience) *in each particular case*" (pp.271-272).

Sport

The particular case of sport must now be examined to determine what it is about sport that tempts us to refer to such activity as **aesthetic**. Best (1978) makes some distinctions concerning sport that prove to be a good starting point. Best distinguishes between sports such as football, climbing, and track and field, which he calls "purposive," and sports such as synchronized swimming, trampolining, and gymnastics, which he refers to as "aesthetic" (p.104). Regarding **purposive sports**, Best states that "[i]n each of these sports the aim, purpose or end can be specified independently of the manner of achieving it as long as it conforms to the limits set by the rules or norms–for example, scoring a goal and climbing the Eiger" (ibid.). (Roberts's [1986] decimation of Best's generalization of ends will not be examined at this time, since for the purpose of this chapter, it is sufficient to distinguish sports where the aesthetic dimension is not fundamental [even though it exists in the particular] from sports where the aesthetic dimension *is* fundamental.) Although, according to Best, an aesthetic experience is unnecessary in the context of a purposive sport, he points out that it is possible to experience aesthetic feelings while participating in such sports. He cites examples such as

> a finely timed stroke in squash, a smoothly accomplished series of movements in gymnastics, an outing in an "eight" when the whole crew is pulling in unison, with unwavering balance, and a training run when one's body seems to be completely under one's control. For many, the feelings derived from such performances are part of the enjoyment of participation, and "aesthetic" seems the most appropriate way to characterise them. (pp.111-112)

The feelings described by Best (1978) should not be referred to as aesthetic. Although they may satisfy the "sensuous" condition for sensuous understanding (in perhaps both the "feeling" and "sense" dimensions), there is no deeper understanding of an expressed aspect of the human experience attained in these situations. It is important at this point to emphasize the notion of an "expressed aspect" of the human experience. Participating in sporting activity *is* part of the human experience. However, there is an important difference between *participating* in a human experience and *expressing* an aspect of that experience. An example from the realm of art will help illuminate this distinction. Levinson (1996, 231-234) cites the example of a controversial art piece displayed on his campus, which he calls *Rape Piece*. *Rape Piece* consisted of a wall erected to display the names of all the male students listed in the campus directory. At the head of this giant poster was the rubric "Potential Rapists." On the surface, this poster looked like a public notice (similar to a "Wanted" poster). If this was the case, the poster would be part of the human experience, that is, an attempt to track down suspected rapists. However, that was not the intention of the artists. In Levinson's words:

> *Rape Piece* is not strictly an item of that category [public notice category], it only resembles such; what it is, at base, is an artistic representation of such an item. That is to say, the creators of *Rape Piece* have borrowed the form of a public proclamation of warning and used it in an image–an image, however, which is knowingly indiscernible from the thing itself, at least if intention and framing context are ignored or left out of account. (p.232)

The importance of "intention and framing context" is evident in the aesthetic realm but not in the sporting realm. The sports person is participating in a human experience but he or she is not intending to express some aspect of that experience by his or her participation in the sport. The experiencing and the expression of an experience is a distinction of fundamental importance when comparing and contrasting sport and aesthetic activities.

By suggesting that the term *aesthetic* not be used to label the feelings involved in sport, that is, Best's "finely tuned stroke ... smoothly accomplished series of movements," and so on, the existence and significance of these feelings are not being denied. In fact, these feelings are critical for the satisfaction one derives from participation in sport. However, the notion of **flow**, which the psychologist Czikszentmihalyi (1975) has coined, would be a better descriptor than "aesthetic" in describing the feelings to which Best (1978) is referring. Czikszentmihalyi (1975), after interviewing hundreds of people pursuing activities such as rock climbing, basketball and dancing, in an attempt to discover what it was about these activities that was perceived as rewarding, found that a majority of those interviewed reported similar experiential states. He described this state in the following manner: "He [participant interviewed] experiences it [the 'flow' state] as a unified flowing from one moment to the next, in which he is in control of his actions, and in which there is little distinction between self and environment, between stimulus and response, or between past, present, and future" (p.36). This "flow" state seems to be what Kaelin (1968) is referring to in his discussion of aesthetic perception in sport when he states that "[t]he feeling of being at one with nature, using it to fulfill our own aims with consummate ease, is a direct aesthetic response of the mover to his motion" (p.25) and Kupfer (1975) in his suggestion that "[c]oncepts such as timing, jelling, flowing, harmonizing, and executing attest to this aesthetic ideal in competitive sport" (p.88). Once again, the term *flow* would seem more appropriate than *aesthetic* in describing this response.

Regarding the sports Best (1978) refers to as aesthetic sports, for example, gymnastics and diving, their purpose cannot be considered apart from the manner of achieving it. Best cites the example of vaulting in gymnastics: "The end is not simply to get over the box somehow or other, even if one were to do so in a clumsy way and collapse afterwards in an uncontrolled manner. The way in which the appropriate movements are performed is not incidental but central to such a sport" (p.104). It is perhaps the aesthetic sport experience that has led many theorists to make a connection between aesthetics and sports. However, the concept of "aesthetic" has been misapplied to these sports. At this point, it must be noted that Best *does* make a distinction between sport and art (p.113). However, this distinction must be pushed further to acknowledge that sport differs not only from art, but also from the more general experience we refer to as aesthetic. In conceiving of the aesthetic as sensuous understanding, it is important to reiterate the condition of attaining an understanding of the human experience. This does not happen in sport, not even aesthetic sports. The fundamental role that form plays in aesthetic sports is not being denied. However, aesthetic experience involves, not only the apprehension of form, but also content. It is how the content of a work of art, for instance, is expressed, that makes a richer understanding of that content possible. Since the content necessary for an aesthetic experience is lacking in aesthetic sports, the term *form sports* would be a more appropriate epithet for these sports.

If one considers various sports to lie on a continuum, we could place "flow" sports at one end and "aesthetic" activity at the other. In between these ends, we would have "form" sports. Now, starting at the "flow" end, we would be adding particular aspects as we moved to the "aesthetic" end. In other words, all sports and aesthetic activity have the potential for the participants in these activities to achieve a state of "flow." As we move along the continuum to the "form" sports, we add an emphasis on form, that is, on "how" certain movements are performed. When we arrive at the "aesthetic" end, where dance forms such as modern and ballet would belong, we no longer have only the possibility of achieving a "flow" state and an emphasis on "form," but also the added dimension of expressing some aspect of the human experience. Such dance forms as folk and jazz dance lie somewhere between form sports and aesthetic activity. In other words, some folk and jazz dance do express some aspects of the human experience, but often these dances are more a series of movements with an emphasis on form, that is, particular steps.

In suggesting that an aesthetic experience involves the expression of some content, one must respond to a counter-example found in the works of Kaelin and Kupfer. Kaelin (1968) suggests that aesthetic expression is evident when "[t]he tempo and rhythm of the game are defined in terms of the building up and the release of dynamic tensions, created ultimately by the opposition of equally capable teams" (p.24). Kupfer (1975) suggests that "[t]he interdependence of team members contesting the opposition yields tensions and resolutions which echo those arising from the circumstances in which real people are situated" (p.89). What can be read into these descriptions is that sport competitions express the concept of tension between players. How would this differ from a dance piece that expressed tension between humans, or humans and their environment? The difference lies in the intention of the experience. In an activity whose fundamental purpose is an aesthetic one, that is, the creation of a dance piece, the expression of tension between humans, or humans and their environment, would be the sole purpose of that activity. On the other hand, in a sporting context, the tension between players is a byproduct of the design of the game. The expression of this tension is not the fundamental purpose of sport. In fact, there are many sports where such overt tension is not evident, for example, individual sports such as diving. The critic could respond by suggesting that, in the case of diving, the tension is between the diver and the standards of the dive he or she is attempting to perform. However, such a perception is stretching the notion of tension.

A similar counter-example is found in the work of Boxill, who proposes that sports *are* concerned with life situations and that sport performances exhibit this concern aesthetically. As examples, Boxill (1985) cites the widening of the 3-second lane in basketball to prevent success without hard work as an expression of the idea of success through effort, and the evolving of the New Games as an expression of the dangers of competition (p.45). In a vein similar to the response made to Kaelin's (1968) and Kupfer's (1975) suggestions that sports express the life situation of tension, if anything similar to the expression of a life situation *is* being expressed, it is purely a byproduct of the design of the game. In Boxill's (1985) examples, her interpretation of the situations is even more tenuous than the notion of games expressing tension. The widening of the 3-second lane in basketball could just as easily be explained by looking at what it means to design a game, that is, imposing limitations to present a challenge, and, realizing that more of a challenge was needed in the game of basketball, a change was made to the 3-second lane. Regarding the New Games, rather than being viewed as a social commentary on the dangers of competition, they could just as easily be viewed as another form of games that presents an alternative to people who prefer non-competitive games, sometimes exclusive from, but sometimes in addition to, competitive games. Thus, sport is not concerned with "life-issues" in the same intentional way that aesthetic activity is concerned with expressing facets of the human experience.

A more damaging criticism to the thesis that aesthetic activity, not sport, is primarily concerned with the expression of thoughts, feelings, and ideas that evoke an enriched understanding of the human condition is the proposal that humankind expresses meaning through sport. Kretchmar (1994) suggests that "games send messages" such as "success is good," "freedom (opportunity) is good" and "justice is good" (pp.218-220). Once again, however, the sending of these "messages" is not the intention of the sports player. They may be a byproduct, but they are not the reason people play sport. However, the sending and receiving of "messages" is an important reason why people engage in aesthetic activity, either as artists or appreciators of art (or appreciators of nature, for that matter). Sport is a meaningful activity, but there is an important distinction between **engaging** in a meaningful activity and **expressing** the meaning in an activity. A good example would be a dance dealing with the physical tension involved in a sport such as football. A football player could play a game of football and experience physical tension. The dancer, however, attempts to express the meaning of physical tension by creating movements that may resemble moves in a football game, but the purpose of these movements is not to score a touchdown, but rather to express the meaning of physical tension. The importance of the distinction between experiencing and expressing an aspect of the human experience cannot be overemphasized.

Although removing the label "aesthetic" from the realm of sports may appear to be devaluing sport to some degree, this is not the case. The potential for flow feelings and focus on form are still being acknowledged. Furthermore, we will now explore an area that traditionally has been reserved for a discussion of aesthetic activity, but that is actually more applicable to sports. This area involves the notion of **intrinsic value**.

Typically, aesthetic activity has been justified on the grounds of its intrinsic value. Crawford (1991) conceives of aesthetic objects as objects "we find perceptually interesting and attractive–objects that can be valued not simply as means to other ends but in themselves or *for their own sake*" [emphasis added] (p.18). Richmond (1989) defines the aesthetic "in its most widely accepted sense as a special kind of perceptual attitude or outlook that involves the apprehension of an object, natural or man-made *for its own sake*" [emphasis added] (p.119). Although aesthetic activity is typically justified on intrinsic grounds, aesthetic activity's greatest value is the potential available through such activity for attaining a rich understanding of the human experience (Bergmann Drewe 1996a, 34). Sport, on the other hand, would appear to be a more likely candidate for justification on intrinsic grounds. Kupfer (1975) acknowledges the notion of "sport for sport's sake" when he proposes that "[s]port is like art in being purposive but without external purpose. We engage in the activity or its viewing for its own sake" (p.89) In another piece of writing, Kupfer (1983) states that "[t]he goals and purposes of sport are not real; they serve no practical need outside the sporting arena. What real use is served in putting golf balls into holes or swatting tennis balls back and forth across a net?" (p.114). Sport is *unique* in being purposive but without external purpose (having dismissed "art for art's sake" in lieu of "art for meaning's sake"). Although critics may propose that sport *does* have an external purpose, that being winning, one should adopt Kupfer's (1975) distinction between a purpose *of* sport and a purpose *within* sport:

> To score or win as the result of shabby play or luck can by no stretch of the imagination be thought of as achieving the "purpose" of competitive sport. Yet this would be of no matter if winning or scoring were its purpose! Scoring (or winning) is valued as a sign of excellence in play because it helps define excellence: it is part of our concept of good play. (p.84)

Kupfer (1983) does grant that the situation is different for professional athletes but he asks, "[W]hy must professionalization infect all levels and appreciations of the game? Why have spectators and amateur players forgotten that it is 'as if' winning were important?" (p.119). The distinction of perceiving winning as important or playing "as if" winning was important is an important distinction and it illuminates the intrinsic value of aesthetic experience. That winning is not the only goal and that intrinsic enjoyment may be found in the engagement of the activity is reiterated by Schacht (1972):

> At the risk of banality, I would suggest that athletic activity consists in engaging in some sport the rudiments of which one has mastered; and that the only "athletic goal" of which it makes any sense to speak, at least where all but the finest athletes are concerned, is simply that intrinsic enjoyment which one may derive from engaging in the activity in question, through winning and/or playing to the best of one's ability and/or playing well. (p.100)

Kretchmar (1972) frames this notion of intrinsic value by referring to the hindrances involved in sport: "I express myself *with* hindrance, not through or in spite of hindrance. It is valued for itself" (p.120). Thus, it is sport and not aesthetic activity that is significant primarily ("primarily" must be emphasized since other motivations may be involved as well) for its intrinsic value.

Conclusion

In conclusion, it would be more appropriate to refer to sports such as football and hockey as flow sports, sports where what we typically refer to as aesthetic moments are actually moments where a sense of flow has been achieved. Sports such as gymnastics and diving, which are typically referred to as aesthetic sports, would more properly be called form sports, sports where the focus is on the form of the activity. Finally, an activity such as ballet or modern dance truly deserves the denotation aesthetic since the purpose of these dance forms is to express ideas, feelings, and thoughts through movement. This expression is an attempt to achieve a sensuous understanding, both on the part of the dancer and the audience. The attainment of a sensuous understanding is what it means to have an aesthetic experience. Removing the "aesthetic" label from sport does not negate the value of these activities. In fact, similar to the way the term *aesthetic* has been misapplied to sport, so has the notion of intrinsic value been misapplied to aesthetic experience. Sport, rather than aesthetic activity, is significant largely as a result of its intrinsic value. Although aesthetic activity has typically been justified on the grounds of its intrinsic value, one should take Abbs's (1989c) position concerning not the justification of "art for art's sake" but rather "art for meaning's sake" (p.209). Sports, on the other hand, are significant because they are played for the sake of the game. Thus, both sports and aesthetic activity are valuable, but for different reasons. A disservice is not done by delineating the distinctions between these different activities. Rather, the distinctions allow us to perceive what is fundamental to and significant in both aesthetic activity and sport.

CHAPTER REVIEW

Key Concepts

- analytic
- postmodern
- aesthetic response
- aesthetic qualities
- sensuous understanding
- aesthetic and artistic
- form and content
- aesthetic and purposive sports
- flow
- engaging and expressing
- intrinsic value

Review Questions

1. How does an aesthetic response differ from an economic or moral response? Give an example.
2. What are some examples of aesthetic qualities?
3. What is entailed by Abbs's reference to the aesthetic as "sensuous understanding"?
4. How is the aesthetic distinguished from the artistic in this chapter?
5. What is the distinction between form and content, and how does this distinction help us to understand the notion of "art for meaning's sake" as well as the aesthetic in nature?
6. What is meant by "flow," and how does this notion relate to the "aesthetic feelings" in Best's purposive sports?
7. What is meant by "form sports" in this chapter, and how does the conception of form sports relate to Best's conception of aesthetic sports?
8. What is the difference between *engaging* in a meaningful activity and *expressing* the meaning in an activity, and how does this distinction help address the question of whether sport can be art?

References

Abbs, P., ed. 1989a. Aesthetic education: An opening manifesto. In *The symbolic order: A contemporary reader on the arts debate.* London: Falmer Press.

——., ed. 1989b. Introduction. In *The symbolic order: A contemporary reader on the arts debate.* London: Falmer Press.

——., ed. 1989c. The pattern of art-making. In *The symbolic order: A contemporary reader on the arts debate.* London: Falmer Press.

Anderson, D.F., E.F. Broom, J.C. Pooley, B. Schrodt, and E. Brown. 1995. *Foundations of Canadian physical education, recreation, and sports studies.* 2d ed. Madison, Wis.: Brown and Benchmark Publishers.

Andre, J., and D.N. James. 1991. *Rethinking college athletics.* Philadelphia: Temple University Press.

Annis, D.B. 1987. The meaning, value, and duties of friendship. *American Philosophical Quarterly* 24 (4): 349-356.

Anscombe, G. 1958. Modern moral philosophy. *Philosophy* 33: 1-19.

Aristotle. 1941a. Nichomachean ethics. In *The basic works of Aristotle,* ed. R. McKeon. New York: Random House.

——. 1941b. Politics. In *The basic works of Aristotle,* ed. R. McKeon. New York: Random House.

Arnold, P. 1988. Education, movement, and the rationality of practical knowledge. *Quest* 40: 115-125.

Arnold, P.J. 1983. Three approaches toward an understanding of sportsmanship. *Journal of the Philosophy of Sport* 10: 61-70.

——. 1988. *Education, movement and the curriculum.* London: Falmer Press.

——. 1989. Competitive sport, winning and education. *Journal of Moral Education* 18: 15-25.

——. 1991. The preeminence of skill as an educational value in the movement curriculum. *Quest* 43: 66-77.

——. 1997. *Sport, ethics and education.* London: Cassell.

Bailey, C. 1975. Games, winning and education. *Cambridge Journal of Education* 5 (1): 40-50.

Bailin, S. 1993. Other people's products: The value of performing and appreciating. *The Journal of Aesthetic Education* 27: 59-69.

Barber, H. 1982. Teaching attitudes and behaviors through youth sport. *Journal of Physical Education, Recreation and Dance* 53 (3): 21-22.

Baron, R.S., D. Moore, and G.S. Sanders. 1978. Distraction as a source of drive in social facilitation research. *Journal of Personality and Social Psychology* 36: 816-824.

Bell, C. 1958. *Art.* New York: Capricorn Books.

Bergmann Drewe, S. 1996a. *Creative dance: Enriching understanding.* Calgary: Alta.: Detselig Enterprises.

——. 1996b. Gold not real Olympic goal. *Winnipeg Free Press,* 26 July, A11.

——. 1999. Acquiring practical knowledge: A justification for physical education. *Paideusis* 12 (2): 33-44.

Bergmann Drewe, S., and M.F. Daniel. 1998. The fundamental role of critical thinking in physical education. *Avante* 4 (2): 20-38.

Best, D. 1978. *Philosophy and human movement.* London: Allen & Unwin.

Bissinger, H.G. 1990. *Friday night lights: A town, a team, and a dream.* Reading, Mass.: Addison-Wesley Publishing Company.

Blum, L.A. 1980. *Friendship, altruism and morality.* London: Routledge & Kegan Paul.

Booth, B. 1981. Socio-cultural aspect of play and moral development. *Physical Education Review* 4: 115-120.

Boxill, J. 1985. Beauty, sport, and gender. *Journal of the Philosophy of Sport* 11: 36-47.

——. (1993-94). Title IX and gender equity. *Journal of the Philosophy of Sport* 20/21: 23-31.

Boyle, R.H., and W. Ames. 1983. Too many punches, too litle concern: With boxing's ills under fresh public scrutiny, new research on brain damage in experienced fighters suggests a road to medical reform. *Sports Illustrated,* April 11, 44-46, 51-52, 54-56, 58, 60, 62-64, 67.

Brackenridge, C. 1994. Fair play or fair game? Child sexual abuse in sport organizations. *International Review for Sociology of Sport* 29 (3): 287-300.

Brandi, J. 1989. A theory of moral development and competitive school sport. Ph.D. diss., Loyola University of Chicago, Illinois.

Bredemeier, B.J. 1988. The moral of the youth sport story. In *Competitive sports for children and youth: An overview of research and issues,* ed. E. Brown and C. Branta. Champaign, Ill.: Human Kinetics.

Bredemeier, B., M. Weiss, and R. Shewchuk. 1986. Promoting moral growth in a summer sport camp: The implementation of theoretically grounded instructional srategies. *Journal of Moral Education* 15: 212-220.

British Medical Association 1993. *The boxing debate.* London: British Medical Association.

Brown, L., and S. Grineski. 1992. Competition in physical education: An educational contradiction? *Journal of Physical Education, Recreation and Dance* 63 (1): 17-19, 77.

Brown, W.M. 1984. Paternalism, drugs, and the nature of sports. *Journal of the Philosophy of Sport* 11: 14-22.

——. 1990. Practices and prudence. *Journal of the Philosophy of Sport* 17: 71-84.

——. 2001. As American as Gatorade and apple pie: Performance drugs and sports. In *Ethics in sport,* ed. W.J. Morgan, K.V. Meier, and A.J. Schneider. Champaign, Ill.: Human Kinetics.

Bunker, L. 1981. Elementary physical education and youth sport. *Journal of Physical Education, Recreation and Dance* 52 (2): 26-28.

Campbell, D.N. 1974. On being number one: Competition in education. *Phi Delta Kappan* 56: 143-146.

Carr, D. 1996. After Kohlberg: Some implications of an ethics of virtue for the theory of moral education and development. *Studies in Philosophy and Education* 15 (4): 353-370.

Chodorow, N. 1978. *The reproduction of mothering.* Berkeley, Calif.: University of California Press.

Coakley, J.J. 1994. *Sport in society: Issues and controversies.* 5th ed. St. Louis, Mo.: Mosby.

Coakley, J. 1986. When should children begin competing? A sociological perspective. In *Sport for children and youths,* ed. M.R. Weiss and D. Gould. Champaign, Ill.: Human Kinetics.

——. 1993. Social dimensions of intensive training and participation in youth sports. In *Intensive participation in children's sports,* ed. B.R. Cahill and A.J. Pearl. Champaign, Ill.: Human Kinetics.

Cohen, T. 1991. Sports and art: Beginning questions. In *Rethinking college athletics,* ed. J. Andre and D.N. James. Philadelphia: Temple University Press.

Colburn, K. 1985. Honor, ritual and violence in ice hockey. *Canadian Journal of Sociology* 10: 153-170.

——. 1986. Deviance and legitimacy in ice-hockey: A microstructural theory of violence. *The Sociological Quarterly* 27: 63-74.

Cordner, C. 1988. Differences between sport and art. *Journal of the Philosophy of Sport* 15: 31-47.

Cordoba, R.D. 2001. In search of a level playing field: *Baca v. City of Los Angeles* as a step toward gender equity in girls' sports beyond Title IX. *Harvard Women's Law Journal* 24: 139-190.

Crawford, D. 1991. The questions of aesthetics. In *Aesthetics and arts education,* ed. R. Smith and A. Simpson. Illinois: University of Illinois Press.

Crouse, A. 2000. Equal athletic opportunity: An analysis of *Mercer v. Duke University* and a proposal to amend the contact sport exception to Title IX. *Minnesota Law Review* 84 (6): 1655-1688.

Csikszentmihalyi, M. 1975. *Beyond boredom and anxiety.* San Francisco: Jossey Bass Publishers.

Cullen, F. 1974. Attitudes of players and spectators toward norm-violation in ice hockey. *Perceptual and Motor Skills* 38: 1146.

D'Agostino, F. 1981. The ethos of games. *Journal of the Philosophy of Sport* 8: 7-18.

Dakin, S., and A.J. Arrowood. 1981. The social comparison of ability. *Human Relations* 34: 89-109.

Davis, P. 1993-94. Ethical issues in boxing. *Journal of the Philosophy of Sport* 20/21: 48-63.

de Grazia, S. 1962. *Of time, work and leisure.* New York: Doubleday-Anchor.

Deacon, J. 2000. Blood sport. *Maclean's,* March 6, 44-48.

Deford, F. 2001. Time bandits *Sports Illustrated,* August 6, 67.

Delattre, E.J. 1975. Some reflections on success and failure in competitive athletics. *Journal of the Philosophy of Sport* 2: 133-139.

DeNeui, D., and D. Sachau. 1996. Spectator enjoyment of aggression in intercollegiate hockey games. *Journal of Sport & Social Issues* 20: 69-77.

Diamondstein, G. 1974. *Exploring the arts with children.* New York: MacMillan Publishing Co.

Dixon, N. 1996. The morality of intimate faculty-student relationships. *The Monist* 79 (4): 519-535.

Dixon, N. 2001a. Boxing, paternalism, and legal moralism. *Social Theory and Practice* 27 (2): 323-344.

Dixon, N. 2001b. Performance-enhancing drugs, paternalism, and harm to others. Paper presented at the International Association for Philosophy of Sport, 27 October, in Williamsburg, Virginia.

Donaldson, T. 1986. *Issues in moral philosophy.* New York: McGraw-Hill Book Company.

Drewe Dixon, S. 2002.To fight or not to fight? That is the debate. *Face Off* (November): 4.

Drewe, S. 2001. The value of knowledge/rationality or the knowledge/rationality of values: Implications for education. *Studies in Philosophy and Education* 20 (3): 235-244.

Dryden, K., and R. MacGregor. 1989. *Home game: Hockey and life in Canada.* Toronto: McClelland & Stewart.

Dumazedier, J. 1967. Toward a society of leisure. New York: Free Press.

Dunlop, F. 1975. Bailey on games, winning and education. *Cambridge Journal of Education* 5 (3): 153-160.

Dworkin, G. 1983. Paternalism: Some second thoughts. In *Paternalism,* ed. R. Sartorius. Minneapolis: University of Minnesota Press.

Dworkin, R. 1977. *Taking rights seriously.* Cambridge, Mass.: Harvard University Press.

Dyer, K.F. 1982. *Challenging the men: The social biology of female sporting achievement.* St. Lucia: University of Queensland Press.

English, J. 1978. Sex equality in sports. *Philosophy & Public Affairs* 7 (3): 269-277.

Fait, H.F., and J.F. Billing. 1978. Reassessment of the value of competition. In *Joy and sadness in children's sports,* ed. R. Martens. Champaign, Ill.: Human Kinetics.

Farber, M. 2001. Two good. *Sports Illustrated,* November 12, 56.

Feezell, R. 1986. Sportsmanship. *Journal of the Philosophy of Sport* 13: 1-13.

——. 1988. On the wrongness of cheating and why cheaters can't play the game. *Journal of Philosophy of Sport* 15: 57-68.

Feinberg, J. 1986. *Harm to self.* Oxford: Oxford University Press.

Ferguson, A. 1999. Inside the crazy culture of kids sports. *Time* (Canadian ed.), 12 July, 36-44.

Festinger, L. 1954. A theory of social comparison processes. *Human Relations* 7: 117-140.

Fielding, M. 1976. Against competition. *Proceedings of the Philosophy of Education Society of Great Britain* 10: 124-146.

Figley, G. 1984. Moral education through physical education. *Quest* 36: 89-101.

Fischler, S. 1974. *Slashing! Hockey's most knowledgeable critic tells what should be done to save the game.* New York: Thomas Crowell.

Flax, J. 1978. The conflict between nurturance and autonomy in mother-daughter relationships and within feminism. *Feminist Studies* 4 (2): 171-191.

Fost, N. 1986. Banning drugs in sports: A skeptical view. *Hastings Center Report* (August): 5-10.

Fraleigh, W. 1982. Why the good foul is not good. *Journal of Physical Education, Recreation and Dance* 53 (1): 41-42.

——. 1984. *Right actions in sport: Ethics for contestants.* Champaign, Ill.: Human Kinetics.

Frankena, W. 1973. *Ethics.* 2d ed. Englewood Cliffs, N.J.: Prentice-Hall.

Gallahue, D.L. 1982. *Understanding motor development in children.* New York: Wiley.

Galvin, R.F. 1991. Nonsense on stilts: A skeptical view. In *Rethinking college athletics,* ed. J. Andre and D.N. James. Philadelphia: Temple University Press.

Gardner, R. 1989. On performance-enhancing substances and the unfair advantage argument. *Journal of the Philosophy of Sport* 16: 59-73.

Gastorf, J., J. Suls, and J. Lawhon. 1978. Opponent choices of below average performers. *Bulletin of the Psychonomic Society* 12: 217-220.

Gerber, E.W. 1972. *Sport and the body: A philosophical symposium.* Philadelphia: Lea and Febiger.

Gombrich, E. 1969. *Art and illusion: A study in the psychology of pictorial representation.* 2d ed. Princeton, N.J.: Princeton University Press.

Gough, R. 1997. *Character is everything: Promoting ethical excellence in sports.* Fort Worth, Tex.: Harcourt Brace College Publishers.

Gould, D. 1987. Understanding attrition in youth sport. *Advances in pediatric sport sciences.* Vol. 2, *Behavioral issues*, ed. D. Gould and M.R. Weiss. Champaign, Ill.: Human Kinetics.

Gouvernement du Quebec. 1977. *La violence en hockey amateur au Quebec: Rapport final.* Quebec: Gouvernement du Quebec.

Griffin, R. 1998. *Sports in the lives of children and adolescents: Success on field and in life.* Westport, Conn.: Praeger.

Grinski, S. 1993. Children, cooperative learning, and physical education. *Teaching Elementary Physical Education* 4: 10-14.

Groff, B.D., R.S. Baron, and D.L. Moore. 1983. Distraction, attentional conflict, and drive-like behavior. *Journal of Experimental Social Psychology* 19: 359-380.

Gruneau, R., and D. Whitson. 1993. *Hockey night in Canada.* Toronto: Garamond Press.

Grupe, O. 1985. Top-level sports for children from an educational viewpoint. *International Journal of Physical Education* 22 (1): 9-16.

Hamm, C. 1989. *Philosophical issues in education: An introduction.* New York: Falmer Press.

Harding, S. 1982. Is gender a variable in conception of rationality: A survey of issues. *Dialectica* 36 (1): 225-242.

Hare, R.M. 1981. *Moral thinking.* New York: Clarendon Press, Oxford.

Harrell, W. 1981. Verbal aggressiveness in spectators at professional hockey games: The effects of tolerance of violence and amount of exposure to hockey. *Human Relation* 34: 643-655.

Hatab, L.J. 1991. The Greeks and the meaning of athletics. In *Rethinking college athletics,* ed. J. Andre and D.N. James. Philadelphia: Temple University Press.

Hellstedt, J.C. 1988. Kids, parents, and sports: Some questions and answers. *The Physician and Sportmedicine* 16 (4): 59-60, 62, 64, 69-71.

Hinson, C. 1993. Children and competition. *Teaching Elementary Physical Education: The Newsletter for Specialists, Teachers, and Administrators* 4 (6): 17.

Hitchcock, D., and E. Baumgarten. 1986. Conflicting affairs. *Teaching Philosophy* 9: 255-260.

Holowchak, M.A. 2000. "Aretism" and pharmacological ergogenic aids in sport: Taking a shot at the use of steroids. *Journal of the Philosophy of Sport* 27: 35-50.

Horn, T. 1993. On competition: What the experts say. *Teaching Elementary Physical Education: The Newsletter for Specialists, Teachers, and Administrators* 4 (6): 8-9.

Hospers, J. 1982. *Understanding the arts.* Englewood Cliffs, N.J.: Prentice-Hall.

Huizinga, J. 1950. *Homo ludens.* Boston: The Beacon Press.

Hursthouse, R. 1992. Truth and representation. In *Philosophical aesthetics: An introduction,* ed. O. Hanfling. Oxford: Blackwell.

Hyland, D. 1990. *Philosophy of sport.* New York: Paragon House.

——. 1991. When power becomes gracious. In *Rethinking college athletics,* ed. J. Andre and D. James. Philadelphia: Temple University Press.

Hyland, D.A. 1980. The stance of play. *Journal of the Philosophy of Sport* 7: 87-99.

——. 1988. Competition and friendship. In *Philosophic inquiry in sport,* ed. W.J. Morgan and K.V. Meier. Champaign, Ill.: Human Kinetics.

Iso-Ahola, S. 1980. Who's turning children's little league play into work? *Parks and Recreation* 16 (6): 51-54, 77.

Jollimore, T. 2000. Friendship without partiality? *Ratio* 13 (1): 69-82.

Jowett, S., and G.A. Meek. 2000. The coach-athlete relationship in married couples: An exploratory content analysis. *The Sport Psychologist* 14: 157-175.

Kaelin, E. 1968. The well-played game: Notes toward an aesthetics of sport. *Quest* 10: 16-28.

Kant, I. [1785] 1959. *Groundwork of the metaphysics of morals.* Trans. L. Beck. New York: Bobbs-Merrill.

Kaplan, M. 1960. *Leisure in America: A social inquiry.* New York: John Wiley.

Keating, J. 1964. Sportsmanship as a moral category. *Ethics* 75: 25-35.

Keating, J.W. 1973. The ethics of competition and its relation to some moral problems in athletics. In *The philosophy of sport: A collection of original essays,* ed. R.G. Osterhoudt. Springfield, Ill.: Thomas.

Keller, H. 1974. Sport and art: The concept of mastery. In *Readings in the aesthetics of sport,* ed. H. Whiting and D. Masterson. London: Lepus Books.

Kildea, A.E. 1983. Competition: A model for conception. *Quest* 35 (2): 169-181.

Koehn, D. 1998. Can and should businesses be friends with one another and with their stakeholders. *Journal of Business Ethics* 17: 1755-1763.

Kohn, A. 1986. *No contest: The case against competition.* Boston: Houghton Mifflin Company.

Kretchmar, R.S. 1994. *Practical philosophy of sport.* Champaign, Ill.: Human Kinetics.

Kretchmar, S. 1972. Ontological possibilities: Sport as play. In *Philosophic Exchange: The Annual Proceedings of the Center for Philosophic Exchange* (summer): 113-122.

Kretchmar, S. 1994. *Practical philosophy of sport.* Champaign, Ill.: Human Kinetics.

Kupfer, J. 1975. Purpose and beauty in sport. *Journal of the Philosophy of Sport* 2: 83-90.

——. 1983. *Experience as art: Aesthetics in everyday life.* Albany, N.Y.: State University of New York Press.

——. 1987. Privacy, autonomy, and self-concept. *American Philosophical Quarterly* 24: 81-89.

——. 1990. Can parents and children be friends? *American Philosophical Quarterly* 27 (1): 15-26.

——. 1991. Waiting for DiMaggio: Sport as drama. In *Rethinking college athletic,* ed. J. Andre and D.N. James. Philadelphia: Temple University Press.

Layden, T. 2001. Ready to rock. *Sports Illustrated,* May 28, 51.

Leaman, O. 1995. Cheating and fair play in sport. In *Philosophic inquiry in sport,* ed. W.J. Morgan and K.V. Meier. 2d ed. Champaign, Ill.: Human Kinetics.

LeBlanc, J., and L. Dickson. 1996. *Straight talk about children and sport: Advice for parents, coaches and teachers.* Gloucester, Ont.: Coaching Association of Canada.

Lehman, C.K. 1981. Can cheaters play the game? *Journal of the Philosophy of Sport* 8: 41-46.

Levinson, J. 1996. *The pleasures of aesthetics: Philosophical essays.* Ithaca: Cornell University Press.

Loland, S. 1998. Fair play: Historical anachronism or topical ideal? In *Ethics and sport,* ed. M.J. McNamee and S.J. Parry. London: E & FN SPON.

Loy, J. 1973. The North American syndrome: Sport for adults-athletics for children. In *Sports or athletics: A North American dilemma,* ed. J. Murray. Windsor, Ont.: University of Windsor.

Loy, J.W. Jr. 1968. The nature of sport: A definitional effort. *Quest Monograph* 10:1-15.

Lumpkin, A., S. Stoll, and J. Beller. 1994. *Sport ethics: Applications for fair play.* St. Louis: Mosby.

Luschen, G. 1976. Cheating in sport. In *Social problems in athletics,* ed. D. Landers. Urbana: University of Illinois Press.

MacIntyre, A. 1984. *After virtue.* 2d ed. Notre Dame, Ind.: University of Notre Dame Press.

Macken, J. 1990. *The authonomy theme in the church dogmatics: Karl Barth and his critics.* Cambridge: Cambridge University Press.

Maquet, J. 1986. *The aesthetic experience: An anthropologist looks at the visual arts.* New Haven: Yale University Press.

Markie, P.J. 1990. Professors, students, and friendship. In *Morality, responsibility, and the university: Studies in academic ethics,* ed. S.M. Cahn. Philadelphia: Temple University Press.

Martinek, T., and D. Hellison. 1997. Fostering resiliency in underserved youth through physical activity. *Quest* 49: 33-49.

Mason, T. 1993. *Only a game: Sport in the modern world.* Cambridge: Cambridge University Press.

May, T. 1994. The concept of autonomy. *American Philosophical Quarterly* 31: 133-144.

McCormick, R. 1962. Is professional boxing immoral? *Sports Illustrated,* November 5, 70-82.

McIntosh, P. 1979. *Fair play: Ethics in sport and education.* London: Heinemann.

McMurty, W. 1974. *Investigation and inquiry into violence in amateur hockey.* Ontario: Ontario Government.

McPherson, B., L.N. Guppy, and J.P. McKay. 1976. The social structure of the game and sport milieu. In *Children in sport and physical activity,* ed. J.G. Albinson and G.M. Andrews. Baltimore: University Park.

Meakin, D. 1981. Physical education: An agency of moral education? *Journal of the Philosophy of Education* 15: 241-253.

Meakin, D.C. 1990. How physical education can contribute to personal and social education. *Physical Education Review* 2: 108-119.

Meier, K.V. 1988. Triad trickery: Playing with sport and games. *Journal of the Philosophy of Sport* 15: 11-30.

Metheny, E. 1977. *Vital issues.* Washington, D.C.: American Alliance for Health, Physical Education, and Recreation.

Meyer, M. 1987. Stoics, rights, and autonomy. *American Philosophical Quarterly* 2: 267-271.

Meyersohn, R.B. 1958. Americans off duty. In *Free time-challenge to later maturity,* ed. W. Donahue et al. Ann Arbor: University of Michigan Press.

Meynell, H. 1986. *The nature of aesthetic value.* Albany, New York: State University of New York Press.

Micheli, L.J., and M.D. Jenkins. 1990. *Sportswise: An essential guide for young athletes, parents, and coaches.* Boston: Houghton Mifflin Company.

Mill, J.S. [1859] 1985. *On liberty.* New York: Penguin Books.

Miller, S., B. Bredemeier, and D. Shields. 1997. Sociomoral education through physical education with at risk children. *Quest* 49: 114-129.

Mitias, M., ed. 1986. Can we speak of "aesthetic experience"? In *Possibility of the aesthetic experience.* Dordrecht: Martinus Nijohoff Publishers.

Munrow, A.D. 1972. *Physical education: A discussion of principles.* London: G. Bell & Sons.

Neal, P.E., and T.A. Tutko. 1975. *Coaching girls and women: Psychological perspectives.* Boston: Allyn & Bacon, Inc.

O'Connor, D.K. 1990. Two ideals of friendship. *History of Philosophy Quarterly* 7 (2): 109-122.

Orlick, T. 1978. *Winning through cooperation: Competitive insanity, cooperative alternatives.* Washington, D.C.: Acropolis Books.

Orlick, T.D. 1973. Children's sport: A revolution is coming. *Canadian Association for Health, Physical Education and Recreation Journal* 39 (3): 12-14.

——. 1974. The athletic dropout: A high price for inefficiency. *Canadian Association for Health, Physical Education and Recreation Journal* 41 (2): 21, 24-27.

Osterhoudt, R.G. 1977. The term "sport": Some thoughts on a proper name. *International Journal of Physical Education* 14 (2): 11-16.

Pangrazi, R.P., and V.P. Dauer. 1992. *Dynamic physical education for elementary school children.* 10th ed. New York: Macmillan.

Parry, J. 1998. Violence and aggression in contemporary sport. In *Ethics and sport*, ed. M. McNamee and J. Parry. London: E & FN SPON.

Pearson, K.M. 1973. Deception, sportsmanship, and ethics. *Quest* 14: 115-118.

Perry, C. 1983. Blood doping and athletic competition. *The Interational Journal of Applied Philosophy* 1 (3): 39-45.

Perry, L. 1975. Competition and cooperation. *British Journal of Educational Studies* 23: 127-134.

Pooley, J.C. 1989. Player violence in sport: Consequences for youth cross-nationally. Part 2. *Journal of the International Council for Health, Physical Education and Recreation* 25 (3): 6-11.

Postow, B. 1980. Women and masculine sports. *Journal of the Philosophy of Sport* 7: 51-58.

Price, K. 1979. What makes an experience aesthetic? *The British Journal of Aesthetics* 19: 131-143.

Rachels, J. 1993. *The elements of moral philosophy.* 2d ed. New York: McGraw-Hill.

Ravizza, K., and K. Daruty. 1984. Paternalism and sovereignty in athletics: Limits and justifications of the coach's exercise of authority over the adult athlete. *Journal of the Philosophy of Sport* 11: 71-82.

——. 1988. Paternalism and sovereignty in athletics: Limits and justifications of the coach's exercise of authority over the adult athlete. In *Philosophy of sport and physical activity*, ed. P.J. Galasso. Toronto: Canadian Scholars' Press Inc.

Rawls, J. 1955. Two concepts of rules. *Philosophical Review* 64: 3-32.

——. 1971. *A theory of justice.* Cambridge: Harvard University Press.

Reddiford, G. 1981. Morality and the games player. *Physical Education Review* 4: 8-16.

Redfern, H. 1991. Aesthetic understanding. In *Aesthetics and arts education*, ed. R. Smith and A. Simpson. Urbana, Ill.: University of Illinois Press.

Richmond, S. 1989. Once again: Art education, politics, and the aesthetic perspective. *Canadian Review of Art Education* 16: 119-128.

Roberts, G.C. 1980. Children in competition: A theoretical perspective and recommendations for practice. *Motor Skills: Theory into Practice* 4: 37-50.

Roberts, T. 1986. Sport, art, and particularity: The best equivocation. *Journal of the Philosophy of Sport* 13: 49-63.

——. 1995. Sport and strong poetry. *Journal of the Philosophy of Sport* 22: 94-107.

Romance, T. 1988. Promoting character development in physical education. *Strategies* 1: 16-17.

Ross, S. 1988. Winning and losing in sport: A radical reassessment. In *Philosophy of sport and physical activity: Issues and concepts*, ed. P.J. Galasso. Toronto: Canadian Scholars' Press.

Russell, G. 1986. Does sports violence increase box office receipts? *International Journal of Sport Psychology* 17: 173-183.

Scanlan, T., and M. Passer. 1981. Competitive stress and the youth sport experience. *Physical Educator* 38 (3): 144-151.

Scanlan, T. 1984. Competitive stress and the child athlete. In *Psychological Foundations of Sport*, ed. J. Silva and R. Weinberg. Champaign, Ill.: Human Kinetics.

Scanlan, T.K. 1996. Social evaluation and the competition process: A developmental perspective. In *Children and youth in sport: A biopsychosocial perspective*, ed. F.L. Smoll and R.E. Smith. Madison, Wis.: Brown and Benchmark.

Schaar, J. 1967. Equality of opportunity and beyond. In *Equality, Nomos 9*, ed. J. Roland Pennock and J.W. Chapman. New York: Atherton Press.

Schacht, R. 1972. On Weiss on records, athletic activity, and the athlete. In *Philosophic Exchange: The Annual Proceedings of the Center for Philosophic Exchange* (summer): 99-103.

Schmitz, K.L. 1979. Sport and play: Suspension of the ordinary. In *Sport and the body: A philosophical symposium*, ed. E.W. Gerber and W.J. Morgan. Philadelphia: Lea and Febieger.

Schneider, A. 2000. On the definition of "woman" in the sport context. In *Values in sport: Elitism, nationalism, gender equality and the scientific manufacture of winner*, ed. T. Tånnsjø and C. Tamburrini. London: E & FN SPON.

Schneider, A., and R. Butcher. 1993-94. Why Olympic athletes should avoid the use and seek the elimination of performance-enhancing substances and practices from the Olympic games. *Journal of the Philosophy of Sport* 20/21: 64-81.

——. 2000. A philosophical overview of the arguments on banning doping is sport. In *Values in sport: Elitism, nationalism, gender equality and the scientific manufacture of winners*, ed. T. Tånnsjø and C. Tamburrini. London: E & FN SPON.

——. 2001. Ethics, sport, and boxing. In *Ethics in sport*, ed. W. Morgan, K. Meier, and A. Schneider. Champaign, Ill.: Human Kinetics.

Schneider, John, and D. Stanley Eitzen. 1983. The structure of sport and participant violence. *Arena Review* 7: 1-16.

Schwager, S., and C. Labate. 1993. Teaching for critical thinking in physical education. *Journal of Physical Education, Recreation and Dance* 64: 24-26.

Searle, J.R. 1995. *The construction of social reality*. New York: The Free Press.

Seefeldt, V., ed. 1987. Benefits of competitive sports for children and youth. In *Handbook for youth sports coaches*. Reston, Va.: American Alliance for Health, Physical Education, Recreation, and Dance.

Shaffer, T.E. 1979. Physiological considerations of the female participant. In *Out of the bleachers: Writings on women and sport*, ed. S. Twin. Old Westbury, N.Y.: The Feminist Press.

Shea, E. 1996. *Ethical decisions in sport: Interscholastic, intercollegiate, Olympic and professional*. Springfield, Ill.: Charles Thomas.

Shields, D.L.L., and B.J.L. Bredemeier. 1995. *Character development and physical activity*. Champaign, Ill.: Human Kinetics.

Shusterman, R. 1998. Interpretation, pleasure, and value in aesthetic experience. *The Journal of Aesthetics and Art Criticism* 56: 51-53.

Siegel, H. 1988. Critical thinking as an educational ideal. In *Philosophy of education : Introductory Readings*, ed. W. Hare and J. Portelli. Calgary, Alb.: Detselig.

Simon, R. 1984. Good competition and drug-enhanced performance. *Journal of the Philosophy of Sport* 11: 6-13.

Simon, R.L. 1991. *Fair play: Sports, values, and society*. Boulder, Colo.: Westview Press.

Smith, M. 1978a. Social learning of violence in minor hockey. In *Psychological perspectives in youth sports*, ed. F. Smoll and R. Smith. Washington: Hemisphere Publishing.

——. 1978b. From professional to youth hockey violence: The role of the mass media. In *Violence in Canada*, ed. M. Gammon. Toronto: Methuen.

——. 1979. Towards an explanation of hockey violence: A reference other approach. *Canadian Journal of Sociology* 4:105-124.

——. 1980. Hockey violence: Interning some myths. In *Sport psychology: An analysis of athlete behavior*, ed. W. Straub. Ithaca, N.Y.: Mouvement.

——. 1983. *Violence and sport.* Toronto: Butterworths.

Smith, M.D. 1988. *Violence and sport.* Toronto: Canadian Scholars' Press.

Smoll, F.L., and R.E. Smith, eds. 1996. *Children and youth in sport: A biopsychosocial perspective.* Madison, Wis.: Brown & Benchmark.

Sorell, T. 1992. Art, society and morality. In *Philosophical aesthetics: An introduction*, ed. O. Hanfling. Oxford: Blackwell.

Stoutjesdyk, D., and R. Jevne. 1993. Eating disorders among high performance athletes. *Journal of Youth and Adolescence* 22 (3): 271-282.

Suits, B. 1977. Words on play. *Journal of the Philosophy of Sport* 4: 117-131.

——. 1978. *The grasshopper: Games, life and utopia.* Toronto: University of Toronto Press.

——. 1988. Tricky triad: Games, play, and sport. *Journal of the Philosophy of Sport* 15: 1-9.

Suls, J.M., and R.L. Miller, eds. 1977. *Social comparison processes: Theoretical and empirical perspectives.* Washington, D.C.: Hemisphere.

Swift, E.M. 1992. The National Hacking League. *Sports Illustrated*, May 18, 76, 86.

——. 1993. A cruel blow. *Sports Illustrated*, December 6, 66-70; 72-74; 76; 79.

Taft, T.N. 1991. Sports injuries in children. *The Elementary School Journal* 91 (5): 429-435.

Tamburrini, C.M. 2000. *The "hand of God"?: Essays in the philosophy of sports.* Goteborg, Sweden: Acta Universitatis Gothoburgensis.

Tännsjø, T. 2000. Against sexual discrimination in sports. In *Values in sport: Elitism, nationalism, gender equality and the scientific manufacture of winner*, ed. T. Tännsjø and C. Tamburrini. London: E & FN SPON.

Tatum, J., and B. Kushner. 1979. *They call me assassin.* New York: Everest House.

Terry, P., and J. Jackson. 1985. The determinants and control of violence in sport. *Quest* 37: 27-37.

Thomas, C.E. 1983. *Sport in a philosophic context.* Philadelphia: Lea & Febiger.

Thomas, L. 1987. Friendship. *Synthes* 72: 217-236.

Tutko, T., and W. Bruns. 1976. *Winning is everything and other American myths.* New York: Macmillan.

Urmson, J. 1957. What makes a situation aesthetic? In *Aristotelian Society Proceedings.* Suppl. Vol. 31.

Vandezwaag, H.J. 1972. *Toward a philosophy of sport.* Reading, Mass.: Addison Wesley Publishing Company.

Vaz, E. 1977. Institutionalized rule violation in professional hockey: Perspectives and control systems. *Canadian Association for Health, Physical Education and Recreation* 43 (4): 6-34.

Vaz, E. 1979. Institutionalized rule violation and control in organized minor league hockey. *Canadian Journal of Applied Sport Science* 4: 83-90.

Veblen, T. 1899. *The theory of the leisure class.* New York: B.W. Heubsch.

Wall, J., and N. Murray. 1994. *Children and movement: Physical education in the elementary school.* 2d ed. Madison, Wis.: Brown & Benchmark.

Warren, M.A. 1983. Justice and gender in school sports. In *Women, philosophy, and sport: A collection of new essays*, ed. B. Postow. Metuchen, N.J.: The Scarecrow Press.

Watson, R., and J. MacLellan. 1986. "Smitting to spitting": 80 years of ice-hockey in Canadian courts. *Canadian Journal of History of Sport* 17: 10-27.

Weiss, P.1969. *Sport: A philosophic inquiry.* Carbondale, Ill.: Southern Illinois University Press.

Wikes, J. 2001. World's bridge players in Toronto for North American Championships. Canadian Press Newswire, July 27.

Whitaker, G. 1991. Feminism and the sport experience: Seeking common ground. In *Rethinking college athletics*, ed. J. Andre and D.N. James. Philadelphia: Temple University Press.

White, P.1990. Friendship and education. *Journal of Philosophy of Education* 24 (1): 81-91.

Widmeyer, W., and J. Birch. 1984. Aggression in professional ice hockey: A strategy for success or a reaction to failure? *The Journal of Psychology* 117: 77-84.

Wigmore, S., and C. Tuxill. 1995. A consideration of the concept of fair play. *European Physical Education Review* 1: 67-73.

Wolff, R. 1970. *In defense of anarchism.* New York: Harper and Row.

Zajonc, R.B. 1968. Attitudinal effects of mere exposure. *Journal of Personality and Social Psychology, Monograph Supplement* 9: 1-27.

Zalk, S. R. 1990. Men in the academy: A psychological profile of harassment. In *Ivory power: Sexual harassment on campus*, ed. M.A. Pauldi. Albany, N.Y.: State University of New York Press.

Zeigler, E. 1984. *Ethics and morality in sport and physical education: An experiential approach.* Champaign, Ill.: Stipes Publishing Company.

Zeigler, E.R., and K.J. McCristal. 1967. A history of the big ten body-of-knowledge project in physical education. *Quest* 9: 79-84.

Index

AGMV Marquis
MEMBER OF SCABRINI MEDIA
Quebec, Canada
2003